READING:
SEVENTY-FIVE YEARS
OF PROGRESS

A 75th Anniversary Publication of
The University of Chicago

READING:
SEVENTY-FIVE YEARS
OF PROGRESS

Proceedings of the Annual Conference on Reading Held at
The University of Chicago, 1966

VOLUME XXVIII

Compiled and Edited by
H. ALAN ROBINSON

THE UNIVERSITY OF CHICAGO PRESS

Supplementary Educational Monographs

Published in conjunction with THE SCHOOL REVIEW and
THE ELEMENTARY SCHOOL JOURNAL

NUMBER 96   DECEMBER 1966

Library of Congress Catalog Card Number: 66-23696

THE UNIVERSITY OF CHICAGO PRESS, CHICAGO & LONDON
The University of Toronto Press, Toronto 5, Canada

PREFACE

*

WHEN, TWO and a half years ago, the University of Chicago's Seventy-fifth Anniversary Committee first met, we were uncertain of the form our celebration of this event should assume. Indeed, we actually received some astonishingly frivolous suggestions from some ordinarily sedate sources and were engaged for some time in discouraging elaborate projects calling for fireworks, striped tents, the growing of beards, or (since so many beards are already grown) the dying of beards a patriotic maroon.

As they have turned out, our anniversary undertakings have involved a certain amount of jollification. They also include important innovations, such as the new Wyler Children's Hospital and the new Public Affairs Academy. But above all, we have felt that the anniversary should be marked, one might say, by our doing what we usually do — only more so. By this we simply mean that serious professional people, from within and without the University, should collectively pursue those problems and enterprises which are the characteristic concerns of an academic community — but that they should do so this year with a heightened awareness of the past, a heightened concern for present self-assessment, a heightened alertness to commitment for the future. And thus we are confident that the most memorable aspect of the anniversary year will prove to be the product of such gatherings as the Annual Conference on Reading, conducted in a spirit of continuing inquiry and addressed to some of the major questions of this moment in academic history. This year's conference was an integral — and highly welcome — part of the anniversary activities.

This reading conference, meeting for the twenty-ninth year, handsomely exemplifies the way in which we have hoped the anniversary would be observed. The members of the University community are deeply conscious of the thoughtful and productive meetings of this body in the past. The reading conference is very properly and happily an element in our anniversary because it is an element in our history — not merely as a series of annual events but as evidence of a sustained, profitable attack, conducted over a period of many years, upon educational problems of very great magnitude. We like to think of the University as a unique pioneer in many areas, and assuredly this conference has pioneered with singular imagination and courage. We like to think that the University has achieved a kind of maturity while remaining youthfully flexible and curious and alert, and again this appears to be the kind of maturity the conference has attained.

The conference this year did its traditional job with its traditional excellence but did so with a special historic consciousness of the achievements of the past, the needs and knowledge of the present, the challenge of the future. Its presence does honor to the University. Its efforts lend wisdom and strength to the University. For this contribution to the anniversary year, the University is profoundly grateful.

EDWARD W. ROSENHEIM, JR.
Professor of English and Chairman of the
Faculty Committee for the Seventy-fifth Anniversary

EDITOR'S PREFACE

*

THE Twenty-ninth Annual Conference on Reading focused on the topic "Reading: Seventy-five Years of Progress." The opening paper dealt with the central theme, and each of the other nine papers delivered at the general sessions was concerned with progress over the years in specific areas of reading instruction. The papers at the sectional meetings, for levels from kindergarten through junior college, were designed to make specific applications to classroom situations. Sectional meetings were also provided for corrective and remedial teachers and for administrators, supervisors, and reading consultants.

The proceedings of twenty-seven preceding conferences have been published under the following titles:

*Copies of titles marked with asterisks are available. All other volumes are out of print.

I wish to express my deep appreciation to the many people who assisted in the execution of this and preceding conferences. My special gratitude is extended to Katherine Wingert, staff associate, and Jerry H. Parsley, research assistant, for the excellence of their assistance over the past two years.

I am particularly indebted to the members of the advisory committee composed of members of the University of Chicago faculty. In the 1965–66 school year the advisory committee consisted of the following members:

> Janet Emig, Education
> Sara Innis Fenwick, Graduate Library School
> Richard Hodges, Education
> Raymond A. Lubway, Laboratory Schools
> Helen M. Robinson, Education
> Edward W. Rosenheim, Jr., English and Humanities
> Helen K. Smith, Education
> Ellen L. Thomas, Laboratory Schools
> Samuel Weintraub, Education

H. ALAN ROBINSON

TABLE OF CONTENTS

✳

INTRODUCTION

✳

H. ALAN ROBINSON

✳

THE THEME of this conference, "Reading: Seventy-five Years of Progress," was chosen for three reasons: (1) the annual reading conference had been selected as one of the activities commemorating the seventy-fifth anniversary of the University; (2) since this was the last of the present series of the conferences on reading at the University of Chicago, it appeared to be especially appropriate to review the progress of reading instruction over the years; (3) with the current strong emphasis on reading instruction and the large sums of money being expended for materials, equipment, and personnel, it seemed most timely to review basic concepts and past history in relation to present events.

In preparation for this conference, a national committee of reading authorities was asked to examine and identify major papers given in previous reading conferences at the University. The reading staff and advisory committee for the reading conference at the University of Chicago then reviewed the papers so identified and chose those listed in chronological order below as particularly outstanding and of current significance.

1. Gertrude Whipple, "Basic Instruction in Reading," in *Co-operative Effort in Schools To Improve Reading*, compiled and edited by William S. Gray ("Supplementary Educational Monographs," No. 56 [1942]).

2. Arthur I. Gates, "Characteristics of Successful Teaching of Reading," in *Classroom Techniques in Improving Reading*, compiled and edited by William S. Gray ("Supplementary Educational Monographs," No. 69 [1949]).

3. Mary C. Austin, "Personal Characteristics That Retard Progress in Reading," in *Keeping Reading Programs Abreast of the Times*, compiled and edited by William S. Gray ("Supplementary Educational Monographs," No. 72 [1950]).

4. A. Sterl Artley, "Mental Capacity, Language Ability, and Experiential Background," in *Promoting Growth toward Maturity in Interpreting What Is Read*, compiled and edited by William S. Gray ("Supplementary Educational Monographs," No. 74 [1951]).

5. Arthur E. Traxler, "Critical Survey of Tests for Identifying Difficulties in Interpreting What Is Read," in *Promoting Growth toward Maturity in Interpreting What Is Read*, compiled and edited by William S. Gray ("Supplementary Educational Monographs," No. 74 [1951]).

6. Jacob W. Getzels, "The Nature of Reading Interests: Psychological Aspects," in *Developing Permanent Interest in Reading*, compiled and edited by Helen M. Robinson ("Supplementary Educational Monographs," No. 84 [1956]) .

7. Paul A. Wagner, "Relationship of Mass Media to Reading Interests,"

in *Developing Permanent Interest in Reading,* compiled and edited by Helen M. Robinson ("Supplementary Educational Monographs," No. 84 [1956]).

8. Arthur E. Traxler, "Values and Limitations of Standardized Reading Tests," in *Evaluation of Reading,* compiled and edited by Helen M. Robinson ("Supplementary Educational Monographs," No. 88 [1958]).

9. Ralph W. Tyler, "What is Evaluation?" in *Evaluation of Reading,* compiled and edited by Helen M. Robinson ("Supplementary Educational Monographs," No. 88 [1958]).

10. William S. Gray, "The Major Aspects of Reading," in *Sequential Development of Reading Abilities,* compiled and edited by Helen M. Robinson ("Supplementary Educational Monographs," No. 90 [1960]).

When possible, the people who wrote and delivered the original papers were invited to bring them up to date and present them. We were fortunate enough to have A. Sterl Artley, Mary C. Austin, Arthur I. Gates, J. W. Getzels, Ralph W. Tyler, and Gertrude Whipple review their original papers and write the present versions. William S. Gray's paper was revised and delivered by Helen M. Robinson. David K. Berninghausen, who delivered the paper on "Mass Media Concepts and Reading Instruction in the World Today," enlarged the scope of Paul A. Wagner's original paper. Frederick B. Davis delivered the paper "The Role of Testing in Reading Instruction," which was based on the two Arthur E. Traxler papers of 1951 and 1958.

Chapter i is the theme paper prepared by Nila Banton Smith especially for this conference. Chapters ii, iii, v, vii, ix, xi, xiii, xv, and xvi are the current versions of the major papers of past conferences. Chapters iv, vi, viii, x, xii, and xiv contain related papers, delivered at sectional meetings, which make concrete application of the major topics to specific grade levels and to corrective and remedial reading instruction. Chapter xvii represents the combined efforts of a number of writers to help administrators, supervisors, and consultants as they face curriculum supervisory problems in reading. In chapter xviii the reader will again find the annual lists of outstanding books published since the previous conference; one for elementary pupils and another for high-school and junior-college students.

Although this proceedings will be the last of this series, other types of publications concerned with research in reading and reading instruction will reflect the thinking and activities of the reading staff at the University of Chicago. We hope that this conference proceedings, picturing the achievements of the past and present, as well as the hopes of the future, will stand in a pivotal position for the seventy-five years of progress to follow.

CHAPTER I

READING: SEVENTY-FIVE YEARS OF PROGRESS

*

NILA BANTON SMITH

*

SINCE THE University of Chicago is celebrating its seventy-fifth anniversary, it is fitting that the theme of this year's reading conference should be "Reading: Seventy-five Years of Progress." This theme is doubly appropriate because of the contributions to reading that the University has made during this period, which have been momentous in volume and inestimable in scope of influence. It is a pleasure, indeed, to discuss this topic in this year that marks the three-quarters-of-a-century milestone of rich educational service that this institution has provided.

READING PROGRESS: 1891 TO 1910

Seventy-five years takes us back to 1891. We will pick up the march of progress in reading at that date and trace it through to 1966. As we roll back the curtain of time to observe the reading scene during the years elapsing between 1891 and 1910, we see a colorful pageant of events and an ever quickening pace of developments.

Perhaps of first importance in this march of progress was the budding of research in reading that occurred in the United States during this pe-

riod (1, 2, 3, 4).* The studies conducted were preponderantly of the laboratory type and were few in number, but they must be recognized as the beginning of an interest which burgeoned during succeeding periods.

Interest in the scientific study of reading began in Europe about the middle of the nineteenth century. Most of the early studies were conducted in France and Germany. A few investigations, however, were made in the United States by Americans who had been stimulated by reports from abroad. By 1910 thirty-four studies had been reported by investigators in England and the United States. Although these studies were not sufficient in number or practical enough in application to have an impact upon classroom instruction, they are historically important because they were firsts in reading research.

Another first in this period was the attention given to reading disability. Men in the medical profession pre-

*This paper is based upon facts presented in the writer's book *American Reading Instruction* (Newark, Del.: International Reading Association, 1965), where interested readers may find a detailed bibliography. A brief bibliography has been provided at the end of this paper, however, and references are made to it throughout by number.

ceded all others in the study of children who had difficulty in learning to read. These men attributed the cause of reading retardation to "congenital alexia" or "word blindness." Many reports on this subject were published between 1900 and 1910.

The first professional book on reading appeared in 1908. The subject had attained sufficient status and content by that time to move one individual to write a book about it. This individual was Edmund Burke Huey, and the title of his book was *The Psychology and Pedagogy of Reading* (4).

As for methods and materials, three developments are worthy of mention. One of these was the development of new phonetic alphabets similar to the Augmented Roman Alphabet of today. The Shearer System, which appeared in 1892, made use of such an alphabet (5), and ten years later the first reader of the Standard Reading Series was printed in another phonetic alphabet, the Scientific Alphabet (6). At first glance, a page in the first reader resembles very closely a page in one of the current books printed in I.T.A., as the Augmented Roman Alphabet is popularly called, except that the former has a few diacritical markings. Neither of these early alphabets was accepted for wide usage. Their development, however, did indicate that even at this time some Americans were striving to invent easier ways of teaching reading.

Two other types of methods and their accompanying materials were developed during this period and used widely throughout the country. One of these was the extremely synthetic and highly organized phonic method, which arose as an answer to criticisms of the word method previously in use. By this method, children spent several weeks working with the sounds of the letters before they began to read. The "family" idea of attaching consonant sounds to common phonograms was also developed at this time. According to this idea, children memorized groups of words such as *ball, call, fall, mall, pall, tall,* and *wall,* and then read readers whose content had been contrived to give practice on these "family" words. Several series of readers based on this method were published and widely used.

Quite the opposite to the synthetic phonic method was the sentence-story method, which was advocated by several educators and which placed heavy emphasis upon literature. This approach was an outgrowth and an expansion of the word method. The essential steps of this method were as follows: first, the teacher told a story or rhyme to the children until they had memorized it or, at least, had become very familiar with it; the selection was then read and analyzed into separate words and phrases; and eventually phonics was applied, although greatly subordinated. The several reading series that were published to implement this plan made use of literature for the most part.

READING PROGRESS: 1910 TO 1925

This was the most exciting period of progress that had ever taken place in reading. It was also the period in which the University of Chicago emerged as an institution of leadership in reading research and in the development of reading as an area of professional specialization.

The dramatic period beginning in 1910 contained the first truly great breakthrough in American reading instruction. This era in the history of reading was marked by the birth of the scientific movement in education. In 1909 Thorndike made the initial presentation of his handwriting scale to a meeting of the American Association for the Advancement of Science, and in 1910 the scale was published. Generally speaking, the publication of the Thorndike scale is recognized as the beginning of the contemporary movement for the scientific measurement of educational products. In the immediately ensuing years, scales and tests appeared rapidly; among these was a reading test — *The Gray Standardized Oral Reading Paragraphs,* devised by William S. Gray at the University of Chicago. This test was published in 1915. Other reading tests, mostly involving silent reading, followed shortly.

With the advent of tests there was an enormous spurt in scientific investigation (3, 4, 8, 9). As previously stated, only thirty-four studies in reading had been reported in the English language up to 1910. From 1910 to 1924, a total of four hundred thirty-six accounts of reading studies were published by investigators in the United States alone.

Although the great preponderance of studies was conducted with the use of the new tests, there were also some very significant laboratory studies.

Foremost among these were several studies conducted by Charles H. Judd and Guy T. Buswell at the University of Chicago and reported in monographs published during the years 1918 to 1922 (10, 11, 12, 13).

The first doctoral dissertations in reading which came to my attention were written at the University of Chicago in 1917: "Studies of Elementary School Reading through Standardized Tests," by William S. Gray; "Types of Reading Ability as Exhibited through Tests and Laboratory Experiments," by C. T. Gray; and "An Experimental Study of the Psychology of Reading," by William Anton Schmidt. Between 1917 and 1924 thirteen additional doctoral dissertations on reading were completed. So it was that a newly emerging and far-reaching educational discipline, namely the scientific study of reading, burst like a bombshell into our slumbers during this short but exciting period.

Remedial reading had a phenomenal development at this time. Interest in it now extended far beyond the medical profession. Beginning about 1910, some psychologists began to concern themselves with reading deficiency, and in the twenties, personnel in the public schools joined in the new movement to help children who were having difficulty in learning to read.

Two outstanding pioneers in developing diagnostic and remedial techniques were William S. Gray and Arthur I. Gates. Both published articles and prepared monographs on this subject in the early twenties. Two of the most notable monographs released by them at this time were Gray's *Remedial Cases in Reading: Their Diagnosis and Treatment* ("Supplemental Educational Monographs," No. 22; Chicago: University of Chicago, 1922); and Gates's *The Psychology of Reading and Spelling: With Special Reference to Disability* ("Contributions to Education," No. 129; New York: Teachers College, Columbia University, 1922). These two giant contributors to reading progress began their important research and writing in this auspicious period and continued to make significant contributions in the many years ahead.

Other innovations introduced during the period were experience charts, individual instruction in reading patterned after the Winnetka and Dalton plans, and the singling out of speed as a reading skill that could be developed through practice.

As for method, the teaching of reading underwent the most drastic change that had ever taken place. From the beginning of reading instruction, oral reading had maintained its supreme and undisputed claim over classroom methods. In marked contrast to the traditional practice, we find a period of years, approximately between 1918 and 1925, in which there was an exaggerated and, in some cases, almost exclusive emphasis upon silent reading procedures. At no time in reading history has a new methodology taken hold so rapidly and been extended so widely.

All of these things happened in the short span of fifteen years. It was a great day when the scientific movement in education began to operate in the field of reading. Even though researchers only scratched the surface during this initial period, it was a momentous epoch in the history of reading. It truly marked our first great breakthrough in the improvement of reading instruction.

READING PROGRESS: 1925 TO 1935

Progress during this next period may be characterized largely as extention and application rather than initiation and innovation. The years between 1925 and 1935 were remarkable in productivity of reading research (7, 8, 9, 14). From July 1, 1924, to June 30, 1935, a total of 654 studies dealing with an extraordinarily wide variety of topics and problems were published, and thirty-five doctoral dissertations in reading were completed.

Throughout these years there were major developments in the diagnosis and remediation of children with reading disabilities. In fact, remedial reading was the chief subject of study during this period. Two new theories were much discussed. Samuel T. Orton associated causes of reading deficiency with left or mixed laterality — handedness, eyedness, and footedness (15). Grace M. Fernald attracted much attention wtih her kinesthetic method, which placed emphasis upon tracing words and letters (16). The terms "reading disability" and "reading deficiency" continued to be used, especially in psychological studies. "Remedial reading," however, came into more general use in connection with reading improvement in schools.

The outstanding innovation of this period was the application of the reading readiness concept. In 1926 the International Kindergarten Union, in co operation with the U.S. Bureau of Education, conducted an investigation of pupils' readiness for reading instruction in first grade (17). This study brought reading readiness problems sharply to the attention of teachers in widespread areas.

It was in 1927 that Mary Maud Reed's research revealed the startling data that one in every six children failed at the end of the first semester in first grade and that one in every eight failed at the end of the second semester in first grade (18). Educators everywhere began to see the need for preparing children to learn to read. The fire once kindled soon became a conflagration that finally enveloped the vast majority of public schools in the country.

The program for teaching reading became much broader during this period than at any time in the past. Part I of the Twenty-fourth Yearbook of the National Society for the Study of Education recommended new and broad objectives in reading (19). The increasingly rapid flow of research revealed new skills, interests, and needs, with the result that the new programs came to encompass both oral and silent reading, both literary and factual material, and much more detailed and explicit plans for teaching skills than formerly.

There was, however, a division in the philosophy of teaching reading during this period. One group believed that children should be given carefully planned sequential practice in skills. These educators continued to use basic readers. The readers no longer placed major emphasis on silent reading, however, but embodied the broader objectives mentioned above.

The other group was convinced that learning took place best when the child was permitted to arrive at and carry out his own purposes — meeting and solving attendant problems within the context of his own experiences and needs. This teaching philosophy was given application under the general title "the activity program." In such programs the children worked freely and spontaneously and actively, following their own interests; and the teachers were intrigued with the new "game" of trying to get all of their subject matter across through "units of work."

The activity program continued into the next period of history. At present we hear no more about teaching reading according to this plan. The short-lived application of the philosophy behind this method, however, had its good effects. The activity program was first to bring quantities of library and reference books into the classroom. It was first to use co-operatively prepared materials other than experience charts. And it was first to point out the practical possibilities of teaching reading in the content areas.

One other mark of progress that occurred during this period should be mentioned. The practice of appointing general elementary supervisors increased rapidly between 1920 to 1928. And by 1930, Detroit and a few other large cities had taken an additional step. They had replaced their general supervisors with special supervisors in each of the basic school subjects — arithmetic, language, spelling, and reading. Thus it was at this point that the special supervisor of reading entered the scene in American schools.

READING PROGRESS: 1935 TO 1950

The entire period from 1935 to 1950 was marked by national and international unrest eventuating in and including another war. Probably the most obvious effect of these circumstances on reading instruction was a reduction in output of research and instructional materials (7, 8, 9, 14, 20). Whereas published research had previously numbered over one hundred reports per year, during the war year 1943–44 only fifty-four appeared. Recovery in numbers was not achieved until the fifties. The number of doctoral dissertations completed was also drastically reduced during this period.

The number of new series of basal readers published between 1935 and 1950 decreased sharply. Whereas sixteen basal series had been listed as new in the preceding period, only four series were published before the war, and during the last two years of the forties two more got under way by publishing their primary programs.

The content of basal reading series did not change drastically. Even in this distressing period, however, there were some evidences of progress. The world-wide tension that was felt at this time caused a few forward-looking educators to start fresh views on the uses of reading in our complex society.

These people set up a new aim for teaching reading — the equipment of individuals with skills they need to live effectually in a world seething with problems. The social effects and uses of reading became matters of concern and were reflected in articles in periodicals and increasing numbers of studies. These emerging and significant viewpoints and concerns about reading were direct outgrowths of social and political stresses.

Interest in reading disability increased rapidly. The multiple-causation theory was developed; informal diagnosis was used for the first time; mechanical aids to reading appeared; and there was the beginning of a trend toward the development of clinics in public school systems.

Advances in method included utilization of the interrelationships of reading and the other language arts, the addition of context clues and structural analysis in word attack, and the extension of comprehension and work-study skills.

Developments in reading supervision also took place. During this period a number of school systems appointed a special person for supervisory service in reading, and the term "reading consultant" made its initial appearance in educational literature. And so reading, in its buoyancy, continued to give evidence of progress even in a period of international conflict.

READING PROGRESS: 1950 TO 1966

In pursuing the progress of reading through three-quarters of a century, we have at last arrived at the era in which we are now living — a stimulating but terror-filled era in human existence, an era of unparalleled activity and unprecedented change.

The vast accumulation of knowledge and the technological revolution have brought problems to our civilization. Other problems have arisen from threats to our democratic way of life from competing nations who would establish world communism. Arising from the recognition of these problems are governmental plans for improving the social and economic lives of our people. The key solution proposed for implementing these plans is education, and since education cannot proceed without reading, there is a compelling motive to increase literacy. Liberal funds are being made available by the government to finance reading research, to buy more reading materials, to equip remedial reading centers, to establish institutes for those wishing to improve their teaching of reading, and to provide fellowships for those wishing to specialize in reading.

Never in the history of our country has reading been the subject of such high interest. Never have opportunities to learn to read been extended to so many individuals at all age levels, in school and out. Truly, reading instruction has grown to entirely new dimensions in the enlarged and important role it has to play in achieving national goals. Without a doubt, the national recognition and support given reading instruction by the government constitute the most salutary and conspicuous mark of progress in the history of American reading instruction.

As a result of these stimulating influences, authors of basal reading series are enlarging their programs with multiple-texts and other methods reflecting the most recent research and trends. Many new approaches to beginning reading are being published. New reading materials are being prepared for teaching those who are illiterate or functionally illiterate. Interest in reading disability is expanding, and increased use is being made of contributions from other disciplines. The demand for well-trained reading specialists is greater than the supply. Several states are now setting up special reading requirements for pre-service and post-service preparation, and several others require certification for reading specialists. Research, the common denominator of *all* progress in reading, is now at an unprecedented high in both quantity and quality (7, 9, 20, 21, 22, 23, 24).

READING PROGRESS IN THE FUTURE

It is not difficult to describe reading progress in the past. The fact that we have records printed in word symbols and that we are able to read these symbols makes it possible for us to review the past whenever we desire. The future is different, of course, since no records have been written and pathways are uncharted. In spite of these handicaps I shall venture a few forecasts.

Undoubtedly, audiovisual materials will play a major role in the teaching of reading in the future — particularly such automated devices as television, films, recorders, computers, and others yet to be invented.

There are some who say that practically all learning in the future will take place through the use of programed material administered by computers. Much experimentation in the teaching of reading by computer is now under way. Computers can, no doubt, be helpful in establishing certain elements of skill that require practice. But to teach other essential processes of reading, such as getting meanings from word symbols arranged in sentences, interpretation, critical reading, and appreciation, which do not lend themselves to predetermined answers, oral dialogue, mental interaction, and exchange of thoughts are required. The teacher will always be essential in teaching the kind of reading skills that will be necessary in our future civilization.

Provisions for meeting individual needs will receive a significant emphasis in the teaching of reading. There will be drastic advances in the preparation of instructional materials that show greater ingenuity and adaptability in coping with individual differences. Since children have different styles of learning, we will find ways of ascertaining these styles early in a child's reading life and in using the materials appropriate to each style.

Teachers will be much better prepared to teach reading, and each class or group will have available several teachers with different special talents that may be called into use. Designs for more flexible scheduling will permit better time distribution to accommodate the gifted readers, the

ordinary readers, and those requiring corrective or remedial instruction.

Clinics will be established in connection with practically all public schools. In college clinics, the facilities will be used largely for research and teacher preparation rather than as a service station for improving the reading of individual students, as is so often the case at present.

There are other possibilities for the future that could be discussed. Within the limits of this paper, however, I will mention only one more — the potential of reading research. We have made tremendous strides in investigation during the last half-century, but perhaps we have only scratched the surface of topics to study and experimental techniques to develop. We shall need fresh, piercing insights to ascertain hitherto unexplored areas for research; we shall need unique experimental designs and new statistical techniques; and withal, we shall need great ingenuity to shape reading methods and materials in the image of our findings.

Such unprecedented progress has been made during the past seventy-five years that we may wonder whether there could ever be another period so productive of reading advancement. There still are many new worlds to conquer, however, and many new contributions to make in this fascinating field. May each of us who is living in the present thrilling age of reading contribute his share to the quickening pace of progress.

REFERENCES CITED

*

1. William S. Gray, *Summary of Investigations Relating to Reading* ("Supplementary Educational Monographs," No. 28; Chicago: University of Chicago Press, 1925).
2. Walter F. Dearborn, "The Psychology of Reading," *Archives of Philosophy, Psychology and Scientific Methods*, I, No. 4 (March, 1906).
3. Walter F. Dearborn, "Professor Cattell's Studies of Reading and Perception," *Archives of Psychology*, IV, No. 30 (April, 1914).
4. Edmund Burke Huey, *The Psychology and Pedagogy of Reading* (New York: Macmillan Co., 1908 [revised 1912, 1915]).
5. James W. Shearer, *Combination Speller* (St. Louis, 1894).
6. Isaac Kaufman Funk and Mose I. Montrose, *Standard Reading Series, First Reader* (New York: Funk & Wagnall's Co., 1902).
7. William S. Gray, "Summary of Investigations Relating to Reading," *Elementary School Journal* (1925–32); and *Journal of Educational Research* (1933–60).
8. U. S. Library of Congress, Catalog Division, *American Doctoral Dissertations* (Washington, D. C.: Government Printing Office, 1913–40).
9. Carter V. Good, Mary Louise Lyda, Glenn Jenson, Stanley Brown, Harold Anderson, Joseph Mapes, Stanley Elam, and others, *Research Studies in Education* (Bloomington, Ind.: Phi Delta Kappa, Inc., 1923–65).
10. Charles H. Judd, *Reading: Its Nature and Development* ("Supplemental Educational Monographs," No. 10; Chicago: University of Chicago Press, 1922).
11. Charles H. Judd and Guy T. Buswell, *Silent Reading: A Study of the Various Types* ("Supplemental Educational Monographs," No. 23; Chicago: University of Chicago Press, 1922).
12. Guy T. Buswell, *An Experimental Study of the Eye-Voice Span in Reading* ("Supplemental Educational Monographs," No. 17; Chicago: University of Chicago Press, 1920).
13. Guy T. Buswell, *Fundamental Reading Habits: A Study of Their Development* ("Supplemental Educational Monographs," No. 21; Chicago: University of Chicago Press, 1922).
14. Emmett Albert Betts and Thelma Marshall Betts, *An Index to Professional Literature on Reading and Related Topics* (New York: American Book Co., 1945).
15. Samuel T. Orton, "Specific Reading Disability — Strephosymbolia," *Journal of American Medical Association*, XC (April 7, 1928), 1095–99.
16. Grace M. Fernald, *Remedial Techniques in Basic School Subjects* (New York: McGraw-Hill Book Co., 1943).
17. *Pupils' Readiness for Reading Instruction upon Entrance to First Grade* (City School Leaflet No. 23; Washington, D. C.: Bureau of Education, U. S. Department of the Interior, 1926).
18. Mary Maud Reed, *An Investigation of Practices in First Grade Admission and Promotion* (New York: Teachers College, Columbia University, 1927).
19. *Report of the National Committee on Reading*, The Twenty-fourth Yearbook of the National Society for the

Study of Education, Part I (Bloomington, Ill.: Public School Publishing
Co., 1925).

20. Dissertation Abstracts (Ann Arbor:
University Microfilms, 1938–65).

21. Helen M. Robinson, "Summary of
Investigations relating to Reading,"
Journal of Educational Research, LIV
(February, 1961).

22. Helen M. Robinson, "Summary of
Investigations relating to Reading,"
Reading Teacher, XV, XVI, XVII
(January, 1962; January, 1963; Febru-
ary, 1964).

23. Helen M. Robinson, Samuel Wein-
traub, and Carol A. Hostetter, "Summary of Investigations relating to
Reading, July 1, 1963, to June 30,
1964," *Reading Teacher*, XVIII (February, 1965), 331–428.

24. Helen M. Robinson, Samuel Wein-
traub, and Helen K. Smith, "Summary of Investigations relating to
Reading," *Reading Research Quarterly*, I (Winter, 1966).

25. Theodore L. Harris, "Summary of
Investigations Relating to Reading,"
Journal of Educational Research, LV,
LVI, LVII, LVIII (February, 1962
through 1965).

26. Theodore L. Harris, Wayne Otto,
and Thomas C. Barrett, "Summary
and Review of Investigations relating
to Reading, July 1, 1964, to June 30,
1965," *Journal of Educational Research*, LIX (February, 1966), 243–68.

CHAPTER II

CHARACTERISTICS OF SUCCESSFUL TEACHING OF READING

*

ARTHUR I. GATES

*

S EVENTEEN YEARS ago at the annual reading conference I presented a paper on the topic "Characteristics of Successful Teaching of Reading." When I was asked to prepare a paper this year, I decided that it was perhaps high time for me to make some assured predictions about the future of teaching reading. After I had sent in a topic, "Reading: In the Years Ahead," I recalled an anecdote that made me change my mind. A pastor observed that an elderly female member of his congregation bowed reverently every time he mentioned Satan. Becoming a little disturbed, the minister finally asked the woman why she engaged in such strange behavior. "Well," the lady said, "it doesn't cost me anything to be polite, and when you reach my age, you realize you can't be too sure what will happen to you in the future." This explains my decision to write about characteristics of good teaching of reading *now*, to contrast the situation today with conditions in a past that I know rather than a future that I can only speculate about.

In the second paragraph of my 1949 paper, I said,

The youngster who finds the general school activities satisfying and who finds himself accepted and respected as an individual has already half learned to read. If the school provides a program which maintains and increases his zest and provides satisfactory equipment and opportunity for doing constructive work, most children will do their part in the process of learning to read.

In the fourth paragraph, I went on to say,

Searching studies of reading retardation and reading disability supply substantial evidence that, generally speaking, children coming from homes and neighborhoods in which reading activities are engaged in and are respected and rewarded tend to become successful readers, but children coming from homes and neighborhoods in which reading plays little or no role and is not well understood or approved tend to become retarded readers.[1]

Since that time many changes have occurred which seem to increase the importance of these views. Investigations by Benjamin S. Bloom[2] and

[1] Gates, "Characteristics of Successful Reading," in *Classroom Techniques in Improving Reading*, compiled and edited by William S. Gray ("Supplementary Educational Monographs," No. 69; Chicago: University of Chicago Press, 1949), p. 8.

[2] Bloom, *Stability and Change in Human Characteristics* (New York: John Wiley & Sons, Inc., 1964).

others have revealed that a slum environment during a child's first six years of life produces mental attitudes and inadequacies which are much more difficult to manage than we had previously assumed. Certain new developments, such as the prodigious growth of television programs for children, seem to increase the resistance of some children to reading even as they attract others. Other factors appear to have enlarged the range of differences among children. Thus the underprivileged child, on entering the first grade in 1940, found fewer than one classmate in five who had attended kindergarten, but today he finds a majority equipped with the advantage of school skills and sophistication that one or more years in kindergarten provide. The six-year-old of today who has enjoyed the advantages of both a good home and a good school life is vastly superior to the child who has had neither. These facts suggest that certain steps be taken as soon as possible.

The first and most obvious step is to get the school and the home together while a child is still very young. Before a child reaches his first birthday, he is beginning to learn to read spoken words. He is learning to distinguish word sounds; he is developing a hearing vocabulary; he is beginning to understand phrases, sentences, and paragraphs; he is starting to use "context clues" and to initiate all the other skills required to read printed words. Reading spoken words and reading printed words are basically the same: they involve substantially the same skills, as I tried to

explain in an article published forty years ago.[3] Reading is largely learned at mother's knee during these early years, which the late Leta Hollingworth called the "Golden Age of the Intellect." Children who have been deprived of minimal home care and learning opportunities during these years suffer limitations which the school at present simply cannot overcome. The home and school must combine forces much earlier. The steps thus far taken by governmental and other agencies are fine but feeble.

The critical nature of the early years should indicate to us the urgent need for making a comprehensive case study of each child at the age of three or four at the latest and then annually for several years. We now have the equipment to make a detailed appraisal of a child's intellectual and behavioral equipment — his readiness to learn to read and acquire other school abilities and his social and emotional makeup — with a degree of validity that rivals the physician's examination. Indeed, a thorough annual educational and psychological case study is as fully needed as a comprehensive annual medical appraisal. It could be a major means of rescuing underprivileged children from educational oblivion and of increasing the educational interests and abilities of all others, even — indeed, especially — the most gifted. In terms of the degree to which it could increase the national level of human competence, it could

[3] Gates, "Methods and Theories of Teaching Reading Tested by Studies of Deaf Children," *Journal of Educational Research*, XIV (June, 1926), 21–32.

be one of the most profitable investments our society could make.

A little book entitled *Elementary Principles of Education*, written by the late E. L. Thorndike and myself,[4] thirty-seven years ago, stated the conviction that a good teacher's time is so precious that he should never be required to do anything which could be done by a few pieces of paper or apparatus, or by a less expert helper, so that his time could be conserved for doing what only he could do. The great increases in school enrollment and in scientific insight and achievement since that time make this policy doubly pertinent today. Indeed, a major conviction of my professional lifetime has been that the teacher is the supremely important factor in the life of the school. And for this reason I shall devote the remainder of this paper mainly to the role which a teacher can and should begin to play.

ROLES OF THE TEACHER

Several speakers and writers have in recent years given the impression that the school of the future will be controlled by computers rather than teachers, by electronic and mechanical apparatus rather than the teacher's voice and actions, by Programing with a capital *P* rather than a teacher's guidance and instruction. I believe that exactly the opposite is the goal to which both scientific research and practical experience of the past half-century direct us. The recent advances in technology should not be regarded as a threat to the teacher's importance

[4] New York: Macmillan Co., 1929.

but, on the contrary, as a promise to make his services far more fruitful.

As our schools begin to take advantage of the advances of technology, teachers should acquire new and more subtle competences. For example, I would recommend that in the near future every teacher in the elementary school, especially in the first three grades, be required to demonstrate the ability to make a comprehensive case study of each child's equipment for learning to read and of those social and emotional characteristics which exert an influence upon his learning. My recommendation is based on several facts. The first is that I have seen many teachers transformed from routine operators to insightful artists by a program of instruction designed for specialists in reading and certain psychological services. I have been told by hundreds of teachers that nothing in their training program compared in fruitfulness with several months devoted to internship in individual case-study work and individual instruction. To ask a teacher without such experience to diagnose and prescribe for a poorly equipped first-grader who is likely to encounter trouble in reading is like asking a physician without experience in treating individual patients to diagnose and treat a subtle disease. What is now done by a reading specialist so late that it requires remedial instruction should be done at the first sign of difficulty by the classroom teacher.

The teacher should learn to teach by insight rather than by rule of thumb. He should be an engineer rather than a mechanic, an artist rather than a draftsman, a physician rather than a technician. It is one thing, for example, to administer a series of diagnostic tests, get the objective scores in terms of age or grade status, count the errors, and note their significance in terms of a standard table and quite another to picture the pattern of the pupil's difficulties as a whole and understand what it means in terms of instruction needs. A good teacher of reading needs to know clearly what interests, skills, and insights are involved in successful reading, in inferior reading, and in all the intervening stages. He should know the reading processes in general and be able to discern them clearly in the activities of a particular child.

Although some children learn to read with little or no guidance, most children need a great deal of individual attention. Indeed, reading is one of those subtle skills that ought to be taught individually. It is similar to learning to sing or play the violin or to acquiring other complex skills in which the activities of the vital mechanisms are not visible to the naked eye. It is relatively easy to see how a child manipulates the pencil or the typewriter or executes a dance step, but in reading, the corresponding skills are hidden beneath the surface, and they are, I believe, much more complicated and subject to more bewildering entanglements and blockings. The reading teacher should be able to provide extensive individual guidance.

This is the great secret of remedial work. The mere fact that the remedial teacher can work with a child face to face, see his difficulties and successes, note his pulses of elation and despair, and give him suggestions at the time they are most needed accounts in large measure for the success of such work. Moreover, the undivided attention itself often causes a child's misgivings and emotional blockings to give way to new confidence and more active attention. So potent is face-to-face remedial work that it usually produces remarkable improvement both in reading ability and in personal adjustment, even when the particular materials and methods are extremely poor as they sometimes are. The past half-century has firmly established the fact that skillful individual tutoring is a most effective form of psychotherapy. Indeed, this fact has been so amply demonstrated that failure to provide skillful diagnosis and individual instruction is now, in our present days of affluence, quite inexcusable.

Learning to read is conditioned by many influences independent of particular materials and procedures. The teacher's success in teaching reading depends upon his ability to provide in his classroom the most fruitful psychological atmosphere. In recent years there has been a widespread call for teachers to get tough. We are urged to cut out the soft and superficial and get down to hard drill and serious work. This admonition has been given despite the fact that a half-century of work in developmental, social, and clinical psychology, as well as in remedial reading, indicates that the situation in which learning flourishes is one in which there is an obvious spirit of friendliness and respect between teacher and pupils and in which learning activity is desired and satisfying — not forced and feared. The teacher's ideal role may be characterized as a leader of a team rather than as a boss sergeant. The teacher must avoid, as he would the plague, any activity or comment which could be interpreted as an assault on the child's self-respect or confidence. The certain response to attack is counterattack.

The best attitude is not one of saccharin sweetness, which a child will immediately recognize as fraudulent and essentially a move for domination. And it certainly is not the laissez faire attitude so frequently confused with the democratic. (The assumption that the pupil will solve his troubles or guide his own learning into the most fruitful channels if the teacher merely leaves him to his own devices is a false one.) Instead, the teacher should show a genuine personal interest but avoid the type of overanxiety which parents so often reveal. Children quickly discover anxiety and become all the more tense themselves.

The most successful teachers of reading I have known are persons who have developed a sensitivity to emotional blockings and a skill in removing or reducing them. Serious emotional blockings develop more commonly in the initial stages of learning to read than in any other subject or at any other time. In the minds of parents and neighbors the crucial test of success in school is whether a child learns to read. If he does, all is well. If he does not, he must be a spoiled brat or a dunce. If a child has difficulty in reading, his parents are likely to become distressed. Learning to read then becomes one of life's greatest trials, since it comes at a time when the child is inexperienced in meeting such exigencies. Young children do not learn best in an atmosphere of tension but in the spirit of lively play.

The successful teacher recognizes the symptoms of typical forms of distress and is skilful in trying to alleviate them. Many cases of failure to learn to read are psychological "escape mechanisms." They are a protest against being pushed out of infancy. They are an appeal from every fiber of a child's being to be taken out of school and put back into the bosom of a sympathetic family. This is merely one of many quite natural reactions that parents often misunderstand and mistreat. It is one of many that the successful teacher understands and handles with the firm, but gentle, hand of an artist.

For this reason I should like to recommend to those of you who wish to become better teachers that you take the time and trouble to familiarize yourself with some of the insights and procedures of modern psychotherapy, as well as with the techniques and understandings needed to make a comprehensive case study of educational abilities and limitations. I consider the insights and arts emerging from certain phases of modern psychotherapy to be indispensable features of the equipment of the reading specialist; and since prevention is more important than cure, these insights and arts should now be regarded as indispensable parts of the equipment of the classroom teacher.

MATERIALS AND METHODS

In general, the past quarter-century has established the validity of certain theories and principles, but it has not proved the relative merits of many specific professional products and practices which are now available or likely to appear in the near future. For example, the possibility of detailed programing, with or without teaching machines, recognized long ago by Thorndike, Pressey, and others, is now widely accepted in theory; but we do not as yet have a number of programed outfits of demonstrated value for everyday schoolroom use. We are still in the experimental stage. The next decade should produce new programs, procedures, devices, and apparatus which are far in advance of anything now available.

At this point I must report with regret that certain recent events have produced a good deal of confusion about reading "methods" in the narrower sense. For several years we have witnessed a series of noisy campaigns to promote particular procedures, such as one or another of a dozen phonic schemes, or of several augmented alphabets, or of machines and types of "individualized" or "experience" approaches. Many of these are in important ways quite new; many are somewhat new adaptations of old practices or principles; and a large number are revivals of old materials and methods with little or no change. A half-century of scientific study and professional experience justifies treating with critical suspicion any method or device which either in practical form or in principle has been tried and found wanting as an all-purpose remedy during years of practical school use in the past. For example, as mentioned in chapter i by Nila B. Smith, many phonic schemes and several types of extended alphabets were used for decades in American schools without receiving anything like sustained widespread approval. Old devices and methods, however, deserve new trials for the reason that some of them may be better suited to the school and home conditions of today than those of yesterday. New materials, apparatus, and procedures need to be tried out thoroughly by reliable experimental studies in the many different school settings and for the many different types of children we encounter today. I believe that teachers would be wise to assume that the relative merits of the many materials and methods now available are not known even for the majority of pupils or classrooms or teachers and that much greater uncertainty exists concerning their value for use with a particular child in a particular classroom by you, a particular teacher. Lest this statement chill you with discouragement, let me hasten to say that the immediate future promises to produce more and better new materials, methods, and insights and more rapid and thorough practical tryouts than have ever before been possible. It is for this reason that, instead of trying to tell you today which of the available methods and materials to adopt, I shall merely attempt to give you a few tips on ways to find out for yourselves in the future.

Let me begin by warning you that if any comparative study — such as a conventional "control group" experiment — of the past, present, or future shows that method A produces better *average* results than B, you should not be misled into concluding that A is better for every pupil and that B is useful for very few or none. An examination of the results of such studies invariably reveals the dominating role of individual difference. The upshot of a half-century of diagnostic and remedial work is that any device which is of great value for certain children is typically mediocre or futile and frustrating for others. A method which is best even for a large majority of a class may be unsuitable for the rest. For example, in my first years in the field, I studied a number of children who had learned at an early age to read words very well by their own form of visual analysis. To have forced one of these youngsters to stop and learn a phonic system might have killed the little psychological goose that was then ready to lay a golden educational egg. I suggest, therefore, that you learn how to use a representative array of the different materials and devices now available so that you may try them out to find when and for what type of child each will prove to be especially serviceable. I regret that we have not as yet developed many tests or short experimental practice-period outfits to reveal objectively to the teacher which of several approaches to learning word recognition in grade one, for example, or to acquiring flexibility in varying the speed and type of comprehension in grade four is best suited to each child. But I am certain that helpful devices of these types will soon appear. Meanwhile, if you will adopt an experimental attitude, you can do this very well for yourselves with informal individual teaching sessions.

I hope that as you observe the reports of future research you will remember that, even when the "experimental method" surpasses the "control" method by a wide margin, the way in which the experimental procedure confused and confounded Johnny and Fred and Mary and Peter is concealed in the mass scores, however high the reliability of the averages may be. A study made by the psychologist Robert Rosenthal has an important bearing on this point.[5] Rosenthal arranged into two groups rats that were of equivalent ability in running certain types of mazes. One group of rats he described as a batch of "rat geniuses," the other as a bunch of "stupid rats." Two groups of laboratory assistants then undertook to teach the two groups of rats to run an identical maze by identical methods. What would you guess happened? You are quite right. The rats described as "geniuses" learned noticeably better than the equivalent rats which had been called "stupid."

[5] Robert Rosenthal and Kermit L. Fode, "The Effect of Experimenter Bias on the Performance of the Albino Rat," *Behavioral Science*, VIII (July, 1963), 183–89.

This little study literally shouts one significant implication, namely, that the different outcomes seem to be the result of something these "teachers" did differently despite the fact that they were trying to teach in exactly the same way. This study proclaims that the role of the teacher is overwhelmingly important even when the pupils are rats utterly blind to most of the things, such as the meanings of spoken words, that teachers habitually use.

This study also illustrates a serious limitation to which the typical control-group method widely used in education is subject. It justifies the conviction that most of the control-group studies of reading methods, especially those made during recent years of turmoil and tempest, have yielded results that are unreliable and often misleading. So-called experiments or demonstrations of methods or materials which have been given great publicity are the least dependable. They are loaded dice. Only very extensive studies —including comparisons of many procedures — carried out for many years in many neutral schools by neutral teachers who are supervised by genuinely competent and neutral investigators will reveal reliably the relative merits of various programs. And this is not the only limitation of control-group experiments.

At a recent conference on educational research, a group of leading American research workers in the behavioral sciences — psychology, sociology, anthropology, education, and so on — agreed upon one far-reaching principal. It was stated as follows: "Seldom, if ever, do differences in learning correspond to variation in a *single* variable." [6] A child's reading interests and abilities depend upon a host of factors which are operating in every reading program — indeed, in every reading period. They are obscured and uncontrolled in the typical control-group study. Not only does the value of a particular device or procedure depend upon the makeup of the child, it also depends on the nature of all the other factors that the device is combined with to make up a particular program of teaching reading. Of these the most important factor is the skill and insight of the teacher himself. One teacher can guide a pupil through an exercise in word analysis in a way that makes it sparkle with the excitement of discovery, whereas another, equally good all-round instructor, may let it become a bewildering bore.

CONCLUDING STATEMENT

I am sure that the future will bring us a host of devices to relieve the burden and increase the effectiveness of teaching many troublesome skills and insights in every school subject and activity, and I am confident that this will enlarge the teacher's opportunity to function at a more expert and subtle level. We must not forget that at no level are the differences in techniques and insights more striking and significant than among the most expert artists — the half-dozen top baseball

6 Guy T. Buswell and T. R. McConnell, *Training for Educational Research* (Cooperative Research Project, No. 51074; Berkeley, Calif.: University of California, 1966), p. 1 (italics added).

players, or portrait painters, or opera singers, or pianists. And, likewise, the more skilful teachers become, the more subtly they will differ in their techniques. Never before has the tide of opportunity for improving the art of the teacher been advancing so strongly. I suggest you all leap in and swim gaily and vigorously with it. I am sure you will emerge on a sunnier professional scene than any you have ever known.

CHAPTER III

THE MAJOR ASPECTS OF READING

*

HELEN M. ROBINSON

*

IT IS WITH extreme humility that this writer will attempt to add to the ideas of William S. Gray, as expressed in his paper for the annual reading conference of 1960, by extracting the contributions of the last six years.[1] The primary reason for reluctance is that Gray developed his model over a period of thirty or more years, during which the writer saw it many times in evolving forms. A second reason is that research and practice of a half-century were incorporated into the earlier paper, whereas only six years have contributed to the changes that will be discussed in the present one. The courage to attempt this paper arises from Gray's frequent revisions of his model and his insistence that a conceptual framework for reading must be fluid and continuously refined. Of special interest is the fact that prior to the publication of Gray's paper, few had written on the aspects of reading. Since that time many writers have attempted to set forth their own notions of reading and of the particular levels or parts of the reading process.

Before exploring this topic in greater detail, it will be useful to ask why a model of aspects of reading is likely to be useful. Albert J. Kingston has said that models are a way of ordering observations to permit the understanding of "underlying relationships between the various components of the phenomena."[2] Models tend to order and simplify knowledge so that both research and instruction can proceed in a more orderly fashion. Furthermore, he points out, models help to delineate what is scientifically known. He states that "it often is difficult to distinguish what we really 'know' from what we 'infer' or 'believe.'"[3] No statement could better characterize so-called knowledge about reading. This mixture of knowledge, inference, and conviction has led to confusion, sharp differences, and debates.

Those who have studied reading or have attempted to teach reading readily agree that it is a complex process. Some identify reading as a "thought

[1] Gray, "The Major Aspects of Reading," in *Sequential Development of Reading Abilities,* compiled and edited by Helen M. Robinson ("Supplementary Educational Monographs," No. 90; Chicago; University of Chicago Press, 1960), pp. 8–24.

[2] Kingston, "Introduction," to *The Use of Theoretical Models in Research*, edited by Brother Leonard Courtney, F.S.C. ("Highlights of the Pre-Convention Institutes," No. V; Newark, Del.: International Reading Association, 1966), p. 4.

[3] *Ibid.,* p. 3.

process," which helps little because thought is equally complex and obscure. Kingston has suggested a possible solution "in the methods of the logical empiricists and in the use of operational definitions. . . ."[4] He indicates that this approach would provide a theoretical framework "in which the components of reading could be treated separately."[5] And this is the precise reason why Gray developed a model of the aspects of reading.

Among approximately a dozen models of reading or some parts of reading, the writer found sharp differences which appeared to defy efforts at reconciliation. Finally it became clear that the confusion resulted from failure to differentiate among (1) the processes required for reading, (2) the skills and abilities used in reading, and (3) the procedures used to teach reading. All three are important and undoubtedly are interrelated. The topic of this paper, however, dictates an operational definition which includes identification of the skills and abilities. Consequently, models of the reading process and of procedures for teaching reading have been omitted. The teacher or administrator who questions the practicality of such an attempt to refine models might be reminded that almost all curricular and instructional decisions are based on some implicit or explicit perception of the components of reading.

In the first part of the paper, views on the broad aspects of reading are examined. In the second part, models of the parts of reading are explored. Finally, an attempt is made to identify the aspects of reading presently recognized.

ASPECTS OF READING

Gray classified the understandings, attitudes, and skills common to reading behavior into four major categories. Recognizing the unity of "the reading act," he cautioned that, although each would be discussed separately, "they are closely interrelated and form a psychologically coherent unit."[6] Gray referred to these four components as word perception, comprehension, reaction to what is read, and assimilation of the new ideas with previous knowledge. He prepared Diagram I to illustrate the relation of the four aspects.[7] The center, called "word perception," includes both the identification of the word and the understanding of its meaning. This aspect of reading is located in the center because without word perception, the other aspects cannot function.

The first surrounding band represents comprehension. According to Gray, comprehension includes, first, the literal meaning, that is, understanding what the author has said; and second, the implied meanings, that is, understanding what the author meant by the word sequences he used. The third aspect of comprehension is concerned with the significance of the communication, including an assessment of the author's purpose, frame of

4 Kingston, "A Conceptual Model of Reading Comprehension," in *Phases of College and Other Adult Reading Programs*, Tenth Yearbook of the National Reading Conference, edited by Emery P. Bliesmer and Albert J. Kingston, Jr. (Milwaukee, Wis.: Marquette University, 1961), p. 103.
5 *Ibid.*
6 Gray, *op. cit.*, p. 8.
7 *Ibid.*, p. 10.

DIAGRAM I
MAJOR COMPONENTS OF READING

DIAGRAM VIII
READING FOR DIFFERENT PURPOSES
AND IN VARIOUS FIELDS

reference, assumptions, and generalizations. Gray summarized these three facets as the "ability to read the lines, to read between the lines, and to read beyond the lines." [8]

The second surrounding band, identified as "reaction," requires the exercise of sound judgment in evaluating what is comprehended. After explaining the skills and abilities required, Gray referred to this band essentially as critical reading or the "acceptance or rejection" of the message.

The outer band, named "assimilation" or "fusion of ideas," represents the integration of information secured through reading with all previous related experience. As new information is processed, wrong concepts are corrected and new insights, broader interests, and rational attitudes are acquired.

In the elaborate diagrams explaining each of the four major aspects of reading, Gray categorized all of the skills, abilities, and attitudes which he considered important to reading. Moreover, he attempted to describe how and when they operated, although this phase of his analysis was incomplete. In Diagram VII of the original article, he attempted to unify and relate the four major aspects of reading and to show their interaction as an intellectual process. His last representation, Diagram VIII, shows the way in which the four aspects of reading are involved in various proportions in reading for content and in reading for other purposes.[9] The application of his model was not detailed at the time

the paper was completed, and he had not yet begun to separate the processes, or factors underlying various aspects, from his operational definition.

Gray's model of the aspects of reading is a way of ordering a mass of skills and abilities that have already been named and described. But according to Elizabeth S. Maccia, "The theory model must be tried out." [10] One way to try out the model is to administer tests of each of the skills and abilities and to determine statistically whether they are dependent or independent and, further, whether they group themselves as the model suggests. Unfortunately, such a procedure is not possible at present since tests for only a few of these skills and abilities have been constructed.

There has been an investigation, however, that adds some plausibility to Gray's model. Mildred C. Letton asked ninth-grade students to verbalize the thought which occurred to them during the reading of a poem. Immediately after the reading she asked the students some questions. A second interview was conducted two weeks later to find out whether the poem had influenced behavior. All responses of the twenty-two subjects were then classified with no a priori system imposed. The elements identified were found to be "consistent with those included in the comprehensive description" by Gray.[11] Additional in-

8 *Ibid.*, p. 17.

9 *Ibid.*, p. 23.

10 Maccia, "The Model in Theorizing and Research," in *The Use of Theoretical Models in Research*, edited by Brother Leonard Courtney, F.S.C., (Highlights of the Pre-Convention Institutes," No. V; Newark, Del.: International Reading Association, 1966), p. 13.

11 Letton, "Individual Differences in In-

vestigations at different grade levels and with other types of materials are needed to test this model.

SUBSTRATA FACTORS

Jack A. Holmes and his associates have carried on a series of studies to determine the skills and abilities which contribute to reading competence. In an early study using college students, Holmes described reading as reasoning and made the assumption that "power of reading" and "speed of reading" could adequately explain the act of reading.[12] "Power of reading" was defined as "the 'power' to *read, comprehend*, and *apply* relatively difficult college textbook material."[13] "Speed of reading" was used "to denote the rate of comprehension of relatively easy material" and was assessed on a speed of reading test.[14] Basing his conclusions upon the previous literature, Holmes identified factors believed to contribute to competence in these two criterion variables; subsequently, he selected or constructed tests that he believed would measure each of the factors. Using his adaptation of the Wherry-Doolittle statistical technique, he calculated the relative contribution of each factor he had selected to the two criteria. Then he used each of these first-order predictors to calculate the magnitude of the contribution of

other factors. Thus he proposed an explanation for reading, based on his statistical model, which included thirteen variables.

In subsequent studies at the high-school level and in fourth grade, Holmes and Harry Singer further developed this model as a means of explaining the reading process at all levels of maturity, or at least, from fourth grade to college. Although their model is designed to explain the process of reading, which is described by Singer as "an audio-visual processing skill of symbolic reasoning,"[15] Singer has stated that the information measured "has been acquired from instruction and learning in such broadly defined areas of reading as word recognition, word meaning, and reasoning-in-context."[16] This analysis appears to be similar to Gray's in some respects. At least, it is not antithetic to it.

Since Singer has described these factors as learned during reading instruction, it seems justifiable to examine them in relation to Gray's model as presented earlier. Many of the tests used by Holmes and Singer were concerned primarily with factors other than the aspects of reading and are not included here because they are related to process.

The aspects of reading delineated by Holmes and Singer appear to fall into some of the classifications of

terpretive Responses in Reading Poetry at the Ninth-Grade Level" (unpublished Ph.D. dissertation, Department of Education, University of Chicago, June, 1958), p. 225.

[12] Holmes, "Factors Underlying Major Reading Disabilities at the College Level," *Genetic Psychology Monographs*, XLIX (February, 1954), 3–95.

[13] *Ibid.*, p. 8.

[14] *Ibid.*

[15] Singer, *Substrata-Factor Reorganization Accompanying Development in Speed and Power of Reading at the Elementary School Level* (Cooperative Research Project, No. 2011; Washington, D. C.: Office of Education, U.S. Department of Health, Education and Welfare, 1965), p. 1.

[16] *Ibid.*, p. 2.

Gray's model and to extend the model in some respects. The following conclusions have been drawn by the writer:

1. It is evident that Holmes and Singer consider rate of reading to be one of the two major components of reading. Nowhere in Gray's article is rate mentioned even as a subskill. It seems clear, therefore, that rate of reading may deserve careful consideration in a revised model.

2. The criterion "power of reading" includes the ability to grasp the central thought and the details, to get an idea that is expressed in several sentences, and to interpret content and to draw inferences, all from single test paragraphs. Each of the foregoing aspects is included in Gray's model.

3. Several of the substrata factors include skills and abilities which Gray subsumed under the rubric "word perception." Of special importance to both speed and power of reading is the ability to perceive, accurately and quickly, letters and words in which minimal clues are given. Some of the word analysis skills included by Holmes and Singer are phonetic analysis; structural analysis, including prefixes, suffixes, and word roots; and context clues. A second aspect of the word perception delineated by Holmes and Singer is the meaning of words in isolation and in context. A third aspect involves word relationships or the ability to generalize about the meanings of words.

4. The substrata factors at the different levels of reading require problem-solving in order that the next step may be identified. In some respects this ability is similar to the organization of ideas to predict outcomes, and Holmes and Singer deem it important to speed of reading.

To summarize, the substrata research began with two criteria which the researchers believed to represent the major aspects of reading and has concluded with models of the interaction of different variables which presumably support or account for the two major components. In this research, no factors could come out which had not been fed in by the tests selected. The tests appear to involve some of the aspects of process — some of the factors basic to teaching reading — as well as some aspects of reading. The aspects of reading not included in Gray's model are rate of reading and the ability to generalize about the meanings of words.

MODELS OF SOME ASPECTS OF READING

Most of the models the writer was able to locate and examine dealt with the process or the sequence of skills of learning to read. Those dealing with the word perception were most numerous; two considered the more complicated aspect of comprehension. Several of the models were based on a communication theory of input, mediation, and output. Others used a linguistic construct, giving special attention to the units of language.

An example of the latter is Eleanor J. Gibson's examination of "the process by which a fundamental intellectual skill is acquired."[17] She postulated three phases, the first of which

17 Gibson, "Learning to Read," *Science,* CXLVIII (May 21, 1965), 1066.

might be called a prereading skill of differentiating graphic symbols. The second, decoding printed symbols to sounds, requires the visual or audio-visual association of letters or words with the vocalized equivalents. In the Gray framework, the second phase might be equated with word perception, although it also involves oral response or oral reading. In the third phase, Gibson considers "word strings" or larger units. She suggests that meaning facilitates dealing with the larger units and that children must learn to deal with constraints of syntactic and semantic patterning. Of special interest in the present context is the mention of oral reading and the use of syntax.

A conceptual model of reading comprehension was described briefly by Kingston, in which reading skills are basic to one of his four postulates.[18] So far, the description of these skills is incomplete, and the remaining postulates deal with processes or correlates.

Donald L. Cleland, in an attempt to explain the intellectual processes in comprehension, included elements of the four aspects of reading postulated by Gray.[19] He referred to perception of words as well as of larger units and to reading for a purpose and selecting or rejecting information relevant to the purpose. He listed validity of ideas, detection of propaganda, and other abilities that are related to Gray's description of reaction, as well as predict-

ing outcomes, drawing conclusions, ascertaining cause and effect relationships, and drawing inferences. Cleland also included making new syntheses or seeing new relationships, which are abilities described by Gray as assimilation. Cleland's final heading is "application," or doing something with the information that has been acquired. Although Cleland's organization and exploration of the processes of comprehension are quite different from Gray's, the essential aspects appear to be similar.

REVISED MODEL

On the basis of research, the more recent models, and accumulated information, the writer will detail the present status of aspects of reading in the remainder of this paper. As explained earlier, only the aspects of reading will be identified and not the processes of reading and the ways of teaching these aspects.

The four major aspects of reading are represented in a new diagram, 1R. Each segment of this circular representation is a different color for easy identification. The area at the top represents word perception, the first aspect. The second major aspect, comprehension, is represented by the yellow area. The green area represents reaction, the third major aspect, and the blue area, assimilation, the fourth aspect. These four major aspects are exactly the same as those shown in Diagram I of Gray's earlier paper. The change in design was made, first, to accommodate a fifth major aspect, which develops along with these four and is dependent on them. A second

---

[18] Kingston, "A Conceptual Model of Reading Comprehension."

[19] Cleland, "A Construct of Comprehension," in *Reading and Inquiry*, edited by J. Allen Figurel (Newark, Del.: International Reading Association, 1965), pp. 59–64.

rates

word
perception

comprehension   assimilation

reaction

rates

reason for the change is the need to portray the unlimited opportunities for growth in competence in all four original aspects. The area of each color is relatively small at the beginning but expands indefinitely.

Colors were used in this representation because they blend into each other leaving indefinite lines of demarcation, which indicates the close relationship among the areas and the interaction of each with all of the others.

The four aspects may develop simultaneously or sequentially. In the mature reader all may function concurrently, but it seems logical to expect that beginning readers acquire and use varying amounts of each aspect at different times. The level of competency in the acquisition and use of each aspect depends upon many factors, all of which are beyond the scope of this paper.

A fifth major aspect of reading is labeled "rates of reading" and is represented by a white band that intersects the four colored segments. Rates of reading are conceived as dependent upon and developing from considerable competence in each of the other four aspects. Notice that "rates," rather than "rate," is used to encompass the range from very slow to very rapid application of each or some combination of the other four aspects of reading.

Although each of the five major aspects may be identified and described separately, they are never conceived as steps but as a coherent whole. The first aspect, word perception, includes word recognition and word meanings.

Words may be recognized instantly by the use of a sight vocabulary which begins with a few words and expands throughout life. Words not recognized instantly may be recognized with the help of one or several of the word identification skills; one of the most common skills is context clues. The context may be words alone or words combined with various graphic representations, such as pictures, graphs, and maps. Other related word identification skills are phonetic and structural analysis, both of which are based on the sound and structure of our language. Phonetic analysis involves the understanding of the correspondence between spoken sounds and their representations by one or more printed letters. Structural analysis is the recognition of parts of words such as roots, and inflected and derived forms. The dictionary provides another means of learning the pronunciation of words.

Words may be identified and pronounced when their meanings are not understood, and therefore, the second part of word perception is fully as important as the first. Word meanings are usually determined by the context, whether the meanings are already known to the reader or must be deduced or looked up in the dictionary. Word meanings may be vague, clear, or precise.

The second major aspect of the revised model is called comprehension. As previously noted, there are differing views concerning its essential elements. Gray delineated two types: (1) the literal meaning, or what the passage says, and (2) the implied meaning, or what the passage really means

Gray characterized these types as "reading the lines" and "reading between and beyond the lines."

In order to secure the literal meaning, the reader adopts a "set" for getting a message from print. He follows the sequence of words, which unfolds the meaning, making full use of all of the linguistic symbols and signals. Helen K. Smith has examined many references to identify the skills essential to comprehension.[20] At the literal level she includes the following: understanding relevant details and facts; securing the main idea or central thought; following directions; recognizing sequence of time, place, events, or steps; and identifying stated conclusions. For comprehension of implied meaning, she includes drawing inferences; determining characterization and setting; sensing relationships among events and characters, cause and effect; anticipating outcomes; determining the author's purpose by identifying the tone, mood, and intent of the passage; making comparisons and contrasts; and drawing conclusions and making generalizations. The reader must follow the logic of an argument, filling in gaps left by the author but being certain that he is securing the author's ideas and not reflections of his own. As the literal and implied meanings are winnowed from the printed representations, evaluative procedures become appropriate.

20 Helen K. Smith, "Sequence in Comprehension," in *Sequential Development of Reading Abilities*, compiled and edited by Helen M. Robinson ("Supplementary Educational Monographs," No. 90; Chicago: University of Chicago Press, 1960), pp. 51–56.

The third major aspect of reading, reaction, may be of two types: (1) intellectual judgment, or what is often called "critical reading," and (2) emotional responses of various kinds and intensities, which are believed to be the foundation for literary appreciation. It should be noted that reaction occurs only as comprehension is fully realized.

According to Gray, the essential aspects of critical reaction were an inquiring attitude and wise selection of facts and relevant standards for making judgment, followed by rigorous checking on the validity of conclusions. Stated another way, critical reaction requires the ability to question the accuracy and validity of what the author said and meant. However, the reader may be unable to answer his own questions unless he has some sound criteria or standards that will provide a base for judgment. Such a basis consists of knowledge of specific facts and established principles. Logical reasoning that can note omissions of information is probably also required.

The second type of reaction, emotional response, has not been extensively studied. From the limited information available, it seems likely that emotional reactions — for example, value judgments — involve attitudes adopted by the reader and his ability to recreate sensory images from unusual or picturesque words and from the particular arrangement of words in a passage. It also seems likely that both intellectual and emotional reactions are used simultaneously, although in some situations one may take precedence over the other.

The fourth aspect of reading is assimilation. Gray explained that this aspect of reading results in revised concepts, expanded understandings, rational attitudes, and new insights and ideas. James M. McCallister described this aspect as "abstracting ideas from the printed page and organizing them into patterns of thinking and action so that generalizations, applications, personal decisions and convictions" may result.[21]

The fifth major aspect has been entitled "rates." Rates of reading are flexible and adjusted to the reader's purpose and to the difficulty of the materials. The most rapid rate might be called "skimming"; it involves reading and skipping in order to get a general idea of what a selection is about, how the author treats a topic, the author's organization, or perhaps the relevancy of the material to the reader's purpose. A slightly less rapid rate is appropriate to light fiction. An even less rapid rate is required for materials in which both vocabulary and ideas, and perhaps also the author's style, are well known to the reader. The rate slows as vocabulary and content becomes less familiar and as critical reactions are involved. Rate may reach a snail's pace as the reader ponders possibile application of ideas and attempts to assimilate those accepted by him. The close interrelationship between rate and each of the other four major aspects of reading should now be clear.

Thus far, no distinction has been made between silent and oral reading. The latter may be described as involving the first four major aspects, with rate adjusted to speaking tempo. In addition, in oral reading the reader projects the author's message in a pleasant voice, using the signals provided on the printed page as well as those implied by the author's mood and tone. Rhythm, stress, juncture, and intonation are influenced by the reader's interpretation of the author's meaning.

In the last of Gray's diagrams, he revealed his awareness of the necessity of adapting the major aspects he had identified to reading for different purposes; instruction was the means he mentioned to achieve competence in making such adaptations. Although he did not state his position, it is clear that he regarded reading for different purposes as an application of the major aspects of reading. In confirmation, Helen K. Smith, in a study of reading for different purposes, found that good readers were often able to choose the appropriate purpose for a selection and make appropriate combinations and adaptations of the different aspects of reading.[22]

Gray also believed that reading in the content areas represented an application of the major and sub aspects of reading. The studies of reading skills and abilities used in various

---

[21] McCallister, "Methods and Materials for Teaching Creative Reading," in *ibid.*, p. 119.

[22] Smith, "The Responses of Good and Poor Readers When Asked To Read for Different Purposes" (unpublished Ph.D. dissertation, Department of Education, University of Chicago, March, 1965).

content areas have shown the necessity for flexibility in adapting the five major aspects of reading to the purposes and expectations in each area. A few additional aspects have been suggested which might be classified as study skills, an area related to reading but also related to writing and other types of abilities.

CONCLUDING STATEMENT

The major aspects of reading, viewed in 1966, differ little from those outlined by Gray in 1960. Probably the most significant contribution of this paper has been the attempt to separate the skills and abilities of reading from the processes used in acquiring them and from the methods and procedures used to teach them. This goal has not been completely realized because many of the behaviors, especially in the reactive and assimilative aspects, have not yet been clearly described. Furthermore, many are so closely related to thought processes, which themselves are so complex, that considerable time will be required to identify them. Nevertheless, the intent of this model is to distinguish between *what* we are trying to achieve and the *processes* for achieving our goals. If this incomplete model helps to order research and instruction, it will have served its purpose.

CHAPTER IV

IDENTIFYING SIGNIFICANT READING SKILLS

*

IN KINDERGARTEN THROUGH GRADE THREE

DOLORES DURKIN

*

WHICH READING skills are of special significance when a child is in the early stages of becoming a reader? Underlying my particular answer are certain assumptions, and since these assumptions affect my answer, I would like to make the more important ones explicit.

SOME BASIC ASSUMPTIONS

My first assumption is that the beginning stages of reading are not confined to a given grade level or age level. Certainly, there are children enrolled in the middle and upper grades who are beginners in reading, just as there are younger children in the first and second grade who are far beyond the "beginner" classification. Basically, then, my first assumption is simply a reminder that a discussion of the initial reading skills cannot be confined to primary-grade children but, rather, must include any child of any age who is just starting to learn to read.

My second assumption is that skill in *silent* reading is what we are trying to teach at all stages of reading development and at all grade levels. Such an emphasis on silent reading should not suggest, of course, that oral reading be eliminated from reading programs. I would still urge teachers, for example, to spend some time every day reading aloud to children, especially to those are still a little uncertain of their own ability to read. Oral reading by one who is skilful, not only provides enjoyment, but also provides the child with a model for his own future reading. It is a kind of concrete demonstration of the fruit he can expect from his current labors to remember particular words, to make careful distinctions between words that look alike, to remember the sounds that are associated with particular letters, to pay attention to punctuation marks, and so on.

Another reason why oral reading can never be totally omitted from the classroom is that certain material — some poetry, for instance — has been written as much for its sound as for its sense. To be fully appreciated and enjoyed, therefore, it must be read aloud — and, it must be added, read aloud by someone who is proficient in oral reading skills. Not to be forgotten either, of course, is the obvious use of a child's oral reading of unfamiliar material for diagnostic purposes. What the child does with the new material can give his teacher specific information both about what has been learned and about the particular problems that impede further progress. However, this kind of reading is not designed to improve oral reading itself, in my view, but instead is a way of reaching the primary goal of our teaching efforts: maximum achievement in silent reading.

At this point it is very possible that those of you who teach young children may consider my emphasis on silent reading as unrealistic. You cannot help but recall, for instance, how your first graders read aloud even when they are reading alone or have been directed by you to "read to yourself." Young children commonly think aloud, and so it is very natural and normal that they should read aloud, even while reading to themselves. All this means in terms of my emphasis on silent reading is that those of you who work with beginners in reading who also happen to be young children must allow for a less clear-cut distinction between oral and silent reading than is possible for those who work with children who are both older and more able readers.

One other assumption that ought to be made explicit concerns materials. Certainly, it is difficult to think about reading skills separate from the materials that will be used to teach them. What I especially want to emphasize here, however, is the importance of having a very broad concept of instructional materials. For example, when I think of reading materials, I do not confine my thoughts to books or, even more specifically, to basal readers. Instead, I include anything that displays the written form

of our language: television commercials, labels on food products, cars, and trucks, street and highway signs, words and numbers on calendars, and so on, as well as the more conventional materials like readers, workbooks, and storybooks. The use of a wide array of materials is, I think, especially important when a child is just beginning to learn to read because it immediately demonstrates that reading is very much related to the world that is already familiar to him. At the beginning, this reassurance may be more important to later achievement and attitudes than a carefully controlled vocabulary.

THE FOUNDATION OF READING SKILLS

Having mentioned a few of the assumptions underlying my view of beginning reading skills, I would like to move on to a description of some of the skills themselves. In describing these skills, I want to emphasize the importance of going back sufficiently far that we recognize the real beginning. With reading, of course, the real beginning is the child's skill in comprehending and using the *oral* form of the language he will be expected to learn to read.

Here, some of you may feel that the basic interdependence of a child's ability in oral language and his subsequent ability in reading its written counterpart is so obvious as to warrant little explicit attention. Although I would agree that this interdependence does seem obvious in theory, in classroom practice one often finds a failure to take it into account. For instance, the teacher who allows a particular basal reader to dictate exclusively the words that will be introduced — even when the vocabulary of the reader depicts places and things foreign to the children — hardly takes into account this interdependence. Nor does the teacher of bilingual children who selects words like "in" and "on" to illustrate vowel sounds, even though her pupils still lack a precise understanding of the meanings of these English words.

I am giving special attention to the interdependence of listening, speaking, and reading because I believe that all classroom teachers would profit from periodically asking themselves the following twofold question: Do my instruction and my choice of materials reflect the fact that reading is an extension of the earlier language abilities of listening and speaking; and, in addition, do my teaching plans include interesting and varied opportunities for the children to add to the reservoir of words currently comprising their listening and speaking vocabularies?

INDEPENDENCE IN IDENTIFYING WORDS

Once reading itself begins, it is almost immediately obvious that the children must be helped to become independent in identifying the many words they are not yet able to recognize in their written form. Available to promote this independence are phonic analysis, structural analysis, and the use of the context in which a new word appears. Although these three sources of help are different, effective instruction in each has some common characteristics. For instance,

with all three, there is not one magically right time to start instruction. The wise practice, stated in a general way, is to initiate instruction — whether in phonics or structural analysis or the use of the context — as soon as the child is ready to understand and to make use of it. In addition, we must remember that the only limits that ought to be placed on instruction are those imposed by the particular abilities of the children.

Sometimes, it must be admitted, the limitations on learning come from other sources. One such source can be indicated by the comment of a very honest teacher who was enrolled in one of my reading-methods courses. After we had spent several class meetings identifying and studying the content of phonics, this teacher came to me and said, "I'm so glad you've spent this time going over what can be taught for phonic analysis because, to tell you the truth, I only know second-grade phonics." This comment came from a person who had been teaching elementary school for fifteen years, the last eleven in second grade. Now, in thinking about what this teacher said, I could only assume that in saying she knew "second-grade phonics" she meant that she knew what was included in the teachers' manuals accompanying second-grade basal readers. With this circumscribed amount of knowledge, two things probably often occurred. The children in her class who were still just beginners in their understanding and use of phonic analysis were probably not given the opportunity to start where they were — at the beginning.

And others who were ready to learn more about phonics than was covered in the second-grade manuals probably were deprived of the chance to gain advanced competency.

What I want to emphasize, with the help of this teacher's comment, is that whether we are giving instruction in basic skills like phonics and structural analysis or whether we are discussing effective techniques of propagandistic writing with advanced students we, as teachers, do bear the responsibility of helping every child assigned to our classrooms begin at the point where his past learnings have taken him and advance as far as his ability and new learnings permit him to go. Perhaps this responsibility suggests still another question for self-scrutiny: Do I, as a teacher, know enough about the possible content of reading instruction that the children in my classroom are never denied the chance to learn all that their abilities allow?

COMPREHENSION SKILLS

Thus far, in my discussion of beginning reading skills, the focus has been on individual words — in particular, on the basic importance of word meanings and of word-analysis skills to a child's success. Even in this early stage, however, reading requires not only the ability to cope with single words but also the ability to grasp the thoughts expressed by the combinations of words that authors select in order to entertain, describe, explain — or whatever other purpose they have in mind. Here, it is again important that we recognize the origin or foundation of these skills, which are commonly referred to as reading comprehension skills. It is important that we understand — in practice as well as in theory — the very close relationship between the child's ability to comprehend language as it is spoken and his ability to comprehend what an author has written. To be more specific, if a child cannot comprehend, for instance, facts or explanations or humor or exaggeration when they are expressed orally, he can hardly be expected to comprehend them when they are communicated through the medium of written language.

I especially want to emphasize and re-emphasize these relationships among the various dimensions of language because it is my belief that failure to recognize them in everyday classroom practice leads to erroneous diagnoses of reading difficulties. I think it would be safe to conjecture, for example, that what is often diagnosed as a reading comprehension problem is, in fact, a deficiency in language comprehension. And what follows from an incorrect diagnosis is inappropriate instruction that focuses on a symptom rather than on the probable causal factor.

SUMMARY

In a sense, almost everything I have emphasized can be summarized in a simple statement, one that may be phrased in positive terms: Reading is an extension of the earlier abilities of listening and speaking. To the extent that there is proficiency and richness in these prior abilities, we can also expect proficiency and richness in reading.

IN GRADES FOUR THROUGH EIGHT

ROBERT EMANS

*

A CHILD entering the fourth grade — whom we shall call Charlotte — has changed in many ways from the time she first entered school. Physically she is larger; she is more co-ordinated; her vision is more mature. She has a richer background of experience, has greater mental and language facility, and has a greater sense of independence. In addition, she brings to the fourth grade reading skills learned in the primary grades, including a basic sight vocabulary and a knowledge of letter sounds.

Not only has Charlotte changed, but so has her world. Now she knows about people and places unlike those she has experienced directly. New ideas and facts from outside her immediate world confront her. The language she hears has become more abstract. She finds herself answering questions, solving problems, and finding means for recreation which she has not done before. She is shifting from story-type to study-type reading, from oral to silent reading. Her school day is divided into special sections such as science, social studies, mathematics, and literature, each with new and special reading demands. In order to satisfy reading requirements she often must go to several different sources.

The school is concerned with the changes in Charlotte and in her world. As Guy L. Bond and Eva Bond Wag-

ner have stated, "The task of the teacher of upper-grade reading is to help the child adjust his reading abilities and skills to meet his purpose and in conformity with varied materials confronting him."[1] By now, Charlotte has already developed many reading skills. This stage, according to Albert J. Harris, is "concerned mainly with the further refinement and improvement of skills already well started."[2]

What are the skills that Charlotte needs to refine further and develop? Identification of these skills has come from at least four sources. One source is the current reading programs as summarized in various curriculum guides. A second is information from the field of child development. (In other words, what skills is Charlotte capable of learning?) Another source is the demands placed upon Charlotte by her world. (For example, what is and will be the nature of the reading material confronting her?) A fourth source is the thinking of scholars of reading such as William S. Gray,[3] Helen M.

[1] Bond and Wagner, *Teaching the Child To Read* (rev. ed.; New York: Macmillan Co., 1950), p. 280.
[2] Harris, *How To Increase Reading Ability* (4th ed.; New York: David McKay Co., Inc., 1961), p. 87.
[3] Gray, "The Major Aspects of Reading," in *Sequential Development of Reading Abilities*, compiled and edited by Helen M. Robinson ("Supplementary Educational Monographs," No. 90; Chicago: University of Chicago Press, 1960), pp. 8–24.

Robinson,[4] and Jack A. Holmes.[5] These four sources are reviewed and a summary prepared of the skills that are needed in the middle years.

For purposes of this paper, the skills were organized around three of Gray's major aspects of reading: perception (which includes word identification and meaning), comprehension, and re-action. Gray's fourth aspect, assimila-tion, was not used, as it requires all the reading skills. Other skills which are relevant to the reading process and seem to reflect flexibility in the use of the fundamental skills are discussed under reading in the content fields and oral reading. Many of the skills could be placed under more than one cate-gory. For example, the use of the dic-tionary could be included under either word identification and meaning, com-prehension, or reading in the content fields.

SKILLS FOR PERCEPTION

With the increase in difficulty of reading materials, Charlotte must identify many new words. Word iden-tification skills learned during the primary years are reviewed and ex-tended. New skills are developed, es-pecially those of syllabication and accent needed for multisyllabic words. When applying identification clues, she should now be able to choose the

4 Robinson, "The Unity of the Reading Act," in *Sequential Development of Reading Abilities*, compiled and edited by Helen M. Robinson ("Supplementary Educational Mon-ographs," No. 90; Chicago: University of Chi-cago Press, 1960), p. 237–44.

5 Holmes, *The Substrata-Factor Theory of Reading* (Berkeley, Calif.: California Book Co., 1953).

most appropriate combination, using fewer phonic and more contextual clues and dividing words into syllables rather than sounding them out letter by letter.

At this stage, Charlotte is more chal-lenged by meanings of words than by their pronunciation since she has al-ready developed many pronunciation skills. Although she needs to continue to explore the meanings of words re-lated to her immediate environment, many new words will be abstract or technical; they will be outside her speaking or listening vocabularies and the things and activities they represent will have been experienced only vicari-ously. Figures of speech may present special difficulties. Not only will she be confronted with words having sev-eral different meanings, but she will also need to apply familiar terms in new settings and will need to distin-guish differences in connotations of words.

If Charlotte is unable to determine the pronunciation of a word or estab-lish its meaning by using the previ-ously mentioned skills, she may use a dictionary. Before this, she probably did not have the word pronuncia-tion skills necessary for using the dic-tionary, and since most of the words she met were within her speaking and listening vocabularies, she felt little need for its use. This, then, is the opportune time for her to learn how to use the dictionary. In locating a word she will need to recall in order the letters of the alphabet; employ guide words; and refer to first, second, third or however many letters are necessary. To achieve the proper pronunciation, she should be able to interpret the phonetic spelling, employ the pronunciation key and accent marks, recognize syllabic divisions, and blend the sounds into word wholes. Finally, to attain the meaning of a word, she should be able to comprehend the various definitions, select the appropriate ones, and adapt it to the text.

SKILLS FOR COMPREHENSION

As Charlotte makes use of the various perception skills, word meanings are combined into a sequence of ideas that must be comprehended. A summary of some of the necessary comprehension skills is contained in a grid developed by the writer (see Table 1. In the left-hand vertical column, various mental activities are identified; and in the top horizontal row are aspects of the reading matter. From the grid one hundred and thirty possible types of comprehension emerge. Prob-

ably many additional rows or columns could be supplied.

SKILLS FOR REACTION

As Charlotte grasps the meaning of the written word, she reacts to the ideas presented. In order to evaluate what she reads, she must have a set of criteria with which to make judgments. These criteria will come from such sources as the facts she has learned, her beliefs, and her purposes for reading, and they will need to be explored and related to the accuracy, recency, and sufficiency of the information, arguments, and conclusions presented. In applying her criteria she must be able to detect suggestions of the author's experiences, biases, qualifications, and purposes. Although not actually a skill, the development of appreciations, tastes, and interests in reading is also a part of reaction and vital to reading maturity.

During grades four through eight is

TABLE 1
COMPREHENSION SKILLS GRID

THINKING ABILITIES	WHAT IS READ									
	Main Ideas	Supporting Details	Sequences	Conclusions	Predictions	Interpretations	Implications	Comparisons and Contrasts	Parts and Wholes	Causes and Effects
Recognizes										
Reproduces										
Distinguishes										
Concludes										
Summarizes										
Generalizes										
Anticipates										
Relates										
Analyzes										
Synthesizes										
Classifies										
Organizes										
Infers										

an appropriate time to stress reaction. Charlotte now has a greater fund of information and more greatly developed intellectual powers. In one sense these years are more fruitful for developing reaction than any later period. As Charlotte goes through adolescence, she will tend to challenge authority and even rebel against it, thus complicating the process for acquiring criteria for judgment. When the reaction process can be one of analysis and self-conscious thinking, Charlotte will be well prepared for the assimilation that is necessary for education.

SKILLS FOR READING IN THE CONTENT FIELDS

As Charlotte progresses through the grades, she is met by increasing demands in the various content areas, such as social studies, science, arithmetic, and literature. All the skills of perception, comprehension, and reaction play a part. Each field has its own specialized vocabulary and its own related complexity of ideas. The reading skills in the content fields are often adaptations of those used in adjusting to new materials and specialized purposes.

Another skill, rate of reading, begins to have relevance when Charlotte deals with different content fields. The appropriate rate is different for reading mathematics and for reading novels, for example. Rate becomes increasingly important as the amounts of required reading increase, as do all of the reading study skills. Charlotte must locate information by various means: discriminating among possible sources (such as books, encyclopedias, dictionaries, atlases, almanacs, and periodi-

cals); searching a library by using a classification system; and using reference guides such as card catalogues and indexes to periodicals. After locating a source, she should know how to find the desired information using aids (such as table of contents, index, title page, preface, headings, footnotes, summaries, bibliography, glossary, and appendixes) and should be able to scan to locate the information on a page. She should then skim the selection to obtain an overview, determine how or whether to read the selection, and establish purposes for reading. In her reading she should answer questions asked by herself and others, use visual and graphic aids (such as charts, graphs, pictures, figures, formulas, tables, diagrams, maps, and globes), summarize through self-recitation, and skim again to review.

As a final step she may need to compile and present a report. Such a report will require reacting to the ideas read in order to select information from one or more sources and establish its relevancy, accuracy, credibility, and sufficiency. The ideas and information will then have to be summarized, classified, and outlined.

SKILLS FOR ORAL READING

On occasion Charlotte may read orally. As in the content fields, oral reading involves many of the skills used in the other areas. Charlotte should read orally in such a way that others will want to listen. To do this she must first determine the purpose of her oral reading (for example, to inform, entertain, or verify a point), prepare by determining the meaning of the selection, and finally, convey the meaning through the expression of her voice, by phrasing correctly, by employing certain tones, pauses, and stresses effectively, and by adjusting to the abilities, needs, and expectations of her audience.

These are some of the skills to be developed in grades four through eight. Educators should remember, however, that "the complex process of reading matures as a unit rather than in a fragmented manner, because each aspect of reading complements and adds significance to all others."[6]

6 Robinson, *op. cit.*, p. 239.

* * *

IN GRADES NINE THROUGH FOURTEEN

FRITZ HJERMSTAD

*

IDENTIFICATION of those reading skills to be taught in grades nine through fourteen begins when a student asks the question, What does the word mean? This question usually arises in relation to the vocabulary found in some fairly demanding reading in a particular content area.

At the simplest level of comprehension, an understanding of individual sentences usually involves those skills commonly associated with word attack and word meaning. If the reader has developed some competence in vocabulary skills through the grades, he will usually employ several methods in order to understand the author's word meanings. He will attack unknown words by using phonic analysis, structural analysis, context clues, the dictionary, or even generalizations based on his understanding of the total context. In other words, he will employ several methods which have proved successful in the past to discover the literal or implied meanings of the words in the selection.

In identifying the vocabulary skills to be mastered in a reading selection, the teacher must be constantly aware that comprehension and speed in reading rest solidly on a substructure of vocabulary. Therefore, it is essential that the teacher identify and promote strong vocabulary skills *before* the students are stopped by a lack of them. Basically, confidence and strength in the area of vocabulary can be gained if the teacher identifies unique or very technical words, helps students attack multisyllabic words, and guides them in using and reading words correctly in a variety of contexts.

IDENTIFYING AND EVALUATING
MAIN IDEAS

If the student has reasonable confidence in his word recognition abilities, his next question usually is, What does the author mean? What the author "means" to the student is usually related to the amount of attention the student has given to the author's paragraph structure and, particularly, to his main ideas. Without the establishment of this basic alliance between reader and writer at the paragraph level, the steps following in the comprehension hierarchy — tracing the author's main ideas through a series of paragraphs, a section, a chapter, and a whole article or book — become much more difficult. A reader should also identify the purpose for which a selection was written; by this means he can establish a general frame of reference on which to center his attention. If he can identify the purpose, he can, at least superficially, find the pattern of the author's thinking and his organization of his material.

As a student attempts to identify the main ideas of the author, he should pay careful attention to the organization or structure of the reading matter. He should attempt to classify main points and subpoints, elaborations and illustrations, and so forth — in other words, to grasp the literal meaning of the selection. By identifying the literal meaning of the selection, the student presumably indicates to his teacher that he has established some contact with the author that can be evaluated. After the analysis at the literal level, the student can begin to evaluate the main ideas stated by the author. At this juncture the student will have to make decisions concerning implications, cause and effect relationships, comparison and contrast structures, and underlying concepts.

The teacher can find some assurance that reading skills have been correctly identified and taught if, after sufficient time has been given for the reading assignment, class questions and discussions deal mainly with the more difficult, implied meanings in the selection and not with restatements of the literal meanings. If the students do not constructively search out the deeper meaning in the reading assignment, it should be clear to the teacher that either they have not mastered the vocabulary of the selection or the subject; or they do not have sufficient background experience to comprehend the assignment; or they have not identified the main elements in the reading that would have allowed them to go on to the deeper levels of interpretation.

CRITICAL READING

Commonly associated with the identification and evaluation of main ideas is an awareness of those structures in reading that are associated with critical reading. To judge whether or not critical reading levels have been achieved, the teacher needs some guidelines. The teacher should first note the types of reading demands in the classroom that are not easily solved by what might be termed "incidental attention." Critical reading should call forth the strongest possible intellectual application on the part of the student as he attempts to explore the depths of the author's reasoning. In abbreviated form, the steps that build critical reading confidence follow a pattern of (1) grasping what the author has said through the identification of the general structure of the material in relation to the use of language and the purpose for which the selection was written, (2) following the chain of reasoning, (3) plotting the implications, and (4) recognizing the inferences and assumptions that arise logically from the selection.

RATE OF COMPREHENSION

Correct identification of reading skills is also important in discussions of the appropriate rates to be used for different materials and purposes. Since rate is governed by total comprehension, the rate the student habitually uses depends on his present reading skills together with his vocabulary ability and familiarity with the context. The identification of the best rates for any student must always be based on the competence he displays when reading a variety of materials. Only by weighing his vocabulary and comprehension skills can the teacher judge the rate that may be expected for a particular selection. The complexity of the material and the purpose for which the material is going to be used should also be kept in mind when rate is being established. One of the three rates will generally be applicable: skimming rate — to find the main idea; scanning rate — to locate a particular subject in the material; and study-type rate — to assimilate at least 75 to 85 per cent of the content.

The demands for competent reading skills in grades nine through fourteen emphasize how essential it is that the student be able to comprehend a vast amount of material at a reasonable speed. Anything that interferes with this process must be identified by the teacher and corrected by sufficient practice in the appropriate reading skills.

VALUES OF PURPOSEFUL READING

The real value of identifying essential reading skills in the classroom is that correct identification enables the teacher to discover individual and group strengths and weaknesses and, in addition, those areas of reading that will need extra time and special emphasis. Thus, if the teacher notes that the students have difficulty in interpretation, he can test the group for the appropriate reading skills — for example, by using probing questions to uncover the sequence of main idea development in a selection.

The teacher is usually confronted with a wide range of interpretations of the printed matter. Some students may still be stumbling over a few of the more complex words; others may be attempting to define clearly the literal main ideas; and still others may be religiously trying to discover whether or not the implications they have discovered have logical merit in relation to the author's purpose.

Adjusting classroom instruction to accommodate each individual's level of reading skill in each reading selection is, of course, impossible. But by identifying the essential skills to be taught in vocabulary, comprehension, and rate, an approach can be established that will give every reading lesson a firm, continuing, flexible basis.

IN CORRECTIVE AND REMEDIAL CLASSES

SISTER MARY JULITTA, O.S.F.

*

THE EMPHASIS in published articles and in discussions on remediation is on deficiencies. As I prepared this paper it became very apparent to me that too frequently the teacher in remedial work tends to look at the underside of the weave — the deficiencies — rather than the upper side — the skills to be developed.

Another disturbing factor is the tendency to identify large, all-embracing abilities such as "gaining a sight vocabulary" or "comprehending" rather than the fundamental skills involved in these reading acts. It is only by developing the fundamental skills that the teacher can actually hope to do corrective work and help the retarded reader gain the power to master the total act of reading. In short, although the emphasis is very frequently placed on large abilities, they can actually be taught only if they are broken down into their component parts.

BASIC SKILLS

Word perception. Because the medium for expressing ideas is the word symbol, the common major concerns in corrective and remedial reading are an adequate sight vocabulary, knowledge of phonics and syllabication, and other similar factors. But instead, attention should be focused on those subskills or clusters of subskills that make these word perception tech-

niques possible. Among these is the skill to discriminate between sounds visually and also to remember sounds. Even this subskill is useless unless it is combined with other subskills: the individual must be able to see the elements within the total word form, mentally hear and discriminate between sounds, and then think the total word as a combination of the individual sound elements.

Certainly, learning about phonic elements and principles of syllabication is often necessary, but utilization of such knowledge is impossible if the previously mentioned subskills are not present. In the entire process of structural analysis, for example, the important thing is to see the parts in relation to the whole and to each other. The use of context clues is even more difficult, for it depends on memory and associational power. Experiences are necessary before the individual can recall them and make associations between the previous happenings and the new reading material.

Comprehension. Several examples from the broad area of comprehension may give an idea of the significance of emphasizing underlying skills rather than the product of a cluster of skills. In what is usually termed "general comprehension" are included such subskills as selection of word meaning to fit the context, proper emphasis on ideas as either major or minor, recognition of the relationship of ideas, and retention of ideas from sentence to sentence so that they can be mentally integrated. Since a student may experience difficulty in general comprehension because of a failure in any one of these factors, as well as many others, it should be clear that in order to help him it is necessary to identify the more specific, underlying skills.

In interpretation, to take another example, the reader must utilize such subskills as being aware of connotations of words; sensing the mood; and making inferences which utilize his experiences, his understanding of the situation, and his ability to see the whole.

For critical reading, proficiency in both literal and interpretative comprehension is necessary. In addition, after comprehending the two kinds of meaning, the reader must utilize reasoning to evaluate what he has read on the basis of standards established through past experience.

Rate of reading. Especially with older students, identification of the subskills involved in rate of reading often is a definite need in order to discover the basic difficulty; important among these are quickness and accuracy of word perception, facility in word analysis, knowledge of meanings of words, ability to spot key ideas, individual reaction time, mechanics of reading, and facility and flexibility in utilizing various reading skills.

STUDY SKILLS

In remedial classes, there is also a need to identify the degree of develop-

ment of study skills because those who have problems in reading will very often have experienced serious difficulties in studying. It is especially important to note whether the retarded reader has the thinking skills essential to study, because if these are developed, they can be transferred to the reading situation when he acquires command over the reading process. Hence, the skills of listening and of viewing pictures should also be identified as essential skills.

In this paper, study skills are restricted to those common to all study, as outlined by Nila Banton Smith. They include: (1) selection and evaluation, (2) organization, (3) recall, (4) location of information, and (5) following directions.[1]

To identify the reader's ability in *selection and evaluation,* the teacher or clinician must go beyond the manifestation of his degree of over-all efficiency to his use of the fundamental skills. At all levels and in various media — studying pictures, listening, or reading — there is a need to identify the subskills of selection and evaluation involved: judging the relevancy of ideas to a certain topic, seeing relationships, and restricting interpretation of printed symbols to the subject at hand. Naturally, these subskills are unified in the actual reading process, but they must be isolated if the remedial teacher is to focus attention on the exact area for development and correction.

[1] Smith, *Reading Instruction for Today's Children* (Englewood Cliffs, N. J.: Prentice-Hall, Inc., 1963), p. 312.

A cluster of subskills are also necessary for the efficient use of the skill of *organization*: abstracting relationships, weighing ideas, making generalizations, and associating ideas. Outlining and summarizing, which are very often used for organizing, utilize the totality of organizing skills.

Although memorization of numerous isolated facts has been minimized in learning today, there must be *retention of ideas* in reading. It is not difficult to identify the general skill of retention but, for effective help, the general skill must be divided into certain subskills, such as association, visualization, or ability to select facts to be retained. Once having identified the subskills involved, the teacher or clinician may easily identify those in which the student is weak in order to improve retention.

One of the greatest aids in study is efficiency in *locating information*, which involves many basic subskills, for example, understanding the sequence of numbers and of letters of the alphabet and a wide knowledge of reference sources. Another subskill of very great importance is knowledge of how to use cross references either in the library or in reference books, which in turn rests on versatility in relating ideas. Many organization skills, such as topical, spatial, or chronological arrangement, are also involved in locating information.

In school life there are many situations in which *following written directions* is required. Similar needs are present in adult life. The subskills involved are literal comprehension, visualization, and retention of ideas while reading so that the total meaning may be grasped.

CONCLUDING STATEMENT

Attention has been focused on the need to identify the underlying or fundamental skills in reading rather than the manifestations of proficiency or deficiency in over-all ability. It has also been noted as important to stress the degree of development of skills rather than the severity of deficiencies in order that the teacher or clinician may utilize the strengths of the individual.

CHAPTER V

ISSUES RELATING TO BASIC INSTRUCTION IN READING

*

GERTRUDE WHIPPLE

*

THE BASIC issues under discussion today do not differ greatly from those that have been of perennial concern. At the 1942 conference on reading held at the University of Chicago, the discussions of basic instruction dealt with such topics as the best method of teaching beginning reading, how pupils should be sorted for differentiated instruction, the value of using basic readers in the middle grades, and whether reading should be taught in college and, if so, how. Though some of these issues have been integrated with new ones, most of them are still being debated. But there is a definite difference today: the problems are more complicated and the proposed solutions far more varied.

WHEN AND HOW TO BEGIN BASIC INSTRUCTION IN READING

The first issue concerns the age when systematic reading instruction should begin. Before 1920 children were taught to read when they entered first grade. With the development of the concept of reading readiness in the 1920's, the time for initiating reading instruction became somewhat adjustable. Reading was postponed for many children until they were ready to learn. Practices recommended in 1942, for example, involved sorting a class of beginning pupils into three ability groups and introducing each group to reading when it showed readiness. Thus, in practice, the concept of reading readiness was implemented only for the immature child.

The findings of certain recent studies have led to a more flexible concept of reading readiness. Dolores Durkin and others have shown that four- and five-year-olds who have learned to read before they enter school maintain their acceleration in reading during the first school year.[1] A Denver experiment by Joseph E. Brzeinski indicated that children who were giving reading instruction in kindergarten made higher reading scores at the end of the first grade than children who were not given such instruction.[2] So today, instead

[1] Durkin, "Children Who Read before Grade I: A Second Study," *Elementary School Journal*, LXIV (December, 1963), 143–48.

[2] Brzeinski, "Reading in the Kindergarten," in *Teaching Young Children To Read*, edited by Warren G. Cutts (Conference Proceedings of the U.S. Department of Health, Education, and Welfare, Office of Education; Washington, D. C.: Government Printing Office, 1964), pp. 50–58.

of asking how late to postpone read-ing instruction, we face the problem of how early to begin it.

Many school people strongly object to teaching reading in kindergarten even to able pupils. Their arguments against early reading, as reported in a recent survey,[3] are (1) that a reading program for kindergarten children is not in accord with the educational aims of the schools, (2) that it is not in keeping with the developmental needs of the five-year-old, and (3) that kindergarten teachers are not trained to teach reading.

Other school people have adopted a more flexible concept and would lower the age of beginning reading instruc-tion. They would introduce up-graded reading-readiness activities and initial reading instruction in kindergarten. These educators point out that little change has taken place in kindergar-ten programs for many years in spite of the fact that entering pupils have wider experiences and larger vocabu-laries than ever before through their contacts with the mass media of com-munication. Those who take this point of view call for the up-dating of kindergarten programs. They do not advocate reading instruction for all kindergarten children but only for those who are socially, physically, and mentally ready to read. Just as it is not wise to teach reading to immature children in first grade, they say, it is equally bad to withhold reading from able children in the kindergarten.

[3] Mary C. Austin and Coleman Morrison, *The First R: The Harvard Report on Reading in Elementary Schools* (New York: Macmillan Co., 1963), p. 14.

If we accept the view that the kin-dergarten program should be adjusted to those children who evidence inter-est and reading readiness, we are faced with deciding the kind of train-ing to provide. Current answers are these: It must be a program that chal-lenges but does not frustrate the chil-dren. The length of the instructional periods must be adapted to their at-tention spans, perhaps twenty minutes daily. The purposes of the program should include the stimulation of lan-guage growth and the development of basic reading attitudes and skills and a rich body of concepts. And when the children enter first grade, their reading program will need to take into account the progress they have already made.

Of all the issues faced by teachers of reading, none is so controversial as that of the method of beginning read-ing. The chief area of disagreement centers on the kind of phonic training to be given and the time for its intro-duction. On the one hand, we find approaches that introduce phonics either before the children have a sight vocabulary or at the time they start to use a beginning reading book. These methods focus on sounds, let-ters, and word elements such as the *at* or *an* family. The phonic materials provide for plenty of drill on letter sounds apart from words. Reading for meaning is postponed until much later in the instructional plan. Exam-ples of these approaches are the vari-ous separate phonic methods, some of the linguistic programs, *Words in Color*, programs using augmented al-phabets such as the Initial Teaching

Alphabet, and Moore's automated typewriter technique. The theory underlying the phonic approaches is that learning to read consists of mastering a code — the correspondence of sounds and their visual symbols — and that since a word is composed of phonetic elements it can best be taught by translating letter forms first into sounds and then into meanings. Advocates of such methods claim that they help children learn to recognize words and phrases in print very quickly. Opponents of the method raise several objections: (1) Too early introduction of phonics promotes word calling; (2) the methods fail to relate the reading to actual reading situations; (3) often a system of words is introduced for practice without regard to the vocabulary the child will meet in his beginning reading materials; and (4) attention to meaning is postponed much too long. Opponents also point out that many of the so-called new methods based on phonics differ only slightly from systems extensively used in the period from 1900 to 1930, which were later rejected in light of research findings.

On the other hand, the point of view about phonics most widely accepted today is that it is only one method of word recognition. Children should learn to recognize words and phrases through the use of picture clues, configuration clues, meaning clues, and general context and phonics; and word analysis skills should be introduced after the child has a small stock of familiar words. Those who advocate this approach integrate phonics with purposeful reading and realize that, though phonics is essen-

tial in improving ability to recognize words, it makes little contribution to silent reading comprehension. Examples of this method are (1) planned sequential reading programs supplemented by the language-experience approach or by individualized reading and (2) many of the basic reader programs.

What position, then, can we safely take toward the "new" methods of teaching reading that are appearing now? Pending careful, objective, and extensive trial in the hands of impartial teachers, we should avoid adopting any of the methods except for experimental use. Rather, we might well follow the recommendation of Austin and Morrison that "continued emphasis be placed on helping children develop proficiency in word recognition through the use of meaning clues, visual analysis of word forms, sounding approaches, and the dictionary."[4]

ROLE OF READING IN SCHOOL AND CLASSROOM

Whatever the method or combination of methods we use to start the children along the reading road, we must decide from the outset on the place of reading in the school curriculum. A few decades ago this question focused on systematic versus incidental instruction in reading beyond the primary grades. Today most educators admit that both these types of instruction are needed. But many hasten to add that reading must be taught in relation to other school

4 *Ibid.*, p. 221.

subjects. They believe that responsibility for reading growth should not be relegated to one period a day or to one teacher but should extend all through the day in all subjects at all levels.

Specifically, two major interrelationships of reading with other school subjects are recommended. One is the integration of the language arts in the curriculum. In support of such integration we are reminded of the fact that early training in listening, speaking, and writing results in more rapid progress in learning to read; and reading, in turn, facilitates progress in the other language arts. The other interrelationship concerns reading in the content fields. Here it is advocated that guidance be given in using, extending, and supplementing basic reading skills; the specialized fields are urged to build upon basic reading instruction in order to help students understand and interpret the languages of these fields, for success in the content areas depends upon reading ability.

In light of the substantial agreement on these interrelationships, is there any disagreement regarding the place of reading in the curriculum? The acceptance of the foregoing views is still largely theoretical; they are not yet reflected adequately in current practices. By way of illustration, consider the teaching of English at the secondary level. Reading is seldom taught as part of a larger communication program. In James R. Squire's preliminary assessment of current practices in high-school English, only 10 out of 118 schools were reported as teaching language skills in a coordinated way.[5] This was true even though half of the schools employed reading specialists on their faculties. Furthermore, the teaching of reading was often limited to remedial instruction for the poor reader, and teachers failed to provide continued developmental training for the remainder of the students. In the 1,617 classrooms visited, it was discovered that teachers gave more than half of their time to the teaching of literature — its history, its authors, the cultures from which it emerged, and the like — and very little time to the development of skills for reading literature. In addition, individual guidance consisted mainly of specifying the number of titles to be read and supplying an approved list. Only a few superior teachers scheduled regular conferences with students, brought in new books for presentation to the class, provided classroom book collections to stimulate reading, and maintained individual reading folders. Similar examples could be given for reading in the content fields. Therefore, if reading is to be allotted its rightful place in the curriculum, the gap between theory and practice has to be closed.

For many years school officials have recognized individual differences among children in the same class in intelligence, reading ability, span of attention, and other characteristics, and they have been convinced of the

5 Squire, "Reading in American High Schools Today," in *Reading and Inquiry*, International Reading Association Conference Proceedings, edited by J. Allen Figurel (Newark, Del.: International Reading Association, 1965), X, 468–72.

need for differentiated instruction. As a result, many different combinations of grouping and individualized instruction have been developed. But which to use and when to use it are very real problems for teachers.

On this issue the lines are clearly drawn between those who would adopt some single form of class organization and those who advocate multiple forms that change with teaching objectives. An example of the single form of organization is whole-class instruction day after day, such as is common at the secondary level. Another example is the two-group plan, which is based on the measurement of reading ability by standardized reading tests and teacher observation; this is a common practice in the elementary school. In support of employing the two-group plan exclusively, it is said (1) that three or more groups would require the teacher to make too much advance preparation; (2) that teacher-direction of three or more groups is difficult, if not impossible, during the short class periods; and (3) that, after all, the range of reading achievement is not wide enough to justify working with more groups. This last objection has been refuted by test results in reading that show a wide range of ability for all classes and an increase in the range as children advance to higher grades.

Quite different from whole-class instruction is the individualized reading approach. Briefly, the main features of this method are the following: children make their own selections of books, read independently at their own pace, keep simple records and

reports of their reading, and have individual or small group sessions with their teachers. Proponents of this plan claim that by allowing children to read at their own rates and use materials of their own choice the children experience fewer frustrations and progress more rapidly. They also read more extensively and become acquainted with a wider variety of reading material. The big disadvantage is, of course, that the amount of time a teacher can devote to the individual child is very small.

The point of view most widely advocated by reading people is that no single pattern of organization is adequate for all teaching purposes. The pattern can best be selected in light of the objective, the skill to be developed, and the nature of the activities that can best promote the teaching purpose. Whole-class instruction can be effectively used, for example, for introducing a new topic for reading or for presenting an oral-reading selection that an individual or a group has practiced in advance. Likewise, small group instruction is best for the introduction and practice of reading skills or for the discussion of a silent reading selection or whenever common needs are apparent. The subgrouping reduces the range of individual differences in some respects, enables the teacher to give more help to each child, and encourages more interaction among the children themselves. In general, good grouping practices never set up rigid lines between good and poor readers; instead, provision is made for flexibility, mobility of pupils according to needs, and a variety of bases for grouping. Individual instruction is also needed; and it can sometimes be given within a group, at other times in a special period set aside for that purpose, or by a special teacher on the faculty.

TYPES OF ACTIVITIES AND MATERIALS ESSENTIAL TO GROWTH IN READING

Another issue teachers face today concerns the kinds of reading activities that should be provided in basic instruction in reading. This issue is far more significant than it may first appear, because it rests on the more basic question of what reading is. As indicated earlier, many present-day critics of reading programs equate reading with word identification. Naturally, teachers who adopt this narrow definition will restrict their pupils' reading activities for the most part to practice in word recognition. At the other end of the scale is the much broader definition of reading that is widely accepted by most reputable reading people. According to this definition, reading involves word perception; word meaning; comprehension and interpretation of ideas; thoughtful reaction, both critical and appreciative; and assimilation and use of ideas. Teachers who hold to this definition stress meaning and interpretation in the students' reading experiences. They encourage students to read between and beyond the lines rather than to believe everything they see in print. They also believe that reading can foster the students' personal and social growth. A well-balanced reading program, according to those who accept this broader defi-

nition, must provide students with many different types of reading activities, such as instruction designed to maintain old reading skills and introduce new skills, help in overcoming difficulties met in reading, improvement of efficiency in study activities requiring reading, occasions for wide reading in which students gain satisfaction through applying their reading skills, opportunities to share the results of independent reading, and evaluation of each student's progress.

The kinds of printed materials for teaching reading are far more numerous than ever before. Almost every day new schoolbooks appear on the market in bewildering variety. There are basic readers of many kinds: linguistic readers, readers printed in I.T.A., programmed readers, multiethnic readers, and readers for less competent learners, for average learners, and for able learners. There are diverse textbooks in various subject-matter areas such as science, social studies, and home economics. There are reading laboratories consisting of series of graded booklets for individualized work and also ready-made collections of books, some assembled for remedial reading and others for recreational reading. There are supplementary books on every imaginable topic. There is an increasing number of trade or library books for every grade level. There are paperback editions of classic and modern authors. There are dictionaries of many degrees of difficulty, ranging from "pictionaries" for first grade to the unabridged dictionaries used chiefly in secondary school and colleges. Likewise, there are encyclopedias for young children as well as secondary-school and college students.

The most important questions, therefore, concerning reading materials are the following two: Considering the objectives of the school's reading program and the characteristics of the pupils to be served, what kinds of reading materials can be used to best advantage? Which are the best of the available materials of these kinds?

In connection with the second question, it is imperative to stress the difficulty of making wise selections from among the flood of new materials. Modern books are so handsome that it seems natural to assume that they are also superior in content and teaching value. But we should be critical of every new volume, for books are subject to the same kind of packaging used in supermarkets. But unlike the supermarket packages, the books are not sealed. Any teacher or school official who has the time and the will can determine what is inside a book. It is not enough to read the deluge of propaganda that comes with it. Real evidence of its characteristics should be assembled and studied before any recommendation for purchase is made.

By way of illustration, here are some of the unexpected findings I obtained in a recent study of fifty primary-grade readers that were either entirely new or recently updated and reissued: *First*, a multiethnic reader is not necessarily an integrated reader as one might suppose; whites may be presented in one section of the book and Negroes in another, with no in-termingling of the races at all. *Second*, a reader that is lavishly illustrated with stylized representations may not appeal to children. We cannot assume that a child looking at the stylized pictures will identify himself, his family, and his neighborhood. In a limited test of stylized and realistic art in primers, I discovered that children preferred the realistic art because the characters had facial expressions and, they said, looked like real people. *Third*, the selections in some preprimers either have no plots at all or have plots that add little interest and excitement to the reading. The selections in such preprimers seem designed merely to repeat words. *Fourth*, a primary reading series constructed for disadvantaged pupils may have a much larger vocabulary load than any of the regular series. In view of the fact that disadvantaged pupils are generally retarded in language development, this is a very serious defect.

Besides reading materials, there are many types of equipment available to teachers today. These include the following: television, tape recorders, earphones, controlled readers, felt boards, overhead projectors, filmstrips, films, slides, pacing devices, and teaching machines. Some types of equipment have been tested and tried, but others are so new that study and careful trial are still needed to determine their relative merits.

READING ACTIVITIES IN THE CURRICULAR AREAS

Most teachers know that students must be helped to become successful, inquiring readers in the specialized areas of the curriculum such as arithmetic, science, and social studies. So the chief issue teachers in these areas face today — and it is a serious one — is how to improve the conditions under which curricular reading is done.

Investigators of current instructional practices have deplored certain conditions found in many classrooms: page-by-page assignments in a single textbook, question-and-answer recitation, parroting of words from the text, failure to set purposes for reading, absence of student interest and understanding, lack of instruction in critical reading, use of textbooks that students cannot read, and failure to adjust the reading activities to individual differences.

In discussing ways to overcome these poor practices, let us use the field of social studies as an example. The substance of the social studies curriculum consists of key concepts and generalizations. Instruction, therefore, should be designed to help the children develop these concepts rather than require them to memorize lists of facts. The acquisition of significant concepts and sound generalizations can best be achieved through the use of problem-solving techniques. According to Clyde F. Kohn, "The development of critical and creative thinking by means of problem-solving techniques depends to a great extent on the reading abilities of the learner."[6] Kohn emphasized the importance of three such abilities: (1) the ability to use accurate terminology in dealing with specific concepts and

[6] Kohn, "Reading in the Social Studies, Especially Geography," in *ibid.*, p. 486.

generalizations at all stages of the problem-solving process; (2) the ability to adapt rate of reading to purpose and content, especially when collecting data to solve a problem and analyzing and interpreting the data; and (3) the ability to keep in mind a series of related ideas in order to draw and test conclusions successfully. For developing this difficult third ability, Kohn recommended the use of outlines, summaries of what has been read, or simple lists of things in the order in which they are presented.

Teachers who are well acquainted with the concepts of a given field and the methods of obtaining knowledge in that field can make reading exciting and interesting. They can help children gain the reading abilities that are needed to apply problem-solving techniques to new situations and gradually to become independent learners in a particular field.

THE NEED FOR BASIC INSTRUCTION

When shall basic instruction in reading end? We know that, as students advance through the elementary school, secondary school, college and university, they require new reading habits and insights, and these, in turn, require new types of reading guidance. Most elementary schools have long provided reading instruction through grade six for all pupils.

Until about 1950, secondary schools in many places limited their teaching of reading to students who were in need of remedial work. Some schools limited it further to the retarded readers in a particular grade, such as the seventh grade. Soon afterward, the concept emerged of teaching developmental reading to all high-school pupils. Not many schools offered such programs until about 1960, when educators became deeply concerned with the high-school dropout problem. Studies showed that most dropouts were reading well below grade norms. High schools and junior colleges were then urged to supply better reading instruction for slower students before they became dropouts.

In the last five or six years, high-school reading instruction has been greatly expanded. Some high schools are giving developmental reading courses that a student may attend for a full semester; others schedule reading for periods that students would ordinarily spend in study halls; still others provide developmental reading as part of the English program. Many experimental reading programs, such as wide reading opportunities and programed instruction in reading, are also underway. In fact, high schools are steadily progressing toward the fourfold reading program now considered essential at all levels: (1) basic instruction in reading; (2) guidance of reading in the content fields; (3) literature, including independent reading of good books for pleasure and information; and (4) corrective or remedial instruction as needed.

Colleges usually teach reading only for selected students in the Freshman year. Almost invariably the course is of a remedial nature. Although some colleges and universities do provide courses designed to promote the student's maximum personal development in and through reading, this is the exception rather than the rule.

Recently much has been done to increase reading-instructional services to adults. The variety of available services include: first, reading improvement centers for adults whose work requires them to cover vast amounts of reading material and who want to learn how to do this faster and to get more meaning from what they read; second, reading classes provided by business and industrial organizations for groups of their employees; third, training in reading given in the schools of the armed services; and fourth, reading instruction for illiterate and semiliterate adults through the use of city, state, and federal resources.

In reply to the question raised at the beginning of this section, basic reading instruction should not come to an end until the student no longer has need for guidance and refinement of his reading skills. Even after a student has left school, reading instruction should be made available to him whenever he wants to improve his reading abilities so that they will be commensurate with his personal needs for reading, as well as with his reading tasks in the world of work.

CHAPTER VI

INSTRUCTIONAL PROCEDURES IN READING

*

IN KINDERGARTEN THROUGH GRADE THREE

LUCILLE MOZZI

*

EVEN THOUGH the primary teacher may have a clear-cut understanding of the objectives of the reading program and be able to identify the significant reading skills of both the individual pupil and the group, she is still faced with the problem of putting this knowledge, information, and understanding into the task of reading instruction. Immediately, a multitude of decisions must be made as to how the classroom instructional program should be organized and conducted. What methods should be used? What can be done about individual differences? What types of learning experiences should be provided? There appear to be two basic elements that must be taken into account in these decisions. These are the individual differences among pupils and the necessity for the classroom teacher to teach, for the most part, more than one pupil at a time.

Despite the pressures of individual differences and the group teaching situation, there are some practical procedures which can insure that balance and proportion are incorporated in the daily classroom teaching program. These procedures are often not included because they are not clearly understood, or they are included but are not emphasized to a great enough extent.

READING SKILLS

It is important that there be a balanced instructional program in the teaching of reading skills. Certain aspects of *all* the reading skills can and should be taught to the beginning reader. Too often the primary teacher becomes so involved with teaching word recognition skills that vocabulary, comprehension, and interpretation are more or less put to one side. Meaning, whether it of single words or groups of words, is de-emphasized and work-study skills completely omitted. The assumption is made that all that is necessary is to recognize words and that meaning will develop as a natural concomitant. This is not true, as many teachers will testify. These teachers are very familiar with the pupils who can call off words with ease but cannot give their meanings.

The ultimate goal of reading instruction is to have pupils understand what they read. This goal cannot be achieved if the teacher does not give the teaching of meaning the same emphasis that the word recognition skills receive. This does not mean that the time allotted for the teaching of various skills must be equal at all times. There are stages in beginning reading when one skill will demand more time than another, and there are pupils who will need a little more time on certain skills. But in general, perhaps over a period of several days or a week, the time devoted to word skills and to meaning should be equalized.

There are several procedures which will insure that the teacher does not unwittingly de-emphasize meaning. One is to supplement the more formal method of teaching reading with the daily use of experience charts or stories. Experience charts can evolve from many sources, use the oral language and understanding of the learner, allow for individual differences in reading ability, and give rise to opportunities for teaching other reading skills besides comprehension.

Another procedure is to use oral reading to evaluate both word recognition skills and fluency. Far too often the primary teacher asks the pupil to read aloud because it is his turn. If a pupils has difficulty with more than three or four words in a selection, it is very possible that he is not understanding what he is reading. This is quite all right if the teacher is only trying to evaluate the pupil's ability in word recognition; but if he is expecting this procedure to improve the pupil's understanding or his fluency in oral reading, he will be disappointed. Understanding can only be achieved if the pupil can read almost all of the words in a selection without difficulty. If the teacher asks the pupil to read a selection silently first, helps him with any difficulties with indi-

vidual words, asks questions about the content, and then asks him to read aloud, understanding and fluency are more apt to result. Oral reading for each individual pupil should be initiated with a definite objective in mind. It is a more difficult task than silent reading because it is an expressive act of language. A pupil must first be successful in the receptive act of language, silent reading, before he can be successful in oral reading. Taking a turn is not a good enough reason for reading aloud. The requirement of having clear-cut objectives in mind for oral reading does not mean that the amount of oral reading need necessarily be diminished in many classroom reading programs. Much depends on how the teacher understands and uses oral reading in the daily instructional periods.

A third instructional procedure which may aid the teacher is the selection of the correct approach to teaching phonics. There are some pupils who cannot grasp the relationship between the sounds of our language and the visual symbols which represent them from the generalization approach. For intellectual, cognitive, and environmental reasons, these pupils may not be able to take generalizations about auditory-visual relationships and apply them to new situations, despite the fact that they can hear, see, and discriminate both aurally and visually. It is very possible that they are part-to-whole learners and must learn the auditory-visual relationship inductively through linguistic patterning rather than deductively through phonic generalizations. The deductive, or generalization, approach is widely used in the phonic programs of many of our basal reader programs. The inductive or pattern approach is used in the many new linguistic materials which are appearing on the market. Most research indicates that a judicious combination of both approaches is likely to be the answer to some of the problems teachers meet in teaching phonics.

A fourth helpful instructional procedure is to make a checklist of skills on which to keep daily track of skill weaknesses and strengths. A checklist is invaluable for setting up groups for special skill instruction, for making sure individual pupils are exposed to learning experiences they especially need, and for determining whether the teacher is teaching all of the essential skills. The checklist should be kept up to date.

LEARNING EXPERIENCES

Three of the most important goals in reading are to understand what is read, to enlarge and enhance one's knowledge of the world, and to develop a positive attitude toward reading. A teacher can insure that these goals will be realized if various types of learning experiences are systematically introduced in the daily lesson plan. One type of learning experience is that which provides for the direct teaching of skills by the teacher. A second type is that which provides for practice and reinforcement of recently taught skills. A third type of learning experience is that in which the pupil must use his reading skills for a purpose. The purpose may range from the

gathering and using of information to the simply recreational.

The level of materials for the first and second types of learning experience should be at an instructional level of difficulty, and the level for the third type at an independent level of difficulty. The reading behavior of the pupils rather than the materials should set the goals for reading instruction.

The inclusion of all three types of reading experiences will provide an opportunity for reaching the goals mentioned at the beginning of this section. With a variety of learning experiences, the demand for a variety of content and levels of difficulty will rise. A large number of appropriate books should be in every classroom.

No means of communication should be taught in isolation. All language skills are of necessity interrelated. Oral language precedes written language, and written or visual language is dependent on oral language.

A child's first experiences with language are aural and receptive. Initial language learning is done through listening. As the motor mechanisms for speech develop, the child adds the expressive or motor act of oral language — speech. As oral language develops there is a constant interplay and reinforcement between the expressive and receptive behaviors. The pupils' oral language must be extremely well developed before he is introduced to the written language because he will be expected to use his oral language skills to reinforce and learn the visual language. If through unfortunate circumstances his oral language is not well developed, the primary teacher will have to take the necessary time to develop it. A well-developed program for listening and speaking is a must for all types of primary programs.

Once written language is introduced, it will in turn reinforce listening and speaking. For instance, reading in the contents fields and then discussing topics that have been raised is an excellent way to develop experiential background and comprehension of ideas. And writing about what one has read is another way to reinforce understandings gained from reading. Awareness of these interrelationships is very necessary, but awareness is not enough. The teacher must deliberately use these relationships in teaching all aspects of language.

* * *

IN GRADES FOUR THROUGH EIGHT

JEAN LAWRENCE

*

BEFORE ANY teacher can plan a successful program, he must be aware of his pupils' levels of proficiency in reading, the skills in which the pupils are deficient, and the pupils' general abilities and interests. A thorough diagnosis by means of standardized and informal tests should help to insure that each pupil will work with materials adapted to his reading level, that he will receive group or individual instruction fitted to his needs, and that he will move along at his maximum rate. Teachers should be able to interpret scores and evaluate test data, or the information will be of little value. Basing one's judgment on one test alone will obviously be unsatisfactory for both pupil and teacher. Ideally, by the end of the first few weeks of a new school year, teachers should have enough information about each pupil to be able to plan the first instructional steps.

Several reading groups should be established to cater to the wide range of reading abilities found in a class. Even though there may be some form of homogeneous grouping or team teaching between grade levels, the teacher will need to divide the class into small groups in order to satisfy individual needs. The teacher must be careful, at first, not to establish more groups than he can successfully handle. The questions usually asked at this point are, Into what groups shall I divide my pupils so that each individual may receive the best kind of instruction to meet his particular needs? And how can I divide my time and attention between these groups in the best possible manner?

Let us suppose that a self-contained

class of thirty to thirty-five children is divided into three or four ability groups. There will be some accelerated pupils who are independent readers. For these, the teacher will act as a guide, diagnosing their needs and fostering their development in all skills while they pursue courses of study on an independent level. The average readers, though needing greater emphasis on all basic reading skills, will also read independently but will require more of the teacher's attention than the accelerated group. Average readers will comprise the greater proportion of the class, and it may be necessary to subdivide them into two groups. The slow readers will need much more help in oral reading, word attack skills, and comprehension than the others. And there may be some extremely poor readers who may need to be referred to the reading clinic.

It is obvious that in order to plan a workable program the teacher must not be needed by more than *one* group at a particular time. The other groups should be engaged in reading activities which are not only meaningful but also constitute a pleasurable experience and which can be pursued independently for part of the total lesson time. A teacher can plan to work with two separate groups during a forty- to forty-five-minute reading period.

MATERIALS, EQUIPMENT, AND
RESOURCES

Much has been said and written about the use of basic readers. There is little doubt that, if enough basic readers are available for three or four different levels within a class, they do provide pupils with good sequential skill-building exercises as well as a variety of types of reading. Used carefully and creatively, they provide the teacher with excellent material in well-organized form. Basic readers can form an integral part of the reading program, but they should not constitute the entire program.

In addition, the following materials should be available in the classroom:

1. Dictionaries. (One should be available for each pupil, if possible.)
2. Sets of several encyclopedias.
3. Children's magazines to supplement those found in the school library.
4. Daily newspaper and children's weekly current events papers.
5. Catalogues, travel pamphlets, guide books, cookbooks, atlases, and directories. (The yellow pages of the telephone book are available in abridged form for school use.)
6. A good selection of books, even if the school has a library. (If the school library is poorly stocked, a teacher can secure books from public, state, and even mobile libraries. Depending on the current projects going on in the classroom, the teacher should see that there is a good supply of books for information or recreational reading on specific topics.)
7. Poetry books, choral reading selections, and plays. (These will be needed for oral reading practice.)
8. Paperbacks. (There is a wide selection of books in paperback form on the market these days. Some schools have set up paperback bookstores to encourage children to choose and buy their own books. A class could raise enough money with a bake sale to purchase several dozen paperbacks.)
9. Supplementary materials. (In addition

to the workbooks which accompany the basic readers, teachers will find it useful to make supplementary materials. Sets of mimeographed sheets for building skills and improving comprehension can be kept in manila folders until they are needed and returned to the folders for later use.)

A teacher can supplement these materials by the creative use of other resources.

Recordings. We cannot expect to motivate individuals to enjoy and appreciate good literature simply by recounting to them the satisfaction good readers receive from such reading. Some pupils have never experienced good reading or heard a good reader. "Good models make for better understanding and interpretation."[1] Recorded works are available in great number and can be used to develop understandings in many content fields.[2]

Filmstrips. There are many excellent filmstrips, which can be used in a variety of ways and with different ability groups. Encyclopaedia Britannica has a series to help pupils learn to use card catalogs, encyclopedias and special reference books.[3] There are also several filmstrips available to help pu-

pils with specific problems in word recognition. Motion pictures on these skills are also easily attainable.

Slides. With a simple camera, a teacher, or even a pupil, can take pictures of a group dramatizing scenes from a book they have been reading. Then the actual dialogue from the story can be taped on a recorder. Later, the slides can be shown and the recording played simultaneously in a group presentation of the book. Almost any good story will lend itself to this use.

Overhead projector. This is one of the most useful audiovisual aids in the classroom. One can make or buy overlays designed to help teach word-attack skills, library skills, and the like. The instrument is quiet, the room does not have to be darkened, and the method is very practical for use with small groups.

Speakers. Every community has people who have interesting things to talk about. A local writer, an illustrator of books, a printer, a bookbinder, a news reporter, someone who has been abroad, a local sports hero, representatives from local industries and occupations, a foreign visitor — each of these can help stimulate interest in a particular book or subject.

Field trips. Pupils profit from firsthand experiences with places, events, or people they encounter in their reading. Visits to national history museums, planetariums, art galleries, local historical landmarks, famous people's homes, and state parks can become a vital part of the total reading program. For Chicagoans, for example, seeing

[1] Arthur W. Heilman, *Principles and Practices of Teaching Reading* (Columbus, Ohio: Charles E. Merrill Books, Inc., 1961), p. 439.

[2] *An Annotated List of Recordings in the Language Arts*, edited by Morris Schreiber (Champaign, Ill.: National Council of Teachers of English, 1964); *Recordings for Children* (a selected list prepared by New York Library Association, New York Public Library, 1964).

[3] *Using the Dictionary, Using Special Reference Books*, and *Using the Card Catalog* (filmstrips by Encyclopaedia Britannica in "Using The Library Series").

Jane Addams' famous settlement house and then taking a tour of the new Jane Addams Center on Chicago's North Side can provide an interesting background to reading Clara Judson's *City Neighbor* (Charles Scribner's Sons, 1951), and Jean Wagoner's *Jane Addams: Little Lame Girl* (Bobbs-Merrill Co., 1962).

GROUPS AT WORK

Not all teachers are fortunate enough to work in spacious, modern classrooms where light, movable furniture facilitates grouping procedures, although even these teachers still have the problem of insulation of working groups from each other. Whenever possible, seating should be rearranged so that each group is able to work efficiently. Bookcases, movable screens, or even pieces of Masonite will provide some degree of privacy. Where it is impractical to rearrange desks and seats, one or two groups can use extra folding chairs in a corner of the room. In some classrooms, groups can sit on the floor. Piles of newspapers make good cushions.

Let us consider the various types of reading activities that could be included in a classroom composed of the three or four ability groups described earlier.

1. *Accelerated readers* — working independently. Initial planning is discussed with the teacher at the beginning of the week; short conferences are planned when needed during the day.

Fourth grade — science project on space. This involves study-type reading, collecting information from weekly periodicals, and using the card catalog to find fiction and nonfiction books. One pupil is reading Madeline L'Engle's *Wrinkle in Time* (Ariel Books, 1962).

Sixth grade. After reading Jean Latham's *Carry On, Mr. Bowditch* (Houghton Mifflin, 1955), one boy is studying the development of navigational aids. The yellow pages help him to find shipping stores where he can see these instruments.

2. *Average readers*

Fourth grade — using basic readers. To improve ability to classify and organize ideas, they are reading a story silently, then listing the actions of the main characters.

Fifth grade — group seated around small table on wheels. Each pupil has earphones plugged into table. They are listening to a recording of Kenneth Grahame's *Wind in the Willows* (Charles Scribner's Sons, 1961). Mimeographed copies of a chapter will be used later for oral reading and comprehension.

Eighth grade — studying technical vocabulary to aid comprehension and clarity attempts in unit on local, state, and federal governments. Words such as *council, representative, veto, constitution, amendment,* and *senate* are being defined and discussed. The group plans a mock session of a city council meeting after field trip to see council in action.

3. *Slow readers*

Fifth grade — "Mississippi River: Father of Waters." Independent readers are acting as leaders of small groups that are working on such topics as folk heroes, folksongs, development of settlements, exploration, industries, and so forth. The teacher works with groups or individuals as required. The unit is linked with language arts, science, and social studies, as well as with recreational reading.

Seventh grade — library skills. Each pupil has been given a written question based on a known interest of his; for example, "which was the first American flag to use stars and stripes? Pupils must think of the proper category in order to use the card catalog and must use the table of contents and index to find pertinent information. Filmstrip "Using the Card Catalog" is ready for individual or group use. Opportunities will sometimes occur for the entire class to work together on a special unit to heighten interest.

* * *

IN GRADES NINE THROUGH FOURTEEN

OLIVER ANDRESEN

*

FOR PURPOSES of instruction, the reading process may be broken down into three major skill areas: vocabulary, comprehension, and rate of reading.

Two types of skills enhance vocabulary growth. First, there are the word recognition skills, those skills by which a reader pronounces a word in print that is already in his speaking or listening vocabulary. Second, there are the word meaning skills, those skills by which a reader determines the meaning of a word in print that is not in his speaking or listening vocabulary.

According to Andresen and Robinson, reading comprehension may be considered as having five levels.[1] Briefly defined, these levels are the following:

1) *Literal level.* At this level the reader recognizes and understands the author's stated ideas.

2) *Interpretative level.* At this level the reader understands not only the stated ideas of the author but his implied ideas as well. In short, the reader sees implications or "reads between the lines."

3) *Critical level.* At this level the reader not only understands the author's ideas, both stated and implied, but passes judgment on them. In light of his own experience, the reader evaluates the author's thinking as expressed in print.

4) *Assimilative level.* At this level the reader not only understands, interprets, and evaluates the author's thinking but adds to it as well with thoughts from his own experience and imagination. Within his own mind, the reader becomes a "co-author" of an idea or experience presented in print. The results of this conjunctive action with the author is an integration of the reader's own judgments and beliefs concerning certain aspects of the author's ideas.

5) *Creative level.* William S. Gray defined his "highest of all the higher mental processes" as involving "the imaginative treatment of ideas in both inductive and deductive thinking" and resulting in "new insights, fresh ideas, and new organizations of patterns of thought."[2]

[1] Oliver Andresen and H. Alan Robinson, "Developing Competence in Reading Comprehension" (address delivered at the First International Congress on Reading sponsored by the International Reading Association, Paris, France, August 8, 1966).

[2] Gray, "The Major Aspects of Reading," in *Sequential Development of Reading Abilities,* compiled and edited by Helen M. Robin-

As is implied, these levels of comprehension are additive. A higher level cannot be achieved without the successful performance of the preceding lower levels. The responsibility for independent and contemplative thinking increases for the reader as he moves from level to level.

The key word in discussions of rate of reading is flexibility. Certainly, a good reader ought to shift gears when he reads. To read in "high gear" within the range of comprehension is called speed reading. To read only for the general idea and with intentional neglect of the details is skimming. To peruse a mass of print in search of only one fact is scanning. Yet, a good reader never exceeds the speed limit determined by his ability to comprehend.

WHAT TO TEACH: VOCABULARY

Occasionally, a student at the high-school or college level will have difficulty recognizing a word in print even though it is already within his speaking or listening vocabulary. In such a situation, it is usually helpful to break the word into syllables. Three basic generalizations for syllabication will usually answer this type of problem: (1) Prefixes and suffixes are separate syllables (exception: *ed* unless preceded by a *t* or *d*); (2) when two consonants fall between two vowels, the division generally is between the two consonants; and (3) when one consonant comes between two vowels, the division generally is before the consonant.

---

son ("Supplementary Educational Monographs," No. 90; Chicago: University of Chicago Press, 1960), p. 19.

Occasionally, a phonic problem arises at this level. This writer recently had as a student a Freshman in college who could not recognize the word *lilac* because he did not know how to sound the *c*. Some instruction on the hard and soft *c* sounds eliminated his problem. An excellent handbook for older students on these problems is Clyde Roberts' *Word Attack* (Harcourt, Brace & World, Inc., 1956).

Although an older reader may outgrow his need for actively exercising word attack skills, he will never outgrow his need for the application of word meaning skills. The first thing one should do when encountering an unfamiliar word in print is to attempt to determine the meaning by the use of the word in context. Unfortunately, this skill doesn't always work; yet, it should be attempted first since it utilizes the material at hand.

If using the word's context fails, the reader should search for clues of the word's meaning by examining the meaning of its parts. For example, if he knows a word with the same root, he may assume that the meanings of the two words are related. It must be admitted, however, that unless the reader is a classical scholar this skill will not work for him readily.

The most certain, but also the most cumbersome, way to determine a new word's meaning is to consult a dictionary. Using a dictionary while reading both interrupts the author's thread of thought and is time consuming. Yet, because the dictionary is the most useful instrument for solving word-meaning problems, its multiple uses must be thoroughly understood and practiced by high-school and college students.

Every student in high school and college should keep lists of the new words he is experiencing on cards or in a notebook. When recording a word, the student should list not only its meaning but its pronunciation, its forms according to the various parts of speech, and its synonyms and antonyms, if any. Once these lists begin to grow, a new problem becomes evident. The student must begin to classify his growing lists of words. Classification should be on the basis of meaning rather than spelling or structure. A good classification method is to determine whether each word is concrete, abstract, or both. Or a word may be classified according to its emotive qualities. Is it "positive," "negative," neither, or both? Such attention to meaning will assist the student in developing his vocabulary.

WHAT TO TEACH: COMPREHENSION

Although a student may understand all the meanings of the words he encounters in a selection, he may still not understand what the author is attempting to tell him. In other words, students who have problems in the area of reading comprehension often need to be taught specific skills by which they can direct their minds toward an understanding of the author's ideas.

One of the most basic, and thus essential, comprehension skills for students at high-school and college levels is the ability to distinguish what is important from what is not important. In other words, the student must be able to recognize key words and phrases.[3] According to their use by the author, certain words and phrases in his sentences will carry the nuclei of his ideas. A student who practices underlining key words under the guidance of a teacher will soon find that his mind emphasizes these key words and gives only a casual glance toward the periphery. The result is that the author's ideas, shorn of excessive verbiage, suddenly loom up plainly within the reader's mind and his understanding is enhanced.

A student at this level should also be able to recognize the relationships among the ideas in a selection. For example, he should distinguish between primary details and secondary details. Once he is aware of these relationships in a selection, he can apportion his intellectual emphasis accordingly. If the author does not state his main idea, and presents it instead as an implication, the student must learn to infer the main idea and to formulate a statement of it within his own mind.

The student should also be able to recognize the different organizational patterns by which the relationships among ideas can be expressed. For example, he should be able to recognize a sequence — chronological sequence, place sequence, or logical sequence — noting with particular attention the order by which the ideas are presented. An alert reader can foresee how a passage will be organized by its heading, its topic sentence, or clue words such

[3] H. Alan Robinson, "A Cluster of Skills: Especially for Junior High School," *Reading Teacher,* XV (September, 1961), 25.

as *first, second, last,* or *best, second best, worst,* and the like.

Two other types of organizational pattern are comparison and cause and effect. When a reader finds his eye entering a selection based on a comparison or on cause and effect, he knows he must look for two subtopics. In comparison, he looks for the similarities and differences of the two subtopics. In cause and effect, he looks for the causal relationship between one subtopic and another. Headings, topic sentences, and clue words such as *whereas* for comparison and *because* for cause and effect would inform the alert reader that one or other of the organizational patterns is present.

A generalization, summary, or conclusion is often presented in a special organizational pattern. Such a pattern contains a main idea (stated or implied) and details, all of which lead or point to a basic statement or opinion of the author. Besides headings and topic sentences, clue words such as *thus, hence, therefore,* and the like will inform the reader that such an organizational pattern is present. The reader's task is to seek out the climactic statement.[4]

WHAT TO TEACH: RATE

One way of breaking the habit of a plodding, inflexible rate of reading is to play the game "Beat the clock." To play this game the student first sets

[4] Oliver Andresen, "Developing Purposeful and Flexible Reading in Grades Nine through Fourteen," in *Recent Developments in Reading,* compiled and edited by H. Alan Robinson ("Supplementary Educational Monographs," No. 95; Chicago: University of Chicago Press, 1965), p. 177.

an alarm clock to ring at the end of fifteen minutes. He then begins to read easy, highly entertaining material as fast as he can but not so fast that he loses the thread of thought. When the alarm rings, he notes the number of pages he has read on a chart. Each day he attempts to increase the number of pages he can read in the same period of time. Occasionally, he should read rather difficult, study-type material in a very slow and thorough manner so that he comprehends in depth approximately 85 per cent of it. By practicing these two types of reading, his flexibility of rate should increase.

One way of helping students to learn to skim is to have them read the first sentence of each paragraph in a selection, continuing until the author's thread of thought is lost. When the thread is interrupted, the reader should peruse the preceding paragraph until he has found the thought again. For scanning — when the reader wishes to find only a particular fact within a mass of print — the student can be helped by taking a moment to decide what "clues" in the material would indicate the proximity of the fact. For example, the reader might want to know the date on which Franklin Roosevelt was married. In a biographical sketch, he would certainly investigate that section discussing postcollege years. He would also look for dates. And certainly, the surest clue that he was near the fact would be the name Eleanor.

A student must learn to shift gears when he reads according to "how well he knows the road," "how difficult the terrain," and his purpose in "taking the trip." If there are no vocabulary problems or comprehension problems present, a person's rate depends primarily on his "mental set." In other words, if he makes up his mind to read faster, he will be able to do so. Only his habit of proceeding more slowly will inhibit him.

* * *

IN CORRECTIVE AND REMEDIAL CLASSES
ELIZABETH P. DAVEY

*

For the past five years, I have conducted one of the twelve remedial reading clinics maintained by the Chicago Public Schools. Pupils selected by psychologists and counselors from neighboring schools come to the clinic, during the school day, for forty-five-minute periods of remedial reading instruction two or three times a week. Last year, 20 per cent of those referred were from below the sixth grade and, for the most part, were non-readers. The others were from the sixth, seventh, and eighth grades and, according to standardized tests, were reading two or more years below their grade level. In this paper, I shall describe the methods of basic reading instruction that I have found useful in teaching those who are two or more years below grade level.

DIAGNOSIS

First, the reading needs of each individual are determined in order to plan an efficient instructional program. Which skills has he mastered and which does he need to develop? At what level should his instruction start? Each youngster is given the *Gray Oral Reading Tests* (Bobbs-Merrill Co., 1963), which are composed of a series of paragraphs of increasing difficulty. General weaknesses, such as poor phrasing, word-by-word reading, and disregard of punctuation, appear and indicate instruction needs. The comprehension questions that accompany the Gray tests are used to measure the reader's understanding of literal meanings and, together with the grade score, partially determine the level of material that he will use in the clinic. The level can be double-checked by having him read silently a short article at the same level as the other materials and then give an oral report. In addition to a check, the silent reading and oral report also provide indications of speech patterns and comprehension abilities.

While he is reading the passages in the Gray tests, a record of his errors — words mispronounced and words not recognized — is kept. If he miscalls common words, he is given a list of Dolch words to identify. And if he is still unable to recognize frequently used words accurately and quickly, instructional time is used to increase his basic sight vocabulary. His attack on unfamiliar words is carefully observed. Does he skip words, or guess at them, or try to work out their pronunciations? A good reader must know not only the many skills involved in word attack but the appropriate ones to use. If he seems to falter in using phonic, structural, and context clues, he is asked to pronounce the fifteen words in the *Botel Reading Inventory* (Follett, 1961). These words are well chosen to test ability to handle vowel and consonant sounds and syllable concepts, and mispronunciations indicate instructional needs. If more information is desired, the supplementary phonics tests in Spache's *Diagnostic Reading Scales* (California Test Bureau, 1963), may be used.

The findings from these tests in the three areas of word recognition, vocabulary, and comprehension are discussed with each pupil. His strengths and weaknesses in each area are explained, and instruction that will meet his needs is planned. Until this time, he has probably only been told that he is behind in reading in terms of grade levels but has received no suggestions as to how to improve. Consequently, he now reacts hopefully to a discussion that deals with the nature of his reading weaknesses and outlines what can be done to overcome them. His reading skills are reassessed frequently, and instruction is modified to meet his changing needs.

Five to ten pupils are scheduled for each period in the clinic. Of the various ways of grouping that have been tried, the most successful has been that which brings individuals with similar word-attack problems together for common instruction. The group works with the teacher for fifteen minutes of the forty-five-minute period on word-attack skills. At the same time, good listening and learning habits that will be helpful in the regular classrooms are given attention. The rest of a period is spent in working with each pupil individually or with two or three together on comprehension and vocabulary. By combining group and individualized instruction, each period can be used to strengthen word-attack skills, to increase vocabulary, and to improve comprehension skills.

INSTRUCTIONAL PROCEDURES

Most of the students who come to the clinic lack good word-attack skills. They guess, skip over, or miscall many printed words. They either are unable to select an appropriate method or are unable to employ effectively the one they have chosen for working out pronunciations of unfamiliar words. They generally know the meanings of many words but are unable to recognize them since they cannot pronounce them correctly. These students have failed to profit sufficiently from the various kinds of training in word analysis they have received in the developmental and remedial classes of their home schools, and therefore, a different approach must be used in the clinic. One way is to start with polysyllabic, rather than monosyllabic, words.

Students actually seem to be more interested in working with long words and find it easier to deal with the separate but combined sounds of polysyllabic words than with monosyllables. Syllabication principles are utilized to divide the words into workable parts. In order to pronounce the parts, instruction and practice in single consonant sounds and consonant blends are often necessary. The effect of open and closed syllables on vowel sounds is noted and practiced. Word roots are located and identified. Pupils are pleased when they can work out the pronunciation of a long word; and the more words they are able to figure out, the more confidence they gain and the more effective they are in using their word-attack skills.

When pupils encounter words in reading that they have never heard or spoken, however, they must consult a dictionary. Frequent practice in alphabetizing and in using guide words is given so that unknown words can be found quickly. Instruction in reading diacritical markings is also necessary. (Pupils who have difficulty with consonant and vowel sounds are often aided by work with the dictionary key to pronunciation.) And finally, instruction and practice in selecting the meaning for a particular context are given.

Reading materials in which pupils will encounter few word recognition or vocabulary problems are chosen to improve comprehension skills. When few unfamiliar words are met, pupils can more readily understand the ideas that the printed words convey. Most of them prefer readings from the content fields — informational subject matter is more popular than fiction. As much as possible, individual tastes and interests are considered in choosing readings. The boy who likes arithmetic reads in a simple mathematics textbook. The girl whose favorite subject is science reads short articles in that field. When an individual reports that he doesn't like any school subject, materials that deal with personal development are suggested. For example, grooming hints for girls and vocational information for boys may be used. Most of the boys and girls respond to comprehension instruction much more successfully if they can read the materials easily and if they are interested in the subject matter.

Instruction in the comprehension skills is started at the factual level. *Who, what, where,* and *when* questions are used to help the readers recognize the facts in the materials. Guidance and practice are given in the assessment of these facts. After the pupils are able to identify main facts, to follow sequences, and to understand literal meanings, instruction is directed toward organizing and evaluating facts, forming generalizations, and drawing conclusions. Instruction at this more abstract level is conducted in both group and individual conferences in which ideas can be discussed. Pupils are encouraged to ask questions about their readings and to find answers. As the instruction advances from simple skills to more complex ones, materials are chosen to move gradually from simple sentences to paragraphs and longer passages.

Most pupils are handicapped by their limited vocabularies. Because they have done little reading, their experience with words is restricted. They need to learn the meanings of new words; they need to learn additional meanings of familiar words; they need to become acquainted with idioms and figures of speech; they need to develop curiosity about words and their meanings. These needs are not fulfilled easily or quickly. The first materials that the pupils read should contain only a few new words. These words should be presented and the meanings discussed when the reading is started. Since all the words that will give difficulty may not be recognized by the pupil or the teacher, training in self-help skills — use of the dictionary, study of the context for meaning clues, and analysis of word parts — should be stressed. Various devices, such as individual notebooks, commercial workbooks, word exercises, knowledge of synonyms, prefixes, and suffixes, and practice in finding root words, should be used to extend their vocabularies.

CONCLUDING STATEMENT

The basic reading instruction for the sixth, seventh, and eighth graders who come to the clinic is planned on the basis of their individual needs. Each pupil's reading needs are studied in order to plan effective instruction. Weaknesses and strengths in recognizing words, understanding meanings, and in comprehending ideas conveyed by combinations of words are determined. Pupils with similar word recognition problems are grouped together for common instruction. New methods of teaching word-attack skills are generally more successful than the ones already tried in their home schools. Pupils improve in comprehension skills if the materials used can be read easily and are interesting and if the instruction they receive develops gradually from an understanding of facts to a consideration of more complex concepts. At the same time, pupils are encouraged to develop an interest in words and their meanings and to enlarge their reading vocabularies.

CHAPTER VII

INFLUENCE OF SPECIFIC FACTORS ON GROWTH IN INTERPRETATION

*

A. STERL ARTLEY

*

FIFTEEN YEARS ago when the topic "Influence of Specific Factors on Growth in Interpretation" was discussed at the reading conference, such factors as intelligence, background of experience, emotional and physical status of the reader, and general language ability were considered. As I reread the paper presented at that time, I was impressed by the fact that the generalizations they contained are as relevant today as they were then. The fifteen years have brought to light not so much in the way of new factors as in further evidence to support, reinforce, and extend what we believed then. I shall attempt in this paper to give an overview of four areas in which findings have been added and thinking extended relative to the interpretive process.

SEARCH FOR THE SPECIFICS OF THE INTERPRETIVE PROCESS

In 1944 Frederick B. Davis reported a pioneer study of the factors comprising one dimension of the interpretive process, namely, comprehension.[1] Through the statistical technique of factor analysis, Davis identified five separate factors. These were vocabulary, reasoning ability, ability to identify the writer's intent, ability to group "detailed statements" in a passage, and knowledge of literary devices and techniques. In subsequent writings Davis stressed the importance of these five areas and pointed up the necessity of their being systematically taught in the upper grades and high school.

Since that time there has been a proliferation of the competencies subsumed under the several dimensions of the interpretive act. Gertrude Williams made an analysis of ten basal reader series current in the 1950's to note what methods were being used to teach critical reading, which she broadly defined as "intelligent reading directed toward the learning purposes of the individual child."[2] In addition to skills identified as necessary to literal comprehension, Williams found thirty-three others that were identified as part of the interpretive process. Only four of the thirty-three were common to all ten of the

[1] Davis, "Fundamental Factors of Comprehension in Reading," *Psychometrika*, IX (September, 1944), 185–97.

[2] Williams, "Provisions for Critical Reading in Basic Readers," *Elementary English*, XXXVI (May, 1959), 327.

71

series, and four were found in only one. Certainly, there was little agreement among the authors as to the identity of the skills.

James F. Kerfoot, in a cogent article, points out that the problems confronting the profession result from a confusion in terminology when interpretation is discussed.[3] With regard to comprehension alone, Kerfoot says, reading theorists have confused their readers by personalizing terms with their own unique labels. What is called "interpretive reading" by one writer is called "elaborative thinking" by another and "creative reading" by still another. He recommends, and I am sure that we would agree, that we dispense with confusing generalized labels and attempt to identify the specific tasks themselves. Further research, Kerfoot suggests, should be directed to the discovery of independent, fundamental abilities involved in interpretation.

It is in accordance with this recommendation that Jack Holmes has directed his work. He has proposed the "substrata-factor theory of reading,"[4] which has been referred to by Helen M. Robinson in chapter iii. From a first-level analysis of his data on reading Holmes found that 78 per cent of the variance was accounted for by four factors—vocabulary in context, intelligence, perception of verbal relations, and eye fixations. Each of these factors underwent a second-level analysis to precipitate out those factors of which it was composed, and each of these factors in turn was analyzed for third-level factors. These analyses yielded such "substrata" factors as general information, word discrimination, and perception of verbal relations.

Though admitting that Holmes's statistical analysis was conducted with "technical excellence and rigorous standards of research," Gus P. Plessas is critical of Holmes's generalizations.[5] Any study employing an intercorrelation technique, he maintains, can yield findings only in terms of the nature of the tests it uses. Plessas points out that, although Holmes's generalizations are predicated on the theory that reading is a reasoning process, his tests are limited in their ability to measure the reasoning function. Moreover, Plessas questions the independence of Holmes's variables. He raises the question, "How *sub* are the subabilities in Holmes's hierarchy of the substrata factors that are mobilized as a psychological working system in reading? Are they the prime factors or primary materials in the reasoning process in reading? Do they have universal qualities?"[6]

The statistical procedure employed by Holmes holds promise. With a broader base of tests that have a substantial correlation with an outside

3 Kerfoot, "Problems and Research Considerations in Reading Comprehension," *Reading Teacher*, XVIII (January, 1965), 250–56.
4 Holmes, "The Substrata Factor Theory of Reading: Some Experimental Evidence," in *New Frontiers in Reading*, International Reading Association Conference Proceedings, edited by J. Allen Figurel (New York: Scholastic Magazine, 1960), V, 116–21.

5 Plessas, "A Critique of the Substrata-Factor Theory of Reading," *Elementary School Journal*, LXIV (January, 1964), 219.
6 *Ibid.*, p. 223.

reading criterion and low intercorrelations, we may be able to sharpen our insights into those factors that contribute in a significant degree to the interpretive process.

Olive S. Niles also believes that the proliferation of interpretive skills is confusing to teachers. She asks, "Is it really necessary to teach all these skills separately? Are they truly basic or are they, perhaps, at least one step removed from those abilities, probably much fewer in number, which are truly fundamental to the process of comprehension?"[7] Niles suggests that there are three abilities which clearly differentiate between the efficient and inefficient reader. They are the ability to find and understand thought relationships, to set specific purposes for reading, and to make "full use of previous learning in attacking new material."[8] Niles believes that these abilities are so important to the interpretive act that they should be taught in all areas where reading is required and on all instructional levels.

And so the search for the basic factors in the interpretive act continues. The fact that there is no unanimity of thought among investigators should not deter teachers from using the best directives they have at hand. Any one of the many excellent texts on reading techniques will contain a chapter or more on comprehension, critical reading, or creative reading. Skill strands will also be indicated, along with suggested teaching procedures. Guide-

books to basal programs indicate the skills that can be taught with their materials and the procedures for the systematic development of these skills from level to level.

A subject-matter teacher at the ninth-grade level who does not have any of these helps available needs only ask himself the following question, What competencies must my students have to carry out the learning tasks in this course as I teach it? The answer to this question may show that the students need to know how to make comparisons between various treatments of a given topic, to detect propaganda devices or slanted writing, to organize ideas in logical sequence, to locate information for specific purposes, to establish those purposes, and to understand a specialized vocabulary. As Kerfoot has suggested, forget the labels and think of the tasks that the students must perform. Those are the skills that must be taught or reviewed regardless of the factors that may emerge from an elaborate research study.

UNDERSTANDING THE LANGUAGE

In the paper presented by this writer in 1951 on the influence of specific factors on interpretation, a section on language ability was included. Primary attention was directed to the importance of a general language factor that appeared to underlie all the language areas — reading, writing, speaking, and listening — and that gave unity to language. This concept is still held as basic.

Since that time considerable water has gone over the dam, and today we

[7] Niles, "Comprehension Skills," *Reading Teacher*, XVII (September, 1963), 2.
[8] *Ibid.*, p. 4.

hear the terms "linguistics," "phonetics," "syntax," and "word patterns" used freely. Truly, something new has been added, or at least we have some new labels. It is difficult to assess the influence that linguistic concepts will eventually have on reading. Linguists themselves are confused about the implications of linguistic science for the interpretive process, and practitioners may certainly be excused if they, too, are confused. Right now there is a spate of "linguistic readers" on the market in which each author has applied his own concept of linguistics with little or no regard to any other program or materials. If the theoretical linguists would confine their efforts to the science of language and leave the application of their discoveries to people in reading, it is possible that much of the present difficulty might be avoided.

To my way of thinking, a knowledge of the language and how it functions is a substantial factor in the interpretive process. Let me suggest several examples. First, I think it is important for the reader to understand that words, spoken and written, are only symbols for experience. Words do not "have" meaning; the reader does not read to "get" meaning; there is no meaning "on the page." Meaning, if there is any at all, is in the reader or listener. It is in his mind or nervous system or wherever it is that memory images repose. The words, spoken or written, serve only as stimuli to the thinking process. The reader creates, or better, reconstructs the ideas that the writer had in mind when he wrote. The

ideas are not in the material waiting to be "grasped" by someone. The ideas of the writer are only represented by printed marks. The reader perceives these marks and uses them to reconstruct meaning out of his own background of experience.

An understanding of language and the way it functions certainly has a contribution to make to oral interpretation. If the printed word is a graphic representation of its spoken counterpart, then the act of oral reading is a transformation of the printed symbols back into the spoken words as they may have been uttered originally. Oral reading is the act of interpreting to an interested listener the ideas, feelings, mood, and sensory impressions of a writer.

One of the main difficulties facing the oral reader is that, in the graphic form, there are only crude indications of how the writer wished to express his ideas. These signals to meaning are in the form of periods, commas, exclamation marks, and the like. Had the writer chosen to speak his ideas instead of to write them, he would have had at hand a much wider repertoire of aids. He could have given vocal stress to important words, he could have used gestures, he could have paused, he could have accelerated or retarded his rate of speaking, he could have changed his pitch, or he could have used various intonational patterns. But the oral reader has none of these aids. What should he do? First, he must endeavor to think, feel, and sense as the writer did; and then he must attempt to project through his voice the ideas and actions that the writer would present were he there to express himself. The reader must serve as a stand-in for the speaker-writer. I am convinced that much of the poor quality of oral reading that we find on all levels is the result of a lack of understanding of what it means to interpret aloud.

An understanding of the language and the way it functions also contributes to our understanding of the use of context in the interpretive act. The words in a passage of connected discourse stimulate meaning, not as separate entities, but through the interaction of one word with another. To explain, one can do no better than to refer to a statement of E. L. Thorndike's written almost fifty years ago, "Reading is a very elaborate procedure, involving a weighing of each of many elements in a sentence, their organization in the proper relations one to another, the selection of certain of their connotations and the rejection of others. . . ."[9] In other words, reading is essentially the process of determining the meaning to be attached to a given symbol *by its relation to other words in a passage.*

In a study of the types of contextual aids that serve as clues to meaning, Wilbur S. Ames analyzed the recorded verbal responses of a group of twenty mature readers who were asked to determine, if possible, the meaning of simulated words appearing in passages of connected discourse.[10] On the basis of 334 contextual situations in which the subjects could attach adequate meaning to the simulated words, Ames was able to identify fourteen separate categories of contextual clues. Among the clues to meaning were synonyms, modifying phrases or clauses, words showing comparisons and contrasts, appositive phrases or clauses, and words or phrases supplying definitions or descriptions. It is interesting to note that Ames's adult readers were able to define 60 per cent of the simulated words correctly, thus indicating the usefulness of the process of reasoning out the meanings of words.

Many of the contextual clues to word meaning that Ames identified apparently have their origin in the reader's almost subconscious understanding of such sophisticated concepts as word order and structure, syntax, and word form-classes. For example, a reader would say while trying to discover the meaning of a simulated word, "It must mean the opposite of the word preceding it, for they are separated by *or.*" In other cases, the reader would attempt first to determine the form-class to which an unknown word belonged, by using as a clue its position in the sentence, and then would reason further about its specific meaning. For example, in the sentence "It isn't economical to try to [simulated word] the computer to do things that the human being does so much better," the reader said, "The word has to indicate causing. The place where it is located in the

9 Thorndike, "Reading as Reasoning: A Study of the Mistakes in Paragraph Reading," *Journal of Educational Psychology,* VIII (June, 1917), 323.

10 Ames, "A Study of the Process by Which Readers Determine Word Meaning through the Use of Verbal Context" (unpublished doctoral dissertation, College of Education, University of Missouri, 1965).

sentence indicates that it must be a verb, and it must mean making or forcing." [11]

The Ames study provides strong arguments for the early teaching of context as a means to more effective interpretation. But more than that, it shows the importance of *teaching language,* in a broad sense, as part of any program on interpretation. An understanding of the functions of words in sentences, word classes, and inflectional and structural components is the foundation of the interpretive process. To understand the meaning of a paragraph, for example, the reader must know more than the lexical meaning of separate words. He must be able to assess each word's weight, value, or significance in relation to the words that surround it. Truly, the teaching of reading is more than teaching children how to pronounce unfamiliar words.

INTERPRETATION AND PURPOSE

At the 1951 reading conference, Paul A. Witty referred to the importance of student attitude to success in reading. He pointed out that reading problems frequently have their origin in indifference toward reading and that when this is the case one must first attempt to create favorable attitudes toward reading before one can work on the specific problem. Most of us who have had experience in a reading clinic will be familiar with the child whose main cause of disability seems to be an unfavorable attitude.

In the last fifteen years, we have

11 *Ibid.,* p. 125.

increasingly come to recognize the potency of motivation, interest, and purpose as contributors to good reading. In some cases a child has difficulty in reading because continued failure causes him to lose interest. The same thing would undoubtedly happen to most of us were we to face failure again and again in some activity considered extremely important. In other cases a child is not motivated or fails to take an interest in reading because there is little or no encouragement of this activity in his home or — unfortunately, in some cases — in the school.

Running through the literature dealing with the culturally disadvantaged child is the recurrent theme that reading is most frequently not prized in his home. There are few if any books, magazines, or even newspapers. There are no bedtime stories or nursery rhymes. Reading plays no part in the lives of the father or mother. When the youngster enters the first grade, he has no burning desire to learn to read, to become independent so that he can experience for himself its pleasure and profit. In many cases, there is no one to care or to be concerned whether he learns to read or not. Unless the school can capture his latent interest early and show him that reading can be fun and that it can help to answer his questions, teaching him to read will be extremely difficult. His interest, it must be added, can hardly be aroused through an initial program of drill on mechanics. His problem will not be the frequently repeated cliché that he "doesn't know his phonics" but rather that he has been given no purpose for learning to read in the first place.

In working with the reluctant reader, it is so easy to become absorbed in the mechanics of the reading act. This fact was observed by the task force of the National Council of Teachers of English while they were preparing the monograph *Language Programs for the Disadvantaged* (a report which all language arts teachers should read whether they are working with the culturally disadvantaged or not):

Some Task Force members found the emphasis on reading to be appropriate and well planned; others expressed concern that, at times — especially on the junior high school level and beyond — instruction in reading was overorganized, stressing mechanical aspects of the reading process rather than the purposes of reading.[12]

Because the reluctant reader so obviously lacks basic skills and interest, we tend to assume that the way to build his interest is to provide more drill on word attack, along with silent reading activities and related exercises in factual recall. Though skills are important, their development can come only after the learner becomes cognizant of their need, not before. Skill practice cannot take precedence over motivation.

Briefly, I would like to refer to the influence of purposeful reading on interpretation in a more restricted sense, as, for example, in a reading assignment in social studies. The materials of social science — textbooks,

12 Richard Corbin and Muriel Crosby (chairmen), *Language Programs for the Disadvantaged* (Champaign, Ill.: National Council of Teachers of English, 1965), p. 29.

encyclopedias, source books — have value for the reader only as they supply answers to questions that seem to him to have relevance and significance. They are resource materials that should be used to supply solutions to problems, bases for judgment, answers to questions, details to support an argument, or causes for existing conditions. They are not materials to be "covered" or recited or regurgitated at some later time. With this contention, I doubt that there will be much argument.

But, if we admit this as the function of textual materials, then we are faced by the unavoidable corollary that their effectiveness can be realized only when they are approached purposefully — with questions to answer, or problems to solve, or a need to find causes for existing conditions. Most of the poor reading that is done, particularly in the content areas, whether in grade five or eleven, may be attributed to purposeless reading to satisfy purposeless assignments. For the teacher to say, "For tomorrow finish the chapter" or "Read to the middle of page 126" is just as useless as to request a student to "go to the library, find it, and bring it back."

Not only do reading purposes predispose the mind set of the reader and make him alert and receptive to new ideas, but they also condition the reading procedure that he will use. Whether he reads intensively or skims, whether he prepares a summary of what he has read or thinks carefully about the content in order to recall a series of events that took place, will depend on his reading purposes. In short, the specifics of the interpretive act are set by the purposes for reading. "Why was the long drive toward world-wide democracy thwarted after World War I?" the teacher asks. "Why do national leaders sometimes turn to dictatorships, as happened in Italy and Germany after 1919?" "Does our text give us a full answer to these questions? Where else could we look?" And later, "Are the reasons given by author A consistent with those of author B?" Such questions as these put the reader in a mental attitude of study, an application of the mind to the acquisition of knowledge through investigation and reflection. The interpretive act becomes an active process of searching out, weighing, reflecting, and reasoning. This is quite different from the passive process of collecting a number of unrelated facts, which so frequently is what the student thinks of as studying.

One of the most illuminating recent studies of reading for different purposes is that conducted by Helen K. Smith. She investigated the methods used by fifteen good readers and a like number of poor readers when asked to read for two different purposes, for details and for general impressions. Briefly, she reports that

most good readers attempted to adjust their reading techniques to the purpose for which they read. They restructured and reviewed the content when their purpose was reading for details; they read for ideas and not for facts when their purpose was for general impression. Poor readers, for the most part, did not adjust

their reading method to the purpose; they read both selections for the purpose of getting details.[13]

Another interesting finding of the Smith study is that "little, if any, direct guidance in reading for different purposes had been given to the subjects" in the study.[14] Apparently, some of the students happened to hit on an idea and a technique they found effective, whereas others did not. Whether the adjustment of reading procedures to purposes can account for good or poor reading, Smith does not presume to answer on the basis of her data. But her study does give evidence of the importance of purposeful reading in the interpretive act.

THE TEACHER MAKES THE DIFFERENCE

Inevitably, when discussing the educative process, whether in the area of mathematics or reading, we must recognize the fact that it is the teacher on the firing line who makes the difference between effective and ineffective learning — in this case, effective or ineffective development of interpretive abilities. How the teacher perceives the interpretive act will determine what he will include in his instructional program and what methods he will use to secure growth. In our joint report to the reading conference in 1951, Witty referred to the teacher and to the part he played in

[13] Smith, "Research in Reading for Different Purposes," in *Changing Concepts of Reading Instruction*, International Reading Association Conference Proceedings, edited by J. Allen Figurel (New York: Scholastic Magazines, 1961), VI, 122.
[14] *Ibid.*

promoting growth in reading. I would now like to add several points.

As pointed out by William S. Gray in a number of his writings (and as explored by Helen Robinson in chapter iii), the complete act of reading has four dimensions — word perception, comprehension of stated and implied meanings, critical and emotional reaction, and application of perceived ideas to behavior. At the conference in 1951 Gray, in introducing the conference theme, stressed the need to train young people to read with "greater breadth and depth of interpretation," to react "more thoughtfully and critically to the ideas apprehended," and to use them "with increasing discrimination as guides to further thinking and action." [15] He raised the question, "What is the concept of interpretation that shall guide teachers?" [16] And in answer, he voiced the hope that the conference would make definite progress in defining interpretation in sufficiently broad terms to meet current demands. Subsequent sessions of the 1951 conference, I feel, proceeded well in this task. But one wonders whether the concepts and suggestions developed at that conference have been woven into the fabric of our thinking about the interpretive process.

As I travel about and meet and talk with teachers and supervisors, it seems to me that their primary preoccupations are still word perception and factual recall. Let there be no doubt about it, these are important skill areas, but this is not the point where the reading process should stop. We seem to be satisfied if the student can pronounce the words and "get the facts" of the story or text. Only a modicum of attention is given to the between-the-lines meaning, to say nothing of critical and emotional reactions. These omissions I feel, have their origin in a limited concept of what it means to promote maturity in interpretation — to teach reading, if you please. It is axiomatic that what we think and believe, we do.

Now, if never before, is the time to teach critical listening and reading, but more than that, to practice it ourselves. There are those who are making pronouncements about the reading act that, if applied, would take us back a half-century in practice. There is a bombardment of all kinds of procedures, devices, machines, gadgets, self-help kits, and workbooks, which, if we were to believe the promotional material, would solve all our problems. Some of these materials and devices are untried, others are based on questionable assumptions, and others are inadequate alone, although they might have a limited use if woven into the fabric of an already sound program.

Though I presume it is a possibility in all professions, it seems to be especially likely in education that unless we are on guard we may be-

15 Gray, "Theme of the Conference," in *Promoting Growth toward Maturity in Interpreting What Is Read*, compiled and edited by William S. Gray ("Supplementary Educational Monographs," No. 74; Chicago: University of Chicago Press, 1951), p. 2.
16 *Ibid*., p. 3.

come "hobbyhorse riders." That is, we may become absorbed with one idea, practice, or device. "If I use this one method of teaching word perception or this one automated device for developing comprehension," we say, "I can rest assured that I will have a sound reading program." But in so thinking, we remove our far-point correction, and our myopic vision permits us to see only a very narrow, restricted reading program. It is to be hoped that we are coming to realize there is no one approach, technique, or device that meets the needs of all readers in the same way. The sound program is one in which we adapt, supplement, and modify in terms of what seems to be effective with a given child. In so doing, we use the best of all rather than restrict ourselves to any one belief while

a generation of readers slips through our fingers.

What I am trying to do is to repeat the wish that Gray made fifteen years ago, that we build a program on a concept of interpretation that has sufficient breadth and scope to meet the contemporary and future demands of society. The kind of program he invisioned is still valid. It should help the reader in

. . . grasping the literal meaning of what is read; securing the additional meanings inherent in a passage; reacting appreciatively or critically to the ideas apprehended . . . and integrating the new ideas with previous experience so that clearer understandings, broader interests, rational attitudes, improved patterns of thinking and behavior, and richer and more stable personalities result.[17]

17 *Ibid.*, pp. 4-5.

CHAPTER VIII

PROMOTING GROWTH IN INTERPRETING WHAT IS READ

*

IN KINDERGARTEN THROUGH GRADE THREE

MARIAN HAMMES

*

DURING THE past television season, Leonard Bernstein, in one of his popular "Young People's Concerts," did a magnificent job of instructing his viewers in the interpretation of music. He did so by showing them how *not* to play Bach, Beethoven, and Brahms. Why? Because he wanted the young people to realize that one needs to know as much about these great men as possible before attempting to interpret their music. He was saying that interpretation of music is more than being able to read notes. Classroom teachers of reading, too, know that interpretation is more than being able to read words.

Teachers should also be cognizant of the following facts: (1) a great amount of interpretation goes on outside of the textbook, even before children have ever had one in their hands; (2) life has taught youngsters to interpret before they ever come to school; for example, they know the meaning or possible meanings that a frown on their father's face may have; (3) ability to interpret can be strengthened by almost any language-experience activity in the primary school; and (4) interpretation of textbook materials will be relatively simple for beginning readers if readiness is encouraged through creative use of existing opportunities in the children's everyday world.

What are some ways of improving skills in interpretation at the primary level? More important than any specific procedure is the provision of appropriate and varied experiences before book reading, during book reading, and after book reading.

PREREADING ACTIVITIES

A discussion with children of what they see in pictures sharpens their powers for accurate observation. A college instructor of a methods class recently proved this point by showing the class a simple picture of a girl and a young horse. In the first comment about the picture, a college Junior called the animal a "pony." Another student corrected her, saying it was a foal or a colt. Someone else asked if it were a filly. Conversation continued, and the class learned the discriminative use of six words — *foal, filly, colt, pony, mare,* and *horse* — during their attempt to accurately describe the picture. Of course, it is important for the teacher to anticipate as many of the children's ideas as possible so that she will not be taken unawares and will be able to utilize each of their contributions. This is a valuable technique in social studies and science, as well as in the teaching of reading, since it encourages children to observe and hypothesize before they attempt to interpret the results of a science experiment, for example, or the meanings of a paragraph.

Map reading is another valuable technique. Maps interest children in kindergarten to grade three, and may well be the springboards to different kinds of interpretation. Weather maps from local television stations are particularly useful. The purpose of the map can be emphasized by having the children write in their own predictions. Or the teacher may read weather reports from various sections of the country and have the children tell how they would dress for the day. Teaching the directions — north, south, east, and west — through dramatizations can also help the children interpret these maps. The children can pretend they are roosters on a weathervane: their beaks point north; their tail feathers point south. They will have a lot of fun being moved by the wind. Deciding on a route to take for scenic beauty by reading a road map can also provide an exercise of interpretive skill.

INTERPRET, WRITE, THEN READ

Sometimes it is necessary to put the cart before the horse, or, as we might say in reading, to put the chart before the book. In the interpretation of science books, for instance, three steps will help: (1) Encourage the children to discover the answer to a problem by experimenting, before they ever see a textbook. (2) Help them write a chart of what they did. They'll have no trouble interpreting the chart since they made the discoveries and then recorded them. (3) Send them off to explore the science books to find proof of their discovery, either in picture or in print. If the project is carefully guided by the teacher, the children will not encounter vocabulary difficulties when they get to the text; and they will have been greatly helped in their interpretation of the printed matter by their experiments.

Interpretation will remain very narrow, however, unless the children have a growing vocabulary. Almost any Sunday paper can furnish a list of interesting words from the articles and pages of advertisements. The words may be clipped out of the newspaper, placed on a plain sheet of paper, run through the copy machine, and then used as a transparency for class discussion. When this method was tried with a group of primary children in our local campus school, the following words were used: *cultured, silhouettes, incredible, glamour, fragile,* and *textured.* Following the discussion, the children were asked to dictate a description of themselves on Easter Sunday to a secretary (a fifth or sixth grader) who needed dictation practice. A youngster's word interest climbs from this type of experience, and parents report their surprise when a new "ten-dollar" word appears in their child's conversation at the dinner table.

Television should not be ignored by teachers; children don't ignore it. In one evening of viewing, and in the space of a few minutes, as many as three words may each be used to mean different things. If a youngster is given a list of such words and directed to be on the alert for their use in his evening's viewing, an interesting discussion may ensue the next day. If pupils learn the use of two, or possibly three, new words, the experience has certainly been productive. Youngsters appreciate this type of homework.

DRAMATIZATION

Meaning plus emotion equals interpretation. After several unsuccessful attempts to dramatize the turkey at Thanksgiving time by saying, "Don't shoot; please don't shoot me," the teacher spoke about emotions and feelings. "How do you suppose the turkey felt? Was he afraid? Imagine you are the turkey. How would you feel?" This generated emotional response, and finally, a first grader named Cliff jumped from his desk, threw up his hands, and said, "Don't shoot; for God's sake, don't shoot me" — a very realistic interpretation.

In dramatizing stories heard or read, children usually present the story precisely as told or written, but can you imagine the fun when they are asked to dramatize Little Red Riding Hood of 1966? Perhaps she will go over to Grandmother's on a Honda; the goodies in her basket may vary from Geritol or instant coffee to pizzas and Toast-em Pop-Up's. Dramatization of the neighborhood version of any basic reader story is also fascinating and a real test of interpretation and application.

A poem, "I Wonder What the Fishes Think," by Aileen Fisher is an excellent one for the development of skills in interpretation.

The lake is glossy now and nice
With winter windows on — of ice.
We use it for a skating rink.
I wonder what the fishes think
When they look up and see us spin
Above their heads and not fall in.
I bet they blink![1]

Poetry is perhaps the most difficult form of writing for children to understand because of the figurative language. Much of the poetry for primary children, however, lends itself to interpretation — by art, dance, dramatization, or oral comment. After reading the poem about the fishes to the children, the teacher might ask them to illustrate the under-ice scene and to finish the line "I bet they . . ." in their own words. The might also be encouraged to interpret the poem in rhythm or dance.

It goes without saying that the illustration of any type of reading will give the teacher insights into how well a child interprets, whether he uses his imagination or whether he sticks closely to the words. Proverbs are especially good for this. What is meant by "A stitch in time saves nine" or "All's well that ends well" or "An apple a day keeps the doctor away"? The class might be asked what these sayings mean to us today and what they may have meant to our great statesmen like George Washington, Thomas Jefferson and Abraham Lincoln. It might be

[1] Aileen Fisher, *Runny Days, Sunny Days* (New York: Abelard-Schuman, Ltd., 1958), p. 114.

equally successful to have a "proverb parley," or a discussion about a proverb, whenever there is a lull of a minute or two before lunch or before the dismissal bell. The only preparation necessary is to have a proverb ready.

IMPORTANT SKILLS

Failing to follow directions often creates a good share of classroom problems, whether the directions have been given orally or in writing. To check on interpretation, the teacher might ask a child to answer the questions What? How? When? and Why? with regard to some specific directions. All good directions should include these four points.

Two other important reading skills are finding the main idea and finding details. Although most manuals give adequate help for developing these skills, they can also be strengthened by other means. Children love to mark up print. They can be given discarded textbooks and told to underline the main idea in each paragraph in red pencil and the details in blue — a good technique for a little variety when the weather outside begins to cut into ordinary motivational techniques.

Oral reading is a significant skill, but it can also become a monotonous time-waster if one child after another reads, merely so that the teacher can see if each knows the words. Too often, oral reading is a vocabulary check rather than an aid to improving in-terpretation. One satisfactory way to use reading is to divide the class into little groups of two and three and to permit the children to read to each other. The "traveling teacher" then moves from one group to another. The opportunity for each child to have his turn is multiplied many times, and the more times he reads, the more he will improve.

CONCLUDING STATEMENT

Let's face it! In order to be enjoyable and functional reading requires interpretation. A good reading program featuring interpretation should be based on the following assumptions:

(1) Numerous language-arts experiences including dramatization, vocabulary development, opportunities for oral reading, and utilization of all unoccupied moments in the school day will clear the air of static and result in improved interpretation.

(2) Through these language experiences, interpretation of textbooks and other printed matter will be improved and will in turn pave the way for more functional and enjoyable reading.

(3) Children cannot be expected to interpret reading material beyond their experiences, real or vicarious. It is the job of the primary teacher to use every available opportunity, and to create others, to strengthen the skills of interpretation, first, through experience and, second, through the printed page.

IN GRADES FOUR THROUGH EIGHT

RAYMOND A. LUBWAY

*

Too often teachers rush in too quickly and expect too much too soon. It takes time for young readers to realize that there is more to literature than plot. Readers with a concept of characterization and the related concepts of motivation and causation have much to look for and enjoy in stories, for these concepts provide a framework which relates and therefore gives meaning to story events. It is only when pupils can see a story as a whole that they have a way of thinking about such questions as the "main idea" or "the purpose of the author." And it is only when they have a grasp of the main idea that they can appreciate figurative language or mood as true embellishments. Some children, the good readers, acquire a conceptual framework on their own. By intuitively applying it to what they read, they discover new ideas and relationships — discoveries that lead to new insights into the world and themselves.

How to reach the others is the problem of the teacher. The task is difficult but not impossible, as I discovered in my sixth-grade English class this year. For the first time in my teaching experience I felt that a class truly came to grips with the question, What is this story all about? At the beginning of the year, their answers to this question were a simple recall of story events.

Two months later, after a reading of O. Henry's "The Gift of the Magi," their answer was, "Love and the part sacrifice plays in it."

The pupils in that class were fairly competent readers. They had a sure grasp of plot and an accurate recall of detail. Whenever I tried to direct the discussion toward the broader significance of a story, I was greeted with silence, puzzled stares, or irrelevant recitals of detail. Clearly my questions had no meaning. The children were prepared to tell me what happened, but I wanted them to speculate on why it happened. I then realized that the context of my questions, the story itself, was too broad. They could not speculate about why characters behaved as they did without a concept of characterization. At this point I changed my strategy.

CHARACTERIZATION, MOTIVATION, LOGIC

I asked the class to read "For Sale: Dragon's Breath," an excerpt from *Young Fu of the Upper Yangtze,* by Elizabeth Foreman Lewis. Young Fu, a bright but naïve apprentice, is flattered into buying an overpriced watch. With the debt due and no money to pay for it, he flees to relatives in the mountains. There he finds snow, which he brings back to the city to sell.

I then asked the class to list the

characters in the story and describe each home. Their responses were accurate enough, if superficial. Young Fu was foolish and clever. (They were not worried about the apparent contradiction.) Fu Be Be, his mother, was poor, weepy, and worried. One child even used the word "cruel." These characterizations were interpretations because nowhere in the text did the author so describe Young Fu or his mother. The pupils had unconsciously risen above literal meaning. My next question was "How do you know?" We then sat down with the text to hunt for support. Sure enough, the class found dialogue and actions to support their descriptions: Fu was foolish for buying the watch and clever for imagining he thinking to sell snow as dragon's breath. My next question was designed to point up the contradiction between foolish and clever. "How does his feeling of obligation to pay the debt fit your description of him as a fool?" This led to a re-examination of the watch-buying incident. One boy offered the word "uneducated" as a better description of Fu. An uneducated person could also be honorable. Although Fu Be Be did not emerge as a finely drawn character in this excerpt, I was able to use one incident to show that, although two interpretations were possible, one concept of the character was more probable than the other. When Fu, pressed for payment of the debt, asked his mother for money, she wailed and scolded, telling him that his foolishness was his own affair; her poor savings were reserved to buy her coffin. Although this action seemed cruel, would a cruel mother

work far into the night to feed and clothe her son? One boy lifted the level of discourse by offering the information that old people in China worried a lot about proper burial; he also observed that old people had concerns which, if not entirely sensible to children, were common enough.

At this point I felt that the class had made great strides. And after three days of discussion, the characters in this story had become more and more real. The class began to look at what was said and done in the story as clues to personality, fears, and dreams. As knowledge of the characters, through inference, became more detailed, the class began to see motives for action and logical consequences of action. Though we spoke in passing of Fu's problem and his solution, it was not discussed as a major aspect of "storyness." This kind of question was reserved for the next stretching step — a discussion of Rudyard Kipling's "Rikki-Tikki-Tavi."

PROBLEMS AND SOLUTIONS

After a reading of the story and a recounting of Young Fu's problem and his solution, I proposed the idea that all stories are about problems and their solutions. To test this hypothesis I asked the pupils to list each character in "Rikki-Tikki-Tavi" and to state his problem. I also asked them to choose the *main* character. Almost unanimously they agreed that Rikki was the main character. There was considerable variance in the statement of his problem: some said it was to bring peace to the garden; some said it was to save the family; some said it was to kill the cobras. The class sensed that these three statements were not contradictory but could not see how they were related until one girl argued that peace in the garden and the safety of the family would be *effects* of killing the cobras. Therefore, the cobras were the basic problem.

Except for a few, all said that the Darzees' problem was to save their babies and that Chuchundra's problem was fear of going into the middle of the room. These interpretations were revised once the central position of the cobras was established. The class ultimately agreed that the cobras were everyone's problem. With the cobras dead, the babies would not be in danger and Chuchundra could go where he liked. Since nowhere in the story does Kipling describe his characters and their situation in these words, the class's conclusions were clearly based on inference. They had already come a long way from their dependence upon literal meaning.

Having risen so far above the concrete, they seemed ready for another push. "Why did Rikki want to get rid of this danger when the task involved so much personal risk?" The text offered little tangible help, and I suspected that my pupils had little personal experience with heroes and matters of life and death. In the discussion that followed they tasted the anguish and delight of pursuing a philosophic question. The clue that led to an acceptable explanation was the reference that Rikki wanted to be a house mongoose. I asked the question "What do you think that means?" Kipling didn't say; but the class, now confident of

their ability to make educated guesses, reasoned that a house mongoose must be like a watch dog. He would protect the family against cobras, a more common danger in India than burglars, and in turn, the family would care for him. As a house mongoose he would no longer have to worry about food, shelter, or companionship. Though they didn't say so, it seemed clear that the pupils felt that Rikki's decision to fight the cobras was a choice of life and security over insecurity or death.

It was not difficult at this point to add another concept to the framework we had been building to give form to interpretive activity. Although Rikki's problem in the story was to kill the cobras and he solved it by doing so, I suggested that he had another problem. It didn't take the class long to identify his long-range problem as one of security.

In the discussion of Rikki-Tikki-Tavi the practice of supporting assertions became usual. This practice served the purpose of keeping interpretations of the text sensible rather than whimsical. The concepts of motivation and problem and solution gradually became more stable and comfortable as a framework for discussion. In addition, the distinction between immediate and long-range problems and solutions not only became useful as a device for viewing a story as a whole but, in the next story, provided a basis for speculating on the author's purpose.

AUTHOR'S PURPOSE

The next story we read was Katherine Mansfield's "The Doll's House."

In the story, the Burnell sisters, from a well-to-do family in a small town, are given a magnificent doll's house — complete even to a tiny oil lamp. This treat is shared, two at a time, with all the girls at school — all, that is, save the Kelveys. The Kelvey girls, for many snobbish middle-class reasons, are not respectable. Kezia, the youngest part-owner, on impulse, lets the Kelveys see the doll's house. For this she is scolded and the Kelveys are angrily chased out of the yard. Though shaken by the experience, the littlest Kelvey crows to her sister, "I seen the little lamp."

It is a good story for sixth graders because they find so much to get stirred up about. Confident of the success of my strategy, I again asked the class to list the characters and their problems. I also asked them to select the main character and her problem and solution. There was no disagreement on the characters and their problems. Incidentally, for the first time, no member of the class listed a minor character. I was not prepared, however, for the outburst of disagreement on the main character. Some said it was Kezia, whose problem was her discomfort about denying the Kelveys a visit to the doll's house; her solution was to allow the Kelveys to see it. Some said it was the Kelveys, whose problem was to see the house and who finally did see it. One boy who obviously missed the point kept insisting that the main character was the doll's house because without it there would be no story.

It was with mixed feelings that I watched the discussion get out of my hands. I was pleased by the class's involvement in the characters and their problems. They asserted positions and defended them by appeals to text, personal experience, and logic. They used as evidence for their arguments not the events themeselves but their import. They were obviously looking at the story as a whole and making the pieces fit together.

On the other hand, they were having difficulty in giving weight to parts of the story. My strategy, which had worked so well in the previous story, clearly could not avoid the factor of personal bias, so much a part of artistics interpretation and criticism. In fact, by asking the class to select a main character I had actually invited haranguing. When I realized this, I stepped in to point out that we were all essentially in agreement about who in the story was important and why. Our disagreement arose when we tried to make one character more important than another. Clearly, Kezio was a a doer, but her action would have had no meaning if the author hadn't created the strong feeling between the girls and the Kelveys. If the Kelveys hadn't been there, would we have seen this side of the town girls? And, of course, if the doll's house hadn't been given to the Burnell sisters, there wouldn't have been a story at all. Instead of looking at individual problems and main characters, I suggested, let's look at the problem of the story as a whole.

Just then a boy raised his hand and said that this story reminded him of the stories of prejudice. The Kelveys were different from the girls in town. It was as though a line were drawn between them. Kezia's letting them see the doll's house was like saying they were equal; the line was cut, and that made everybody mad.

The boy's metaphor immediately made all the pieces fall into place for me and the class. The immediate problem of the story was solved when the Kelveys saw the house. The long-range problem of prejudice was not solved in the story, only exposed. Was this the author's purpose? My class thought so.

I was proud of this class. I could have stopped there, but I had one more story, "The Gift of the Magi," that I thought would be useful as a final exercise. After I read it to them, I asked what this story was all about. One boy, who hadn't been particularly active in previous discussions raised his hand and said, "I guess you could say that it is about love and the part that sacrifice plays in it." There it was. Thirty minutes of the period to go and the lesson was over. No lists, no questions, no analysis of problems. A very different response from one I would

have received at the beginning of the year: "Well, it is about a woman who wants to buy a present for her husband but she doesn't have any money and her husband wants. . . ."

CONCLUSON

As a result of this year's experience, I learned several things about developing the ability to interpret what is read:

1. If your questions are met with stares or irrelevant responses, find new questions.

2. Don't start with big questions; start with small ones.

3. Don't rely upon workbooks or written materials to do the job; discussion allows for more freedom and is more stirring.

4. Keep asking "Why?" and "How do you know?" until the practice of supporting opinion becomes usual if not habitual.

5. Keep reminding yourself that in the middle grades and in junior high school we can only promote, not teach, the ability to interpret what is read.

*   *   *

IN GRADES NINE THROUGH FOURTEEN

JAMES M. McCALLISTER

*

IN ARTICLES dealing with high-school and college reading programs, the word *interpretation* is seldom defined. The definitions that do appear are those of mental processes ranging all the way from the ascertaining of lit-

eral meaning to the application of ideas in creative thinking. In this paper we shall consider interpretation as that aspect of reading which occurs when the reader has ascertained the literal or sense meaning of what an author is saying and begins to utilize that meaning in his own thinking. By this definition, interpretation enters into the reading act at the point the reader begins to think about or do something with what the author has said.

Although research has not identified the components of interpretation or determined the sequence in which they operate, it can at least be said that these components are called into operation when the reader exercises associative abilities. For practical purposes, these abilities may be considered in four groups: (1) relating the reader's own experience to what the author has said, (2) selecting the meaning that conforms to the reader's purpose at the moment, (3) objectively evaluating the author's point of view, and (4) synthesizing two or more meanings to compose new ideas or opinions. These four items do not comprise a complete list of the components of interpretation, but they suggest approaches that the teacher can make in attempting to promote interpretation as an accompaniment of reading in his classes.

RELATING THE READER'S EXPERIENCE TO MEANING

Interpretation is a thinking process. All that the printed page can do is assist the reader to weave a fabric of meaning out of his own experience. We know that the members of any high-school or college class will vary greatly in the experiential content that they can apply to any reading situation. Because of variations in experience, we cannot expect the same interpretation from all members of a class. One of the disappointing discoveries that teachers, especially inexperienced teachers, frequently make is that students do not independently arrive at the interpretations that the teacher, who is familiar with the subject, expects.

These shortcomings in experience may be minimized by providing in advance some of the necessary background before students begin independent reading. This procedure will be especially necessary in content subjects if the teacher expects the students to arrive at particular interpretations. Even when a variety of interpretations is desirable, appropriate background will be essential to assist students in their thinking. The different techniques the teacher may use include questioning, laboratory experimentation, class demonstrations, discussions, and assistance in selecting appropriate materials.

As a high-school or college student advances in the study of any content field, he naturally grows in experience in the field; but unless he receives guidance from the teacher in acquiring the prerequisite understandings for interpretation, he will probably get farther and farther into material unrelated to his experience. The cumulative effect of outdistancing his experience will generally inhibit his interest and progress. In most cases, it will be desirable to delay reading assignments until the essential concepts have been developed and explained through other classroom procedures. The need for prereading instruction will vary with individuals, but will always be necessary to some extent. When experiential background is limited, biased, or completely missing, the level of interpretation will be limited accordingly.

USING PURPOSE TO GUIDE INTERPRETATION

Intelligent interpretation is always influenced by the purpose in reading. First of all, the reader searches for the writer's original intent. Misinterpretation is always possible if emphasis is placed on the literal meaning of the words instead of on the writer's purpose. Sometimes purpose is definitely stated by the author; at other times it must be detected by "reading between the lines."

One approach to discovering the author's purpose is to examine the organizational pattern of the material. The reader should note the introductory statements, if any, to ascertain whether the writer gives a clue to the pattern he will follow. If no pattern is indicated, the purpose must be detected as the organization unfolds during reading. Patterns vary with the character of the selection, of course.

To determine purpose, it is also especially helpful to be acquainted with the devices that writers often use to influence the reader's interpretation. Reference has already been made to the use of introductory statements. Does the introductory statement relate the new material to something studied previously? As the writer develops his discussion further, does he introduce problems or questions to guide the thinking of the reader? Does he follow a logical sequence? Does he follow a time sequence? Does he introduce concrete examples to illustrate principles or processes? Does he discuss cause and effect relations? Are factual definitions of new terms included? These questions should remind us of the many such devices commonly found in textbooks.

In literary works different devices may be used. Russell B. Thomas suggests that literature may be approached as an expression of the personality of the author, as an instrument of communication between the author and the reader, as an account of the past, as a poetic construction, or as a demonstration of knowledge about things.[1] The purpose of the author will determine the special devices and manner of writing.

Whenever a reader encounters a writer's device and recognizes it as a sign of his purpose, his thinking is changed or directed accordingly. For the mature reader, this happens more or less automatically. The teacher may aid students in developing this ability by being sure that they are prepared to recognize and respond to such devices effectively.

Often a student will need to read to discover not the exact purpose of a writer but his contribution to some topic or problem in which the student is interested. For example, in preparing a report or a paper, the student may read several references; as he discovers ideas or thoughts which are

[1] Thomas, "Relation between the Nature of the Material Read and Methods of Interpretation," in *Promoting Growth toward Maturity in What Is Read*, compiled and edited by William S. Gray ("Supplementary Educational Monographs," No. 74; Chicago: University of Chicago Press, 1951), pp. 62–66.

useful, he makes note of them. In this way he is disregarding the author's purpose and substituting his own purpose. As opportunities for such selective reading are provided, the reader will grow in purposeful interpretation.

OBJECTIVE EVALUATION AS AN ASPECT OF INTERPRETATION

After a reader has determined his purpose for reading and has begun to extract ideas or information from a selection, he must of necessity evaluate the usefulness, authenticity, accuracy, and truthfulness of what he is reading. The first step in evaluation is naturally the reader's personal reaction. If the reader relies on personal reactions alone, however, he will not go beyond traditional attitudes, prejudices, and false-to-fact information. The teacher has the opportunity — and the necessity — of providing objective standards or habits which will act as a corrective for the shortcomings of personal reaction. An objective approach is implied in such questions as the following. (1) Do I understand what the writer is trying to convey? (2) Do I think about what I have read before accepting it? (3) Should I check the accuracy of the author by reading other sources? (4) Am I aware of facts that the author may have omitted? (5) Does the author's background indicate that he is competent to write on this subject? (6) Which of several writers is the best informed and the most competent to set forth a position on this subject? (7) What proposition or position is consistent with the welfare of the greatest number of individuals? (8) Which propositions are consistent with accepted standards of value? Of course, the questions asked will vary with the purpose of the reader and the character of the selection, but it is important that the reader know what kinds of questions to ask in a given situation. By asking such questions, the reader practices the skills of weighing and considering data, detecting false inferences and unsubstantiated facts, testing the authenticity of sources, suspending judgment, and formulating valid conclusions.

The type of interpretation described in the preceding paragraph is the slowest and most difficult kind of reading. It requires active, careful reflection on the ideas expressed and a rigidly exacting analysis before arriving at conclusions. It may involve a search for the mood or tone of the author, a recognition of any devices of propaganda, and an understanding of the time and locale in which the writing occurred, among other considerations. Years of directed practice are necessary to develop the attitudes and thinking essential to this type of independent reading.

INTERPRETATION THROUGH CREATIVE SYNTHESIS

If reading is defined as a thinking process, interpretation cannot really be considered complete until the reader synthesizes or integrates the new meanings into his own experience. Of necessity, much instruction emphasizes efficiency in identifying, recording, memorizing, and repeating facts; but once students have the information, they need practice in such activities of independent thought as extracting and organizing meanings common to two or more statements, supplying or anticipated meanings not stated precisely, speculating on what happened between events, anticipating what will happen next, and reasoning from cause to effect.

The teacher's questions may be one of the most effective means of developing this kind of interpretation. A teacher who primarily asks questions requiring factual answers will get literal responses with little or no creative thinking on the part of readers. On the other hand, the teacher who asks questions which demand some form of organized thinking will be able to see the growth of abilities in synthesis and integration. Oral discussion is also a useful device to promote interpretation because associative responses are enhanced by an exchange of ideas. Through skilful questioning and directed discussion, the formulation of original ideas may be stimulated, mis-conceptions may be clarified, and information may be integrated with other learnings for future use.

CONCLUDING STATEMENT

As conceived in this discussion, interpretation is a cumulative ability which develops with a student's increasing experience. Its promotion is a function of all teachers — not just reading or English teachers. Whether intentionally or not, most teachers probably contribute to its growth, since it results from varied learning activities which bring into play different mental processes. Therefore, students in grades nine through fourteen are going to develop some power of interpretation regardless of what their teachers can do. The question is, "Can teachers enhance or accelerate growth by trying to direct it?" They undoubtedly can, and the most effective means is by purposeful guidance of reading activities.

*   *   *

IN CORRECTIVE AND REMEDIAL CLASSES

JAMES F. McCAMPBELL

*

IN HIS pamphlet "Literature and Social Sensitivity," Walter Loban gives an interesting example of misinterpretation of narrative. The narrative in this case was the story "That's What Happened to Me," in which a high-school boy with an inferiority complex daydreams that he high-jumped twelve feet "with only a short run." Loban quotes a student's written response to this story: "It was wonderful for him to win the high-jump game as many times as he did. That sure must have been thrilling to see. Even more thrilling to do." [1] The student has entirely missed the daydream element and, consequently, has grossly misinterpreted the story. And, of course, you are all familiar with the student who wrote a theme on Wordsworth's poem "Intimations of Immortality" and mistakenly called it "Imitations of Immorality." Or the teacher who misvalued a student because he had mistaken in his folder the student's locker number for his I.Q. score. We all make similar mistakes. Why? Is it because we are in a hurry or because we are human? I do not know, but your interpretation of the significance of such errors will determine what you try to do about preventing them.

INTERPRETATION SKILLS

Basic to skills of interpretation are literal-meaning skills. Yet, perhaps the greatest error we teachers of corrective reading make is the error of teaching these skills to the exclusion of others. "To interpret" means something more than "to know." "To interpret" has something to do with "understanding the significance of," something beyond literal understanding. Although we may often focus our teaching on *either* the skills of literal reading *or* the skills of interpretation, underneath such a focus should be the explicit understanding that neither is sufficient without the other. Insofar as our teaching implies that the student can do one *or* the other, we are giving the student an incorrect view of the act of

[1] Loban," Literature and Social Sensitivity" (Champaign, Ill.: National Council of Teachers of English, 1954), p. 20.

reading. If the student understands a work on the literal level, the next step is to help him see the implications beneath the surface of the work — to make inferences. One important kind of inference skill is the ability to recognize the connotations of words.

For any one object, we have available a variety of words. The difference among these words is not in their referent, since that is the same for all of them; the difference is in their connotations — the feelings, emotions, and attitudes that are associated with them. To be aware of these connotations is to be a better interpreter.

Also necessary for interpretation is an understanding of structure — the relationships of the various parts to each other and to the whole. Since problems of structure are well-known concerns of reading and English teachers, further discussion is unnecessary here. Other examples of common concerns are recognizing purpose and understanding thematic statements.

Likewise, most teachers commonly relate reading to students' personal experiences. Teachers may sometimes overlook inductive approaches, however, as they help students understand relationships among written materials. Induction is the process of inferring generalizations from specific examples. After students have read two newspaper articles on a related topic and have discussed each separately, the teacher may ask, "How are the two articles the same?" After the students have had the opportunity to make generalizations from closely similar examples, they may be asked to extend the process by comparing four articles, and so on, using their past reading experience to understand new experiences. The goal of the inductive approach is for the teacher to remove himself from the reading act and allow the reader to deal independently with the material.

None of these skill objectives is ever fully accomplished. Everyone continues to learn new words. Everyone continues to grow in his understanding of internal structure and relationships. Everyone has an ever widening range of experiences against which he weighs and evaluates each new experience. In other words, the ability to interpret *Oedipus Rex* is in this sense merely an extension of the ability to interpret the most banal paragraph in a basal reader. We can define rather precisely the skills involved in simple reading tasks. Our failure lies in our inability to define the skills necessary for complex reading tasks and to develop strategies to teach these skills. Nearly all of the skills can be introduced one at a time, simply and clearly enough for use in the corrective classroom.

TEACHING INTERPRETATION

Here is a specific example to serve as one model for the teaching of skills involved in interpretation. It begins with material suited to students' interests and abilities as well as to the teaching of a particular skill. The lesson includes, in order, vocabulary help, questions at the literal level, questions about implications, questions requiring comparisons, and questions involving evaluation.

Suppose that we want to teach stu-dents to recognize symbols in litera-ture. Where do we start? Our first step is to find materials that match our students' interests and abilities. Fables seem to fit this criterion. Short, simple, and interesting, they use non-human figures to represent human characteristics. So we choose one for our students to read — "The Lion and His Three Counselors." We lessen the number of problems at the literal level by telling the students the meaning of difficult key words, for example, *counselor* and *irritable*. Then they read the fable. Next we check on literal understanding: "Tell me briefly in your own words what happens in this story. Is the lion's breath really unpleasant? How do we know? Why does he not kill the fox? Why did he kill the sheep? the wolf?" Then we ask for inferences about symbols and theme: "Is the story really about animals? What makes the animals like people? What kind of person does each animal represent? What is the story really about?" Next, comparison: "Have you ever had someone ask you a question when they did not really want an honest answer? How did you answer? Which of these characters were you like? What kind of answer does the fable suggest is best?" And finally, evaluation: "Do you agree with the fable? Is not honesty the best policy? What do you think?" Even though the objective was recognition of symbols, the teaching did not stop at that point. It continued through the entire range of skill objectives, ending with evaluation.

A second fable might be used and the teaching process repeated. The second time, however, there should be two differences. The first is that another comparison is added: "How are these two stories alike?" The second is that the skill on which we are focusing has now been further developed in depth. The depth of penetration and amount of time spent on any one fable depend upon the students' responses, but for maximum effect the process should be continued until, after many fables, the students have learned the following:

1. Each animal represents a particular human characteristic.

2. The animals are flat characterizations; rather than complex creatures, they represent only a single quality of human character.

3. If one thing stands for or represents another, it is called a symbol.

4. Inanimate objects as well as animals may be used as symbols of human characteristics.

5. Some symbols are common to our cultural knowledge; others are developed by the author.

6. As symbols, the figures in a fable imply a meaning that is not directly stated in the fable.

What happens next? Well, that decision depends upon the teacher's estimate of the situation. He could continue to pursue literary symbols by moving to simple allegory or simple symbolic poetry. He could pursue more "consumer-oriented" symbols by turning to political cartoons or to advertising trademarks. He could shift the focus to some other basic skill. The choice will, of course, be determined by his estimate of the students' needs, interest, and abilities.

CONCLUDING STATEMENT

The teaching of essential, specific skills is the *sine qua non* of good reading instruction. And yet, it is not sufficient by itself and should not be isolated from the total act of reading. The teaching procedures presented in this paper are repeatable again and again for the teaching of skills within the context of interpreting what is read.

CHAPTER IX

THE PROBLEM OF INTERESTS: A RECONSIDERATION

*

J. W. GETZELS

*

I BEGAN MY paper of ten years ago by saying that my area of specialized competence, if any, was not in the field of reading. This remains the same today — perhaps even more so. I went on to say that from my limited point of vantage, work on reading interests seemed peculiarly deficient in three important respects: precision of definition, rigor of theory, and depth of analysis. I do not know whether there has been any marked alteration in this over the period. But today I would add to my initial list a fourth item — exactness of observation — which at the time seemed to me so self-evident that I neglected to mention it, an omission for which I have since been taken to task and which I would now rectify.

I then proceeded in my original paper to a formal examination of the concept of *interest* by placing it in the context of motivation theory and differentiating it from other motivational concepts like *preference, attitude,* and *drive,* with which it is often used interchangeably. Is an interest psychologically the same as a preference? an attitude? a drive? or is it in some significant way distinguishable from these?

I took the position that not only are interests, preferences, attitudes, and drives distinguishable as motives but that they *must* be distinguished if we are to understand the unique function of interests in the psychic economy of the human being. By way of illustration, I distinguished between an interest and a preference. We have a preference for broccoli over asparagus, but we may have absolutely no interest in either. We would not expend a minuscule effort to learn more about one than the other. The child faced with a choice of subjects already available in school may admit to a *preference* for one subject over another. But he may have no *interest* in either. A preference is a disposition to *receive* one object as against another; it does not induce one to seek out the particular object for acquisition or study. In contrast, the basic nature of an interest is that it does induce us to *seek out* particular objects and activities.

Similarly, I argued that there is a significant distinction between an interest and merely a positive attitude, although the two are often used synonymously. We may, for example, have a positive attitude toward the Eskimo and yet have no particular interest in them. By contrast, we may have a decidedly negative attitude toward the Soviets but have a very keen interest in them. An attitude is a disposition to react in a particular direction with regard to a given object or event. We do not ordinarily speak of being driven by an attitude; we are necessarily driven by our interests.

Finally, I distinguished between a drive and an interest. A drive has its source in a specific physiological disequilibrium, and the individual seeks conditions that will reduce the drive. An interest has its source in experience and challenges us to exert ourselves even though there is no necessity in any biological sense. Technically speaking, we may say a drive is a function largely of our *instinctual* processes, an interest largely of our *ego* processes. Against this background, I attempted to formulate a working definition of interest. An interest, I said, is a characteristic disposition, organized through experience, which impels an individual to seek out particular objects, activities, understandings, skills, or goals for attention or acquisition.

It is a punishing experience to reexamine what one has perpetrated in the past, especially what one has had the temerity to put in writing — in the present case, to observe the now self-evident omissions, to say nothing of the shoddy thought and awkward rhetoric. I am, for example, chagrined to discover that I neglected to distinguish between an interest and two other important types of motives, that is, *needs* and *values*. I can also rectify this now. A need is a disposition or force within a person which impels

him consistently toward one type of activity as against another. Thus we may speak of an individual as having a high or a low need for achievement or for affiliation. Insofar as a need is not necessarily biological but may have its source in experience, it is distinct from a drive; insofar as it disposes the individual toward a general type of activity rather than toward a specific object or goal, it is distinct from an interest. The need for achievement may, for example, find expression in the school situation in the arts, sciences, athletics, or extracurricular activities. The need is the same; the interests are different. An interest may also be distinguished from a value. A value is a conception of the *desirable* — that is, of what ought to be desired, not what is actually desired — which influences the selection of behavior. Thus, it is possible for an interest and a value to be quite incompatible; an interest disposes us toward what we *want* to do, a value toward what we believe we *ought* to do. And in fact, we have not paid sufficient attention to the discrepancies between our values and our interests and, more especially, between *our* values and *children's* interests.

Despite these and other omissions, I would maintain that *within the assumptions about human behavior I made at the time* there is not much I would change in the original paper. The definition of *interest* I gave is tenable, and the determinants of interest which I cited are not unreasonable. But if we *alter the assumptions about human behavior*, then a number of the formulations about interests must also be altered. It is my contention that the basic assumptions about human behavior have undergone change during the past decade, and therefore we must rethink our prior conceptions of motivation and the nature of interests. Or rather I should say more carefully, my own assumptions have undergone change, and accordingly my conception of motivation and of interests has also undergone alteration. It is the nature of these transformations and their consequences for thinking about education that I should like to consider in this paper.

I.

Stated most simply, my basic assumption a decade ago was that human activity could best be explained in terms of a combination of the homeostatic model of self-maintenance and the drive-or-tension-reduction theory of behavior.[1] According to this theory, the organism's optimum state is held to be one of rest and equilibrium, and the organism is said to act in such a way as always to return to the optimum state of rest and equilibrium. Hunger raises the organism's level of tension and drives it to seek food; the organism ceases to seek food when it has eaten, that is, when the tension produced by the hunger

[1] Parts of this section are based on J. W. Getzels, "New Conceptions of the Learner: Some Implications for the Classroom," in *Reading and Emerging Cultural Values,* Twenty-eighth Yearbook of the Claremont Reading Conference, edited by Malcolm P. Douglass (Claremont, Calif.: Claremont Graduate School and University Center, 1964), pp. 10–21.

has been reduced. Fear raises the organism's level of tension and drives it to seek cover; the organism ceases to seek cover when the danger is over, that is, when the tension produced by the fear has been reduced. And so on. With respect specifically to learning (or thinking, problem-solving, and other forms of intellectual activity including reading), the organism is said similarly to be driven or stimulated (we call it "motivated" in education) as it is into any other behavior. As Ernest R. Hilgard in his famous book *Theories of Learning* states Hull's position, "Without drives the organism does not behave and hence does not learn."[2] Learning always involves the reduction of a drive state, a decrease in tension. In these terms, an interest could also be conceived as a tension-producing state which impels the individual to action and stimulates him to behavior that reduces the tension raised by the interest.

During the past decade there has been a growing discontent with this homeostatic model of the human being and the drive-or-tension-reduction theory of behavior, at least as they are applied to the problem of learning and other forms of intellectual activity. It is felt that learning, thinking, and problem-solving may indeed be means of reducing certain drives but that they are not only that. They may also be ends in themselves, the organism acting to *increase* stimulation as well as to *decrease* stimulation. The optimum state of the human being may not be *passivity* but *activity*;

[2] Hilgard, *Theories of Learning* (New York: Appleton-Century-Crofts, 1948), p. 78.

and although he may be threatened by what is unfamiliar, by what he does not know, by what he has yet to learn, he is often challenged by what is new, intrigued by what is strange, and will go out of the way to encounter, explore, and master it. He seems to be *interested*, if I may put it this way, even when there seems to be no apparent drive or specific tension that is being reduced. The organism is said to act not only to *avoid* stimulation as previously assumed but also to *seek* stimulation. That is, the human being is not only a *stimulus-reducing* organism but also a *stimulus-seeking* organism.

Once pointed out, the evidence of this comes from so many sources that it is surprising this view is not more firmly established in academic psychology and in education. One of the most obvious features of the behavior of animals, for example, is the tendency to explore the environment, that is, to be "interested" in their whereabouts. As Robert W. White has put it, "Cats are reputedly killed by curiosity, dogs characteristically make a thorough search of their surroundings, and monkeys and chimpanzees have always impressed observers as ceaseless investigators."[3] Indeed, in a series of beautifully executed experiments, Harry F. Harlow and his associates at Wisconsin have shown that monkeys who are viscerogenically sated — that is, are not hungry, thirsty, or otherwise driven, at least by any recognizable drive — will

explore apparently just for the sake of exploring and will learn to unassemble a puzzle of some complexity with no other motive than, as Harlow has said, "the privilege of unassembling it."[4]

We who are humanistically inclined may be quite skeptical about the relevance of animal experiments, and more especially about the direct applicability of animal learning experiments, for human education. And in fact, the model of the hungry rat as the prototype of human learning and behavior has done harm enough. But at least for animals, the homeostatic drive-reduction model of behavior is being put to severe question. As Harlow points out, the learning behavior of the animals in his experiments reduced no recognizable primary drive, decreased no identifiable tension or stimulation. Indeed, far from trying to reduce tension or stimulation, the animals seemed to be seeking it.

Discontent with the orthodox concepts of motivation and behavior has not been restricted to the animal laboratory, as White shows. It is increasingly being argued that the central motive in the growth of children is not food satisfaction or thirst satisfaction or some other so-called primary-drive satisfaction but effective interaction with the environment as exemplified by the child's curiosity and exploratory activity. Consider, for example, as White suggests, the readily observable play of contented chil-

---

[3] White, "Motivation Reconsidered: The Concept of Competence," *Psychological Review*, LXVI (1959), 298.

[4] Harlow, "Motivational Forces Underlying Learning," in Kentucky Symposium, *Learning Theory, Personality Theory, and Clinical Research*, (New York: John Wiley & Sons, 1954), pp. 36–53.

dren. A child all of whose bodily needs have been satisfied does not, as the stimulus reduction theory of human motivation and behavior would suggest, remain at rest. On the contrary, it is just then that his play is most active; it is just then that he seems most *interested*. Careful observations by Piaget and others show that as early as the first year of life the child gives evidence of curiosity, exploration, and even experimentation. He has the capacity for being interested. And, of course, later it is almost impossible to keep up with the normal child's incessant questioning. Why is this, how is that, he wants to know. If I may put it this way — and this, I think, is the crux of our changing conception — there seem to be not only the familiar viscerogenic drives such as hunger and thirst to be satisfied by *satiation* but also neurogenic needs to be gratified by *stimulation*, that is, needs for excitement, novelty, and the opportunity to deal with the problematic.

There are numerous lines of evidence for this more recent conception of the human being as a stimulus-seeking and not only a stimulus-reducing organism. Donald O Hebb, of McGill University, for example, directs our attention to such common human interests as mystery or adventure stories, skin-diving, exploring caves, climbing dangerous mountains, traveling to strange places — all of which seem to provide pleasure by raising the level of tension and stimulation rather than by reducing it.[5]

[5] Hebb, *The Organization of Behavior* (New York: John Wiley & Sons, 1949), pp. 227–34.

In order to examine this apparent human need for stimulation systematically, Hebb instituted a series of experiments on the effect of "stimulus deprivation." He asked the question, What would happen if we provided the human being with everything he needed — food, water, shelter, bodily comfort, and so on — that is, if we satisfied all his primary drives, but deprived him of varied environmental stimulation, that is, deprived him of the opportunity to be interested.

To cite only one of the studies, Bexton, Heron, and Scott paid subjects more than they could otherwise earn just to do nothing.[6] The subjects were well fed and comfortably housed — all they had to do was to remain in bed. But there was one experimental condition: stimulation was minimized. The arrangements were such that they could not see, hear, touch, or communicate with anyone. At first nothing happened; quite sensibly, the subjects merely slept. But soon they could not sleep, became restless, and displayed constant random behavior. They would sing, whistle, and talk to themselves. Their thinking and problem-solving abilities deteriorated, so that they could not answer questions which they had had no trouble answering before the experiment started. The experience became so unpleasant that, despite the high pay for presumably doing nothing, it was difficult to keep the subjects in the experiment for more than two or three days, and

[6] W. Harold Bexton, Woodburn Heron, and Thomas H. Scott, "Effects of Decreased Variation in the Sensory Environment," *Canadian Journal of Psychology*, VIII (1954), 70–76.

some subjects left even sooner. More than this, upon leaving and for some hours afterward, the subjects reported feelings of confusion, headaches, mild nausea, intellectual lethargy, and physical fatigue.

As Hebb and his colleagues argue, the maintenance of normal, intelligent, interested behavior requires a continually varied sensory input to cope with. It is well known that the organism may become disorganized through too much stimulation — we call it *frustration*. But the organism can also become disorganized through too little stimulation — we call it *boredom*. And it is said people have "died" of it, or at least they can be permanently crippled, intellectually and emotionally, by such a condition. Indeed, is not the effect of prolonged solitary confinement often just this? From this point of view, if we may use an analogue for the sake of brevity, the human being is not, as the preceding dominant concepts would have it, like a calculating or information-processing machine that may lie idle indefinitely and respond only when the electric motor is triggered, so to speak, by some drive or stimulus; he is more like a machine that is perpetually in motion and must be permitted to keep working — in fact, he must be given something to work on — if he is to function effectively and remain in good repair.

In these terms, interests may be seen as serving a vital function beyond those usually attributed to them: they assure that the organism will seek or at least remain open to the continuous sensory input needed for

optimum functioning over and above the input required by the primary bodily drives like hunger and thirst.

II.

Recent studies of culturally deprived and segregated children show that a crucial characteristic of these children is just this: their capacity to be interested has been impaired.[7] These studies have a theoretical and practical significance beyond the children themselves, significant as they are, of course. For just as we learned a great deal about the nature and development of mental health by studying its loss, so can we learn a great deal about the nature and development of interests by studying the loss of interests. Lower-class status places the child in an inferior position physically, intellectually, and emotionally. Physical surroundings are dispiriting, intellectual stimulation is lacking, and family life is unstable. Empirical evidence shows that the motives and interests of lower-class children do in fact reflect these experiences. They tend to have lower need-achievement than middle-class children;[8] their educational and occupational aspirations tend to be depressed;[9] they respond more to material than to non-

[7] See J. W. Getzels, "Pre-School Education," in *Contemporary Issues in American Education* (U.S. Office of Education, Bulletin No. 3 [1966]; Washington, D.C.: Government Printing Office, 1966), pp. 105–14.

[8] Bernard C. Rosen, "The Achievement Syndrome: A Psychocultural Dimension of Social Stratification," *American Sociological Review*, XXI (1956), 203–11; "Race, Ethnicity, and the Achievement Syndrome," *American Sociological Review*, XXIV (1959), 47–60.

[9] William H. Sewell, Archie O. Haller, and Murray A. Straus, "Social Status and Educa-

material rewards as incentives for learning, whereas the reverse is true for middle-class children;[10] their time-orientation is shorter,[11] and they are less willing to defer gratification than are middle-class children.[12] That is, their interests are focused on the present rather than on the future.

If we take the extreme case of cultural deprivation as represented by the segregated status of the Negro, the conditions become extremely adverse: well over 50 per cent of Negro families live at the very lowest level of the lower-class standard.[13] But segregation has implications for emotional and mental development going well beyond the conditions of lower-class membership. The segregated child perceives himself as socially rejected by the prestigeful elements of society and develops a sense of his own *worthlessness*. Others may hope to escape and surmount their surroundings, even if the hope is often illusory; but the stigma of segregation is seen as inescapable and insurmountable. Un-

der these circumstances, what does it mean to be interested — interested in what and for what?

As Ralph Ellison writes for the Negro, "I am an invisible man. No, I am not a spook like those who haunted Edgar Allen Poe, nor am I one of your Hollywood-movie ectoplasms. I am a man of substance, of flesh and bone, fiber and liquids — and I might even be said to possess a mind. I am invisible, understand, simply because people refuse to see me. . . . When they approach me they see only my surroundings, themselves, figments of their imagination — indeed, everything and anything except me."[14]

What, then, do children growing up in these conditions tell us about interests? Unfavorable socialization experiences, dispiriting physical surroundings, unequal school opportunities, manifest occupational discrimination, a sense of personal worthlessness, all conspire to depress not only the range of interests but the *capacity to be interested*, and especially to be interested in what we are likely to value. In this regard, these children are not unlike the subjects in the experiment who were deprived of stimulation or, perhaps better, like the children in Wayne Dennis' study of the Teheran orphanages, where stimulus variation was minimal, who despite good physical health were retarded in other respects.[15] The condition of cultural deprivation or segregation like the condition of minimum

tional and Occupational Aspirations," *American Sociological Review*, XXII (1937), 67–73.

[10] Glenn Terrel, Jr., Kathryn Durkin, and Melvin Wiesley, "Social Class and the Nature of the Incentive in Discrimination Learning," *Journal of Abnormal and Social Psychology*, LIX (1959), 270–72.

[11] Lawrence L. Leshan, "Time Orientation and Social Class," *Journal of Abnormal and Social Psychology*, XLVII (1952), 589–92.

[12] Louis Schneider and Sverre Lysgaard, "The Deferred Gratification Pattern: A Preliminary Study," *American Sociological Review*, XVIII (1953), 142–49.

[13] David P. Ausubel and Pearl Ausubel, "Ego Development among Segregated Negro Children," in *Education in Depressed Areas*, edited by A. Harry Passow (New York: Bureau of Publications, Teachers College, Columbia University, 1963), pp. 109–41.

[14] Ellison, *Invisible Man* (New York: Modern Library, 1952), p. 3.

[15] Dennis, "Causes of Retardation among Institutional Children: Iran," *Journal of Genetic Psychology*, XCVI (1960), 47–59.

stimulus variation or stimulus deprivation prohibits the effective functioning of the organism by impairing the capacity to be interested. The etiology of this impairment was suggested by Piaget: "The more a child has seen and heard, the more he wants to see and hear." [16] We have already indicated that an interest is a disposition organized through experience, that is, through seeing and hearing, and that the capacity for interests is retained through stimulation, that is, through continued seeing and hearing. Cultural deprivation, segregation, minimal stimulus variation, stimulus deprivation, all act to restrict the child's opportunity to see and hear and thereby not only limit the range of interests he can acquire but may damage the capacity for interests itself.

The central pedagogic question raised in my paper and in the entire conference of a decade ago was: How can pupil interests be fostered? The assumption was that the teacher could not expect children to be interested; he had to instil interests in them. Classroom strategy was based on this assumption. Lesson plans, no matter what the nature of the lesson, often automatically began with a statement of the steps the teacher would take, the devices he would use, and the rewards and punishments he would

16 See J. McVicker Hunt, "The Psychological Basis for Using Pre-School Enrichment as an Antidote for Cultural Deprivation," *Merrill-Palmer Quarterly*, X (July, 1964), 226; and J. Piaget, *The Origins of Intelligence in Children*, trans. Margaret Cook (New York: International Universities Press, 1952 [originally published, 1936]), pp. 276 f.

mete out in order to motivate, that is, to interest, the pupils.

All this was founded on the conception of the human being as exclusively a stimulus-reducing organism. That is, the child would not be interested if the teacher did not take steps to interest him. But if we now add the conception of the human being as also a stimulus-seeking organism, then instead of posing the question as we did formerly, How can we interest children? we may now begin with the more fruitful question, Why is *this* child not interested?

The altered conception of the human being and the consequent transformation in our basic pedagogic question changes the anticipated teacher-pupil relationship in a crucial way: from a relationship in which the teacher expects pupils not to be interested to one in which she expects them to be interested. To be sure, many children are not interested, and no amount of expectation is by itself going to create interest. But our conceptual reformulation has two important practical results. First, if there is anything that may be said about human beings with any certainty at all, it is that they ordinarily try to live up to the expectations of others who are significant to them. Although the expectation that children will be interested may not make them interested, the teacher's expectation that they will not be interested surely creates the likelihood of a self-fulfilling prophecy: the pupils will live up to her expectation not to be interested. The reformulation mitigates against the possibility of this type of self-fulfilling prophecy. Second, and more important, the change in the basic question from how we can instil interests in children to why this child is not interested leads us to look at the individual child rather than children in the mass, to focus on causes rather than on symptoms, and to think of ways to prevent the loss of interest rather than to deal with the lack of interest as if lack of interest were the child's natural state. This is a signal gain not only theoretically but practically, for in the long run it may be easier to head off the loss of capacity to be interested than to try to instil interests after the capacity for interests has been damaged.

I have purposely said very little about reading. I am not a reading specialist or a reading teacher, and I do not pretend to be one. I am not sure what the implications of what I have been saying about the human being and his interests are for materials and methods of instruction in reading — if any. Nonetheless, I wonder whether current materials and methods are immutable, whether they are "givens of the natural order," so to speak. My own inclination is to believe that some radical transformations must be made in the light of our changing conceptions of the human being and his interests, at least for the disadvantaged child, if not for all children. I wonder, for example, whether the first activity of a school in a disadvantaged area cannot be, say, breakfast in small family-type groups rather than a garbled recitation of the pledge of allegiance — and

this not because the children may be hungry but because it is a situation which many children have learned the uses of responsible give-and-take ("please pass the salt"), gained insight into the nature of quantity ("how many cups in a quart"), and perhaps even acquired an interest in the idea of reading ("from colorful cereal boxes"). More than this, since the critical characteristic of some children is not only that they do not have an "interest in reading" but that their "capacity to be interested" at all has been damaged, I wonder whether the early portion of their school experience might not be directed more imaginatively at repairing the damaged capacity to be interested than at drilling so-called reading readiness skills in conventional workbooks.

These suggestions are naïve in the extreme and are intended to prime the pump for useful ideas rather than to be useful in themselves. But in view of the results with current materials and methods, there seems to me so pitifully little to lose in trying something else that almost anything reasonable is worth the risk. I cannot help recalling that, despite seventy-five years of progress, I was recently told that in one urban junior college the average student who comes to them from a disadvantaged school reads at the fifth- or, at best, sixth-grade level.

These children tell us something about the need for reconsidering what we have been doing or, perhaps more exactly, what we have not been doing. And it seems to me that what they are telling us is that this is a time for

boldness — boldness in conceptualiza-
tion and boldness in practice.

III.

Two final comments: A colleague
of mine who saw a draft of this paper
objected that human nature had not
changed during the past decade. This
is a misapprehension of my argument.
I am not arguing that human nature
has changed during the past decade
or the past ten decades. We know very
little about this. It is the *conception* of
human nature, like the conception
of the universe, or of space, or of
matter, that is, how we *think* about
human nature, that has undergone
change. Another colleague agreed
with my argument but wanted to
know how I dared admit I had altered
my views within a ten-year period.
Would not this imply that I might
alter my views again? The answer is
yes, of course. We cannot do without
conceptions of the human being, for,
explicitly or implicitly, educational
practices are founded on *some* conception of what the human being is
like. But we must hold these conceptions as hypotheses to be retained,
altered, or discarded in the light of
never-ending observations of the children themselves. Ultimately, it is only
they who can tell us; and we must be
ready to reconsider our conceptions
and the consequent educational practices, no matter how long or dearly
held, in the light of what they tell us.

CHAPTER X

FOSTERING INTEREST IN READING

*

IN KINDERGARTEN THROUGH GRADE THREE

MARGUERITE BOUGERE

*

According to Webster, the word *foster* comes from an old Middle English word for food or nourishment and as a verb may mean to develop, stimulate, promote, or cherish. The teacher who fosters interest in reading will nourish and stimulate children's learning so that they not only learn to read but learn to love and seek out reading as a pleasurable and rewarding activity.

The teacher who lays the groundwork for a lifelong interest in reading must know, first of all, the children themselves. What are their feelings about themselves? What are their interests in the world around them and in the world of fantasy and play? What do they want to know about? What do they like to do best? What do they value? Studies of the reading interests of primary children indicate that, as a group, children in this age range tend to prefer stories in which there are elements of humor and surprise, stories of animals and make-believe, stories of children's experiences, and stories of triumphs over obstacles. Such studies are useful in pointing out what young children in general are apt to like and in showing the wide range of their preferences. But general knowledge of preferences cannot take the place of specific knowledge of the very special individuals with whom the teacher works every day. Knowledge of child development and of children's general interests must be supplemented with well-kept records and careful, sympathetic personal observations that will tell the teacher something of each child's background, his present level of maturity and ability, his loves and fears, his enthusiasms and aversions. Primary teachers who keep a notebook with a page for incidental records on each child find that ten minutes or so each day spent in jotting down observations can pay rich dividends in cumulative knowledge of individuals and successful teaching.

THE TEACHER SETS THE STAGE

The child's school environment can do much to foster interest in reading, and perhaps the most important part of this environment is the teacher herself. The teacher who reads widely, who knows and loves children's literature, and who wants to share her own joy in reading with children will think of many ways to nourish reading interest.

A room library collection, well stocked with a variety of books, is a basic requisite for fostering interest. Whenever possible, access to the school library or to a public library should supplement and add variety to the room collection. Eye-catching bulletin board displays centered around new acquisitions or books of topical interest and art work by the children that is related to current reading will help stimulate interest in exploring the book corner.

Time for free reading should be set aside as part of the weekly program. Incidental provision for "looking at books" to occupy spare moments is not enough to make recreational reading satisfying or important in children's eyes. The specially planned free-reading period should be a time of quiet absorption in the book or magazine of the child's preference and of unobtrusive but thoughtful teacher guidance in matching children's interests and abilities to reading choices. And there should be planning for regular story times, when the teacher reads aloud or tells stories — perhaps a well-loved tale, perhaps tempting bits of a new book, perhaps a serial presentation of a longer selection to be savored and discussed by the class over a period of time, perhaps some carefully selected poems or a bit of nonsense verse.

A lifelong interest in reading is best built upon a firm foundation of opportunities to relate reading to ongoing personal needs and interests. The teacher who wishes to lay such a foundation is always on the alert for ways to make reading meaningful and satisfying in children's daily lives. Does the class have a new turtle? Wilfred Bronson's *Turtles* (Harcourt, 1945) is an example of the kind of book that can be shown, and perhaps read aloud, when interest in the new pet is at its height and then left prominently displayed in the book corner for later perusal by interested children. Do the children in the class come from diverse racial and ethnic backgrounds? Folk and fairy tales of many lands and cultures speak to the children's love of make-believe, and, when selected for the purpose, may serve to build a bridge between a particular child's home background and his school life. Is some recent space adventure a focus of attention on television and radio? Class-dictated stories transcribed on charts by the teacher can help to foster the habit of reading for information about current events. The children's weekly newspapers can serve the same purpose.

Young children usually love action, and their interest in reading and hearing stories can be developed and extended by giving them many opportunities to actively recreate and share their enjoyment through talk, writing, art work, and spontaneous dramatizations of many kinds. "Story riddles" composed by children (with or without teacher help) can be a source of pleasure to the whole group. For example, one child may say, "I am a naughty little monkey. I got a new bike for a present. Who am I?" The delighted response of "Curious

George" from classmates who know and love H. A. Rey's appealing *Curious George Rides a Bike* (Houghton, Mifflin, 1952) can establish a happy sense of sharing among many of the children and stimulate others to become acquainted with the "naughty little monkey" who appears in a series of easy-to-read books. Making simple stick puppets or fist puppets of favorite characters, manipulating flannel board figures to accompany a well-known story, and creating a mural of storybook scenes are but a few of the activities a primary teacher may use to permit children to act out and share their growing interest in reading.

INSTRUCTIONAL PROCEDURES CAN FOSTER OR IMPEDE INTEREST

For many children, the teacher need only supplement the encouragement and incentives to reading ability and interest they receive in their homes. For many others, the teacher is the prime reading model as well as the reading instructor. Lifetime interest in reading can scarcely be nourished when discouragement and fear surround early reading experiences. Special care must be taken to build readiness, to encourage the slow beginners, and to plan activities related to reading in which they can find pleasure and support before they read "on their own."

The especially able child, the one who learns to read before first grade or who makes such rapid progress that he is soon reading far above grade level, often needs teacher help to develop interest in reading for personal enjoyment and information. It is sometimes erroneously assumed that the very able reader "just naturally" has an absorbing interest in free reading, but he, too, can profit from an individualized supplemental program tailored to his special abilities and needs. Such a program may be centered around free reading, with teacher guidance through conferences; or it may be a group project featuring informal book reports of many kinds — individual oral reports, panel discussions of book characters, themes, and plots, dramatizations, or illustrations.

The primary teacher has a heavy obligation to supplement the basal reading program and to nourish the reading interest of *all* readers by making fullest possible use of the manual's suggestions for relating the lessons to wider reading. Sometimes teachers, in the press of time and because of their zeal to promote growth in skills, overlook or neglect the aids to reading interest that are included in basal manuals. Most of the commonly used reading manuals are full of suggestions for introductory and follow-up selections from children's literature to accompany units in the readers.

PARENTS ARE IMPORTANT

Effectively fostering children's interest in reading requires the co-operation of many people. We have spoken of the problems that can arise when children's homes do not provide the necessary background for reading. And we are all aware that, even with the best efforts of the school to teach the child to read and to love reading, few children can entirely transcend adverse home influences to reach their full potential for permanent interest in reading. What can schools and teachers do to help? First of all, they can recognize all parents as valued allies and make special and sympathetic efforts to reach out to those parents whose behavior may seem at odds with school purposes. Many schools provide prekindergarten conferences with parents to lay the groundwork for home-school co-operation in building reading readiness as well as in other important matters. Follow-up conferences throughout the primary years help to promote parent-teacher understanding which can benefit the child. "Good news notes" sent home to highlight the child's progress in reading and individual reading records that apprise parents of the extent of a child's reading are but two devices which can help build co-operation between home and school. Teachers can encourage parents to take their children to public libraries and can help them discover the inexpensive editions of fine juvenile books that can be used as gifts for young readers.

Some schools, in co-operation with parents' organizations, have an annual book fair to stimulate interest in ownership of books. Sometimes these fairs are viewed chiefly as money-raising enterprises, but thoughtful school personnel in low-income areas use the book fair as a way to bring excellent low-cost books to families who tend to think of juvenile books as expensive luxuries or who patronize the supermarket bookshelves exclusively.

An alternative project to the annual book fair, and one which promises to be a continuing aid to teachers in fostering interest in reading, is the school managed paperback bookstore. In very recent years, a number of schools have arranged for children to purchase paperback books at or near cost. This may be a mail-order arrangement, or it may be a "bookstore" staffed by parent volunteers and open one or more days each week at convenient hours. Such projects are excellent means of arousing parent and child interest in good reading and in building an inexpensive, but well-selected, home library. Teachers can help in book selections, thus extending their influence on children's reading growth beyond the confines of the classroom.

IN GRADES FOUR THROUGH EIGHT

DOROTHY P. HEIDER

*

PRESENT-DAY reading interests of children are indeed a riddle for many teachers. How can they best help their pupils develop into readers who will read? Since we know reading interests are acquired and learned, a first step is to determine present interests by means of some type of evaluation. Any of the following methods would be revealing: teacher-prepared questionnaires, individual conferences, interest biographies, or teacher observations of reactions to a book. The interests revealed by these means may then serve as a starting point for expanding interests in reading. Once the nature, scope, and quality of a pupil's reading interests has been determined, it is imperative that a wealth of appropriate materials, at various levels of reading ability, be readily available for each of the content areas and for personal reading. Patricia Jean Cianciolo suggests that a well-balanced library of adequate size can satisfy to a significant degree a wide variety of interests at each maturity level, can keep abreast of changing interests, can be used to facilitate the teaching of content and skills, and can help teachers capitalize on immediate interests and thus promote wide reading.[1]

STIMULATE WIDE READING

One of the best ways teachers may stimulate and improve interests and tastes is by reading to pupils at all levels. The reading ability of middle graders frequently lags behind their appreciation level and vocabulary. Teachers can fill this gap as they read stories that stretch minds, extend interests, and make pupils aware of the good things that literature offers. Enthusiasm is contagious; therefore, the teacher must be a good oral reader! Only when a teacher demonstrates day in and day out his own belief in reading as an enjoyable and useful pursuit can he expect to help each individual build lifetime reading habits.

It is not enough to surround pupils with books, whether in the classroom or in the central library. Teachers need to schedule regular periods during which both pupils and teachers read. We may be more successful in producing readers who will read if we make it obvious that personal reading is held in such high esteem that it is worthy of school time.

Pupils can help prepare book orders and suggest books or types of books to order each year for the classroom library. Then, when the books

[1] Cianciolo, "Encourage Human Variations by Using Children's Books" (Delta Kappa Gamma Bulletin, No. 32; Austin, Tex.: Delta Kappa Gamma Society, 1965), pp. 23–24.

arrive, committees of pupils can open the packages, make a record of the books, and help get them on the shelves. This is a good way to get pupils to read, as is a visit to an all-city book fair or exhibit in the fall or spring, where pupils can actually browse and compile lists of interesting books to suggest for purchase.

A comfortable rapport should be established with school and public librarians. They can and will be of tremendous help in guiding pupils to greater reading independence.

Many teachers create interest through the use of unit study. It is important to recognize that pupils are interested in the scientific wonders of the world, in the cultures of the present and the past, and in problems of everyday living. Through unit study, pupils can demand quality in factual presentations as well as in narrative ones.

Games are another means of stimulating interest. A fifth-grade social-studies class, for example, studied the important people in its state's history by devising a game called "Personality Clues." Each pupil chose five heroes and made up three clues about each. In order to make up good clues, they did research. The game was such a success that it was used again with cities of the state.

Anthologies were mentioned by one as the cause of lack of interest in reading at this particular level. Her recommendation was to use them only for certain purposes. If, for example, there was to be a unit on "Courage," the appropriate stories in the anthologies should be supplemented by the use of other available books.

ATTRACT PUPILS TO BOOKS

At the beginning of a reading unit, teachers should have a planning day. The students should be allowed to select ideas for study that involve reading. In the Ginn fourth-grade reader *Roads to Everywhere*, for example, for the unit "Wheels and Wings," committees are suggested for the study of various aspects of transportation — early and present-day balloons, trains, automobiles, and planes. These committees report to the group, draw a mural, and write on the mural a summary of all the reports.

One might try at the end of a unit a "Surprise Day," for which students may, if they wish, present something to the class: a poem, a story, a pantomime, or perhaps a dramatization of a situation or scene from an interesting book. Often even the pupils who have read a particular story share in the surprise. Teachers should always be pleased with a creative approach, as the following fourth grader's teacher undoubtedly was: after she had read her own stories to the class to set the mood, she said, "Now I'd like you to think of my stories while I play these musical selections on the piano."

During a "fun and nonsense" unit try having a Joke Day. This is a time to share jokes and riddles and to write some. Humor brings enjoyment and offers release from tensions. A great part of the opportunity for enjoying humor comes from the printed page. Published cartoons and comic material may be used to stimulate ability in appreciating the ridiculous or funny. Pupils eagerly co-operate in collecting cartoons to share during a current events period. Teachers may keep files of humorous pictorial materials to be read by pupils either silently or orally. When the teacher or pupils meet humor in their reading, time should be allowed for its appreciation. For an example of how humor may be turned to other purposes, let's look at a recent episode of a comic strip intermediate-grade children enjoy: Hollyhock informs Priscilla that there is something she holds more dear than money. Priscilla's mother overhears the girls and thinks Hollyhock must mean good health and good friends. Hollyhock, however, in her emphatic manner announces to both that what she really means is her library card. This strip might well lead to an interesting discussion of how individuals feel about their library cards. Do they really realize what a privilege it is to be able to have one's own library card? Have their teachers taught them how to use the library and showed them the opportunities and interesting reading that it makes available?

Most intermediate-grade pupils are willing and eager to pretend. Once over their initial self-consciousness, they have an excellent time. They quickly become able to pick out the events of a story that can be portrayed easily and those that must be narrated or changed. As they develop an interest in dramatics, they begin to read stories from the point of view of dramatizing them. Interestingly enough, the best readers are not always best in dramatization; slower readers often have the better imaginations.

A Storyteller's Club that reads orally or tells a story to the kindergarten and first-grade children is an activity boys enjoy as much as girls. The obvious pleasure of the younger children is very rewarding to the older readers. They also like to read stories over the intercom system as "radio programs" for other grades or for other reading groups in their classroom.

Charlotte Huck feels that many children in the middle grades enjoy sharing their reaction to books, provided teachers do not require them to write or give orally a detailed report on every book they read.[2]

One way of insuring creativity is to have individuals choose books and and then read and share them with their classmates in whatever way they wish, perhaps using flannel board characters, dressing in costumes to set the mood, or writing coded messages. Making a diorama of a favorite book for a central library book-week display is another activity enjoyed by many pupils.

Another interesting way of reporting on books involves group work. One pupil in each group reviews a favorite part of a book for a panel of experts listening to him. All in the group may ask questions, and then, as a group, they decide whether or not this person has done a good job in presenting his review.

[2] Huck, "Instead of Book Reports," in *Middle-Grade Activities*, Bulletin No. 3, Vol. 29 (Chicago: Scott, Foresman & Co., 1964), p. 1.

READING IS A PERSONAL AFFAIR

A fourth-grade teacher has found that the following idea brings good results. At the first parent conference in the fall, she explains her "Star Reader" plan to the parents. Each child is expected to read one-half hour each night at home from any source he wishes. A dittoed weekly form indicating his time record is brought back each Friday signed by the parent. If the child has completed his assignment, he receives a star and is listed as a star reader for the week. This teacher reports that the children have been honest in reporting and indicate they like this project.

Another procedure for increasing motivation is to prepare short book lists for various occasions of the year for both pupils and parents. Summer reading lists are helpful, too, if they are prepared with each individual in mind. The reading lists can be put inside the front cover of a "Vacation Reading Booklet," and the books may be checked as read. The following pages can be used for reports, titles and authors of favorite books, lists of characters, amusing quotations, illustrations, and criticisms. The booklets should be brought back to school in September and shared with others.

After having read many books for such units as "Books Too Good To Miss," "Books That Stretch the Mind,"

or "Books about People Who Have Ideas," each student in the seventh and eighth grades in one school wrote and illustrated his own book. For example, after having read numerous essays, one eighth-grade boy wrote twelve essays of his own and compiled them under the title *Seek and You Shall Find, or A Guide to the Crises of the Day*.

Allowing books to be taken home is another incentive for wide reading. The arbitrary categorization of materials into "basic" instructional texts, supplementary readers, and recreational or library books, with major emphasis on the use of instructional materials has often retarded the free development of wide interests. In individualized reading, there should be no such categorization of materials. Through teacher guidance in making appropriate selections, pupils will come to know the great enjoyment that may be experienced in reading. By challenging them to think about what they read, we will help them approach reading creatively. Pupils need to be given wide latitude in their choice of reading matter. A balanced fare is desirable, but, for the reluctant reader, interest in what he is reading is paramount. All forms of encouragement the teacher can think of should be used. A smile, a gesture, or a word may occasionally serve as the strongest incentive.

IN GRADES NINE THROUGH FOURTEEN

FRANCES M. BECK

*

ALL GOOD teachers feel they know their students. But some probably know them only narrowly — as personalities, already unalterably shaped, to be coped with. Others have observed each developing characteristic carefully and have turned to the professional literature to help them enrich their teaching with more knowledge of their students' particular age group. Reports of recent surveys and inventories are also invaluable to teachers who want to learn more about their students.

If you haven't yet read it, I'm sure that you will be interested in the article "The Teen-Agers" in the March 21, 1966, issue of *Newsweek*. I learned from this article that *Seventeen* was the favorite magazine of adolescent girls and *Hot Rod* the favorite of adolescent boys; that *16* magazine had some eight hundred thousand readers; that some adolescents read five to six books a month; that, although some were serious scholars, librarians found that the tastes of most were heavily influenced by movies and television; that sex was one of students' primary interests; and that there was so much pressure on "grades" that even the good student did very little reading on his own.

In my research for this paper, I asked students if they remembered the ways in which their teachers had intrigued, coaxed, led, or forced them into reading. There were various kinds of responses, but generally they took the following forms: "He asked us to make suggestions to each other about what we should read." "She asked us to choose readers for the roles in the class play." "She listened to our ideas." "He made the book he was reading so important and so interesting that we all wanted to share it."

SUGGESTIONS FROM TEACHERS

I also asked a number of teachers what they did to cultivate better reading habits and enrich interest in reading. One, Mrs. Helen Smith of Bradford (Pennsylvania) High School, a teacher of "reluctants" this year, told me of many ingenious ways of catching and sustaining interest. They included the following:

1. Sharing my thumbnail sketches. Every two weeks I select about five books, display them on my desk, and after briefly commenting about each (by describing a character, reading aloud an amusing incident or crazy predicament, or asking, "What would you do if . . . ?"), I pass the books around the class.

2. Inviting our librarian to roll her book cart into our room and talk about some of the books we have selected together.

115

3. Arranging book jackets on the bulletin board. Sometimes these are on special themes — careers, foreign countries in the news, hobbies, teen-age problems. I try to enlist the aid of students interested in art or design. The Wilson Library Bulletin contains some good suggestions.

4. Making available membership information about TAB or Campus Book Club. I take class time to read the monthly news aloud with my classes and often display some of the listed books on my desk or window sill. I'm amazed at the number of students who avail themselves of this opportunity to purchase books.

5. Encouraging students to share something they have enjoyed reading — an idea expressed simply, a description, words that create a mood. Some times we form a circle. I start the sharing but never insist that everyone should contribute, but I'm pleased when they all do. Before the end of the period, we vote on the books with the greatest appeal.

6. Helping students to design book covers and murals or to write a skit based on the books.

7. Providing a guided free-reading period once a week for those students scheduled five days a week. I move about the room and discuss the books with individual students. If I find someone not too happy with his book, we try to find a new one together. I never require a student to complete a book he doesn't like, but I ask him to be fair and read a few chapters. I call it "tasting."

8. Providing browsing days in the library. A few students use the card catalogue to find books on their hobbies or careers. Some have excellent lists which other students may use.

9. Widening their horizons by discussing the "quote-of-the-week" written on the board or by introducing "round-the-world teen-agers" with their problems. So often the reluctant reader lacks self-confidence, and this seems to help.

10. Suggesting that three or four students read the same book and give a panel report.

Other teachers suggested several sources of ideas to promote interest in reading: the publications of the National Council of the Teachers of English and the International Reading Association and the proceedings of the annual reading conferences at the University of Chicago.

USEFUL CLASSROOM ACTIVITIES

Every good librarian sometimes uses a "book talk" to catch the interest of a group of potential readers; and, as we can observe from Mrs. Smith's ten suggestions, good teachers do, too. As an illustration of some of the characteristics of this device, let me share with you a most engrossing book I've recently read. It is one I chose for myself in a local bookstore. This element of personal choice is supposed to be extremely important and to indicate immediate self-involvement; but note what happened next. My work, my family, my other reading — all of these combined to make time unavailable, and three months passed without an opportunity to read this particular book. Finally, the time came to write this paper. I *thought* myself still very busy; but in my reluctance to begin writing — for what new ideas could I present to experienced teachers in the field — I wrote long overdue letters to my family and friends; I put up hems in all my summer dresses; and I turned to this book.

In a sense, then, this book might be called an "escape" book, but it is more than that. It is really a collection of lectures by the artist, Ben Shahn,[1] who is also a truly gifted writer and teacher.

Although I've read most parts of this book at least twice, I feel that in the future I'll return to it often. Some parts of it I feel I have fully comprehended, but other parts — since I am really not very knowledgeable about the history of art, the artist and his craft, and the like — I have only half-understood. It is the kind of understanding one has when, with no ill intent, one happens to hear a whole conversation between two persons who are strangers to one's self on an unfamiliar but immediately intriguing topic.

You will want to read Shahn's lecture "The Biography of a Painting." Shahn wanted to try to assess, for his own enlightenment, "what sort of things go to make up a painting . . . to what extent I could trace the deeper origins, the less conscious motivations."[2] Since the particular painting, "Allegory," was based upon a report of a Chicago fire, it had great interest for me as a Chicagoan and as a city-dweller.

In "The Education of an Artist"[3] Shahn revealed some provocative ideas about the artist and the student artist, which also have a general application to the profession of education and to the teaching of reading:

Attend a university if you possibly can. There is no content of knowledge that is not pertinent to the work you will want to do. But before you attend a university work at something for a while. Do anything. Get a job in a potato field; or work as a grease-monkey in an auto repair shop. But if you do work in a field do not fail to observe the look and the feel of earth and of all things that you handle — yes, even potatoes! Or, in the auto shop, the smell of oil and grease and burning rubber. Paint of course, but if you have to lay aside painting for a time, continue to draw. Listen well to all conversations and be instructed by them and take all seriousness seriously. Never look down upon anything or anyone as not worthy of notice. In college or out of college, read. And form opinions! Read Sophocles and Euripides and Dante and Proust. Read everything that you can find about art except the reviews. Read the Bible; read Hume; read Pogo. Read all kinds of poetry and know many poets and many artists. Go to an art school, or two, or three, or take art courses at night if necessary. And paint and paint and draw and draw. Know all that you can, both curricular and noncurricular — mathematics and physics and economics, logic, and particularly history. Know at least two languages besides your own, but anyway, know French. Look at pictures and more pictures. Look at every kind of visual symbol, every kind of emblem; do not spurn sign-boards or furniture drawings or this style of art or that style of art. Do not be afraid to like paintings honestly or to dislike them honestly, but if you do dislike them retain an open mind. Do not dismiss any school of art, not the Pre-Raphaelites nor the Hudson River School nor the German Genre painters. Talk and talk and sit at cafes, and listen to everything, to Brahms, to Brubeck, to the Italian hour on the radio. Listen to preachers in small town

[1] Ben Shahn, *The Shape of Content* (Cambridge, Mass.: Harvard University Press, 1957).
[2] *Ibid.*, p. 31.
[3] *Ibid.*, pp. 128–51.

churches and in big city churches. Listen to politicians in New England town meetings and to rabble-rousers in Alabama. Even draw them. And remember that you are trying to learn to think what you want to think, that you are trying to coordinate mind and hand and eye. Go to all sorts of museums and galleries and to the studios of artists. Go to Paris and Madrid and Rome and Ravenna and Padua. Stand alone in Sainte Chapelle, in the Sistine Chapel, in the Church of the Carmine in Florence. Draw and draw and paint and learn to work in many media; try lithography and aquatint and silk-screen. Know all that you can about art, and by all means have opinions. Never be afraid to become embroiled in art or life or politics; never be afraid to learn to draw or paint better than you already do; and never be afraid to undertake any kind of art at all, however exalted or however common, but do it with distinction.[4]

As you may well surmise, I regret that Ben Shahn was unknown to me before I read his book; but let me tell you of the "bonuses" I've reaped since learning of him. Recently I went into the home of some friends. There on the wall was a reproduction of a Ben Shahn poster. I spoke at length with the owner, Francis Lloyd, who told me that his interest in Shahn had been sparked by a student of his who derived considerable inspiration from Shahn.

I discovered another bonus in the acknowledgments of permission to reproduce the pictures used in the book; there I learned that a local alderman, Leon Despres, was the owner of three of the drawings. The pleasure I derived from this knowledge was as important as the pleasure I later felt when I received an invitation, in response to my letter to the alderman, to visit his office to see the drawings.

Next, I spoke of reading this book to the most literate, articulate (at least on literature and art) family that I know. The wife immediately handed me a current issue of *Ramparts*, the cover of which displayed a Ben Shahn sketch of Senator Fulbright.

Now you see the broadening directions in which the reading of one new book can lead — deeper friendship, more social and political awareness, and even a new magazine to become acquainted with, to say nothing of the new learning from the content of the book itself.

Another useful device that many good teachers use is the comparison or contrast of two or more books. Since Ben Shahn represents the professional creative artists and can serve as a prototype for male students, we might wish to contrast his book with a book by Phyllis McGinley.[5] Here is a lady, a professional writer of charm and wit, who is proud she is a woman. One may want to talk back to her as one reads, but one cannot deny that she has a gift for writing and living.

Although their styles vary greatly and their intentions in writing are not identical, we can compare selections from each of these authors — McGinley's "The Consolation of Illiteracy" with Shahn's already mentioned "The Education of an Artist." McGinley's is just loaded with the books you all have

[4] *Ibid.*, pp. 130–31.

[5] For example, see *The Province of the Heart* (New York: Dell Publishing Co., Inc., 1959).

read; but her special delight in them is the delight of self-discovery by a literate (despite everything she says to the contrary), mature reader. Two other selections may usefully be compared:

Shahn's "Biography of a Painting" and McGinley's "The Other Side of the Shield: A Note to the Reader"; [6] both have addressed themselves to the same question. "Why do you devote your skill, your creative talent to a particular production which is later available to the scrutiny and contemplation of others?"

And if you will turn to the 1964 Proceedings of the Annual Conference on Reading, you will find a number of other suggestions of book pairs,[7] which may encourage a wider range of interest and contribute to the development of taste and discrimination.

THE CONGRESSIONAL RECORD

Another useful source of material to interest the too-busy-for-much-reading

[6] *Ibid.*, pp. 7–10.

[7] Frances M. Beck, "Motivating Students To Read: In Grades Nine through Fourteen," in *Meeting Individual Differences in Reading*, compiled and edited by H. Alan Robinson ("Supplementary Educational Monographs," No. 94; Chicago: University of Chicago Press, 1964), pp. 68–69.

adolescent is the *Congressional Record*, which, among other qualities, is a serious contender for the "best buy" in terms of words-per-penny. It is published every day that the House of Representatives and/or the Senate meet. Many days it must publish three hundred thousand words. The range of materials, when one considers the boundless appendix, is wide — a tiny poem, sections of novels, and speeches, in addition to the daily proceedings — and may, indeed, meet the interests of many students. If your school does not receive a complimentary copy, the subscription fee is $1.50 a month.

One successful technique for using the *Record* is to distribute a copy to each student with a sheet of general questions that could apply to any issue. Each student then skims quickly to secure answers to questions about present church-state relationships, proposed bills and their content, and other legislative concerns. Although my students generally skim quickly and find answers to these questions, they usually reward me further by reading many other items (possibly noted in peripheral vision while looking for a small detail I may have asked for) and sharing them with their neighbors.

IN CORRECTIVE AND REMEDIAL CLASSES

JEAN HOGE

*

FOSTERING INTEREST in reading among retarded, and usually reluctant, readers presents a special challenge. A sincere effort should be made to identify individual interests through class discussion, individual interviews, close observation of the books selected at the library, and inventories of children's interests (such as *What I Like To Do* [Science Research Associates, 1954]). When identification of interests has been made, materials should be carefully selected to take advantage of these interests on the level of ability of each student.

PRIMARY GRADES

For the poor reader in the primary grades, developing the desire to read may be the teacher's first consideration. One boy who had been in the first grade for two years was having little success with a standardized word-recognition test; but he seemed to have excellent motor co-ordination. His teacher kept him after the test session and asked him if he liked school. His answer was in the affirmative. When asked if he liked to read, he responded that he thought he did, if he just knew the words. "I like to go to school" was printed by his teacher, and the boy was asked to copy the sentence and then read it back. He did this haltingly; but the next sentence, "I like to read," was copied and read fluently. The boy's eyes brightened, as he suddenly realized that he could read the sentence. Experience stories composed from the boy's talking gave him his first successful experience in reading.

For a group of pupils having difficulty in reading, interest was kindled when action words were used as a basis for experience stories. Their favorite was the word *jump*, which was introduced in relation to a story they had read about frogs. A four-sentence experience story was then acted out, with the boys and girls jumping like frogs around the room. They then went on to copy the sentences and to draw pictures as illustrations of the story.

One teacher found that some of her poor readers were reluctant both to read and to express themselves verbally. By using a primary typewriter and having these pupils dictate individual experience stories (they were fascinated to see the stories come to life on the typewriter), she succeeded in interesting them to such an extent that they spoke quite freely and enjoyed reading their own stories. These stories, typed on colorful half sheets of construction paper, were then illustrated by the children.

Using the totality of the senses in many ingenious ways will awaken interest. Books with accompanying records on which the words in the book are read slowly and then sung co-ordinate the visual and auditory approaches. Stories may also be traced, using tracing paper or dotted lines.

Cereals made in the shapes of the letters of the alphabet can be used to form words and then eaten as a reward. Word cards can be sprayed with different colognes for students having difficulty in identifying a group of words.

Occasionally, there may be a boy or girl who care nothing about the lives of "Jack and Janet," "Dick and Jane," or "Susan and Pete." Perhaps the latest space adventure will interest him. Since his basal reader is unlikely to tell him anything about this important subject, the teacher and pupil may have to compose their own book, using material from television, newspapers, and news magazines that can be put into simple language. Or they may use high-interest and low-vocabulary trade books.

INTERMEDIATE GRADES

In the intermediate grades, students have wider interests and consequently more learning situations. Hero worship is prevalent and should be capitalized on with books ranging from Michelangelo to Mickey Mantle. One fourth-grade corrective reading class had pamphlets on the lives of famous people at an easy reading level, and such remarks as "I'll trade Michelangelo for Alexander the Great" were quite common. Such biographies, together with a box of play-acting clothes, can be the impetus for creative

dramatics, which in turn can create a deeper interest in the subject matter.

The backward reader, in the middle grades, is expected to cope with concepts he may have encountered all too rarely in the primary grades. Why should he learn about longitude and latitude or electric circuits? If these concepts are related to definite situations, the teacher will have a much better chance of luring him into reading and enjoying it. For example, the pupil may be asked, Where will you eat breakfast if you start the night before at Chicago and go west, or east, and cross a longitude line? What will the weather be and what clothes should you wear if you cross a latitude line? To answer the question, How does a circuit produce heat from a dry cell? a bit of copper wire with a dry cell can safely be used. Concepts for the retarded reader need to be made as concrete as possible for understanding and enjoyment. The teacher should explain why a unit is important, what its purpose is, and exactly how many of the details are important enough to be remembered.

One girl in the middle grades had little interest in the subject matter being studied in her class but was interested in clothes, good grooming, and boys. She was given the A, B, and C books of "Teen Age Tales" (Heath, 1966) and enjoyed the stories. These stories were then related to social studies by suggesting to the girl that she find out about the hula skirt and muu-muu of Hawaii, the clothes worn in Japan, or the treatment of women in India.

In grades four through six, easy-to-read books of high interest are important for the retarded reader. Content should be mature (that is, on a level with chronological age) and exciting, whatever the subject matter. Television shows should be exploited, with the teacher viewing the currently popular programs in order to use them as a base to extend their interests to better programs and to encourage further study of subjects that are particularly interesting in encyclopedias and other written sources of factual material. Comics may also be used to build interest in reading. These exciting, easy-to-read escape materials can lead the way to adventure stories.

Students having trouble in reading in the intermediate grades can also be helped by a familiarity with library procedures, so that they can find what they want the moment they want it. However, books of fiction usually have titles that don't give much indication of what will be inside the book; so a helping hand by either librarian or teacher is usually most gratefully received. Thumbnail sketches of books by one librarian were so successful that all books she mentioned were immediately checked out.

UPPER GRADES

In the last years of high school, students' interests have expanded to such a wide range that a teacher has difficulty keeping in touch with all of the areas involved. Nevertheless, she should try to be attentive to all indications of interests. For example, even though one boy's intricate diagram of a hot-rod engine was quite incomprehensible to his teacher, it was clear that this was his main interest and that he would enjoy books by Gault or Felsen. Similarly, a severely retarded reader who was a deep sea diving enthusiast found *City beneath the Sea* (Benefic Press, 1962) absorbing. To cope with this wide diversity of interests, paperbacks provide great variety at a minimum cost.

Newspapers are useful for interesting adolescents. The girl who rarely reads on her own may turn to the women's section, to the columnist who answers teenage letters, or to the styles in the advertisements. Some boys may look at the sports section, and others may be intrigued by the descriptions of autos for sale in the used-car section or by the help-wanted ads.

Factual material often appeals to boys in this age group. Such materials as the books from the "Life Science Library," picture magazines such as *Life* and *Look*, or *Hot Rod* magazine and *Geographic School News* may open areas of interest previously unrecognized. They may also be attracted to fiction which emphasizes a hero with whom they can identify.

CONCLUDING REMARKS

Students may learn to enjoy reading through hearing good literature read by the teacher. After they listen to stories, they should be encouraged to enter into lively discussions directed toward involving them in the story's plot, characters, mood, and so forth. Purposeful listening and an interesting discussion afterward may prompt some students to read the story or one like it, which the teacher should be ready to suggest.

Many other devices that may take advantage of the right moment for an individual student should be used. A teacher may interest some poor readers by suggesting that they prepare bulletin boards about the stories they have read or scrapbooks on their hobbies, doing choral reading, tape interesting material, or write stories and poems immediately after an exciting or moving event (a nearby tornado, a race riot, the latest journey of an astronaut).

* * *

THROUGH STORYTELLING

SARA INNIS FENWICK

*

THE CONTRIBUTION of storytelling to many aspects of reading development and language-arts skills has been acknowledged in the literature throughout this century; but, in the past, it has been discussed most frequently as a practice technique for children.

Recently, however, the re-examination of ways to provide enriched experiences with language and literature has led to the renewed recognition of the potential of storytelling. This potential is directly related to the intensity of the emotional involvement in the drama of the story. This more direct involvement, because of the absence of a physical barrier between listener and teller, sets the stage for a greater concentration of attention and, therefore, a more enriched listening experience.

COMMUNICATION WITH ALL

Storytelling, of course, is not a new exercise. Down through the centuries since man began keeping records of his history — personal history as well as group records — storytellers have gathered in many different settings. In early years the storyteller would have been found in tribal ceremonials, beside war-campfires, in baronial dining-halls, in the more sophisticated throne rooms and drawing rooms, beside cottage fireplaces and peddlers' caravans, and among the people of every region. One characteristic of the audience that could have been observed in all times and places was the range in age, a range from the youngest to the eldest. In a simple society with a large segment of its ceremonials, its literature, its genealogies, and its history preserved in oral form, the storyteller was the custodian; and storytelling was truly a process of communication, not primarily an activity for entertainment. When, at a higher level of literacy, storytelling became a valued form of entertainment, it was an occasion shared by all members of the household or community. In our society we seem to have lost this dimension of storytelling. For decades storytelling has been kept alive mainly in the children's rooms of our larger public libraries, in the kindergarten and primary classrooms at school, around campfires, and in the playground programs of recreational organizations. We have long overlooked the value of storytelling in building a common background of experience. Television ought to be providing opportunities for such experiences; but it almost never serves as a medium for the folk art of storytelling.

The direct communication of the storyteller with each individual listener through the medium of a shared experience sets the stage for a greater emotional and intellectual involvement; through the shared experience communication of the beauty of language, the originality of the conception, the suspense of the plot, is more likely to occur.

In telling stories to children the teacher or librarian may aim for growth in the communication skills that are the objectives of reading and language-arts programs: listening ability, vocabulary development, sentence formation, anticipation of events and plot, and understanding and appreciation of figurative language. The child who smiles with pleasure at the sound of a new word and silently "tastes" it with his own tongue; the child who later repeats phrases and sentences from the story; the child who recognizes story parallels in his reading and who is sensitive to varieties of folk-

story plots and style factors; and the child who shows his understanding in his face, his laughter, and other overt reactions — each of these is not only demonstrating responsiveness to the imaginative content of the story but also exercising listening and language skills. The identification of the oral story and its book is clear to the children when the storytelling experience is a sharing of literature, and often provides a valuable stimulus to independent reading.

Specialized needs for which storytelling holds especially rich potential are those of children with low cultural horizons, children who come from homes where standard English usage is minimal or where English is a second language. These children are disadvantaged in their command of a school-accepted vocabulary and sentence skills, as well as in their acquaintance with literature in English. For them, a careful selection of well-known stories presented orally beginning in nursery school and continuing throughout their school life, can be effective in providing them with the background they lack.

THE ART OF STORYTELLING

It is the *telling* in storytelling that should be emphasized. This is not to say that reading aloud is less useful, but the values discussed above are more likely to be realized in a situation where the adult has continuous eye contact with his audience, where he shares his own reactions to the story elements, and where he can be instantly aware of his listeners' involvement, their puzzlement, their wonder, their joy, their fears, and their understanding.

The major requirement for any storyteller is a worthwhile story that the teller believes in and wants to share. The selection of the story is the most important ingredient in the process. Preparation should include a thorough mastery of the story and a saturation with the events, language, mood, and setting. Storytelling then becomes a process of effectively sharing the story, simply and directly. Storytelling is a different art than the dramatic monologue; the teller endeavors to keep himself "out of the way of the story." He is neither performing it nor talking remotely about it; he is the medium through which the story is communicated.

Since the selection of a story is of utmost importance, the storyteller needs to develop a considerable familiarity with a wide range of stories that are worthy of telling. This means that the teacher and librarian must become acquainted with a great body of the best of children's literature. Padraic Colum has described the characteristics of a good story for telling: ". . . I learned that a story that is to be told has to be about happenings. That it has to be in sentences that can be easily and pleasantly carried over by the human voice. That it has nothing to say about states of mind . . . That its characters should be explicable at every moment, even though they do odd and unpredictable things."[1]

Useful aids for storytelling include the following:

May H. Arbuthnot, *Children and Books* (3d ed. rev.; Chicago: Scott, Foresman, 1964).

Ruth Sawyer, *The Way of the Storyteller* (New York: Viking Press, 1962; Compass, 1965).

Marie Shedlock, *The Art of the Storyteller* (rev. ed.; New York: Dover, 1951).

Ruth Tooze, *Storytelling* (Englewood Cliffs, N.J.: Prentice-Hall, 1959).

Helpful lists of stories are the Carnegie Library of Pittsburgh's *Stories To Tell to Children*, the New York Public Library's *Stories*, and the Enoch Pratt Free Library of Baltimore's *Stories To Tell*.

The person who learns a story that is memorable to him and shares it effectively with an audience of one or hundreds has joined the long line of traditional oral tellers of tales who have helped to create and preserve living literature.

[1] Colum, *The Fountain of Youth* (New York: Macmillan Co., 1927), p. 194.

CHAPTER XI

MASS MEDIA CONCEPTS AND READING INSTRUCTION IN THE WORLD TODAY

*

DAVID K. BERNINGHAUSEN

*

There is an island in the ocean where in 1914 a few Englishmen, Frenchmen, and Germans lived. No cable reaches that island, and the British mail steamer comes but once in sixty days. In September it had not yet come, and the islanders were still talking about the latest newspaper which told about the approaching trial of Madame Caillaux for the shooting of Gaston Calmette. It was, therefore, with more than usual eagerness that the whole colony assembled at the quay on a day in mid-September to hear from the captain what the verdict had been. They learned that for over six weeks now those of them who were English and those of them who were French had been fighting in behalf of the sanctity of treaties against those of them who were Germans. For six strange weeks they had acted as if they were friends, when in fact they were enemies . . . .[1]

Walter Lippmann's *Public Opinion* began with this story of "The World Outside and the Pictures in Our Heads." He noted that the news of our environment comes to us now fast, now slowly; but that whatever we believe to be a true picture we treat as if it were the environment itself.

[1] Walter Lippmann, *Public Opinion* (New York: Macmillan Co., 1922), p. 1.

PERCEIVING THE WORLD

This story was chosen to illustrate the first concept for consideration in this paper, which might be labeled: *perceiving the world*. As Lippmann so dramatically reminds us, we interact with our world according to the picture of reality that we hold in our heads. As we perceive our world, so we decide how we shall act.

In light of the concept of *perceiving the world*, consider the aim and the function of the teacher. In the early years of school, the successful teacher produces in his pupils a skill which was not there before, the skill of reading. But why does the teacher, and the school system, think this is important? Because reading opens up the universe for the pupils — encourages them to explore the world into which they have come and gives them a very important tool for exploration. Undoubtedly, young people will explore their environment with or without teachers, and with or without the ability to read, for man is an organizing creature, responding to the stimuli in his environment (at least to some of them), trying to understand the clues that he notices, and making for himself a picture of reality that has meaning to him. In Lippmann's terms, he is building a picture of the world in his own head, and he perceives the world, so will he act upon it.

In exploring our universe, we get many different clues as to the nature of reality. Noticing the size, the brightness, or the color of an object helps us to "see" what is there. Noticing that part of a tree in the distance is not visible because a house seems to blot it out tells us that the tree is farther away than the house. These clues to the nature of our environment do not actually tell us the nature of the object or its precise location; but we add those clues we have noticed all together, draw some inferences, and then "guess." We also seek to give the object a significance, that is, we try to answer the question, What meaning does this object have for me?

Sometimes the clues to which we respond mislead us. For example, you may recall a certain model of the Studebaker car which looked very much the same from the front as from the rear. Once, on the highway, I pulled out to pass a slow-moving car, thinking that except for a Studebaker going away from me the road was clear. Just in time I realized that it was not going away but was coming toward me, and I dropped back into my lane. The concept illustrated here is that of *point of view*. If I had been on the second floor of a building, safely removed from any possible physical contact with the Studebaker, my faulty perception would not have mattered very much. But in the driving situation, my life was endangered because

I had misread the clues as to the nature of reality.

Whenever we are confronted with strange social mores or taboos or other unfamiliar phenomena, we cannot help perceiving them as having meaning. But the meaning we assign may not always be correct. For example, a savage who has never seen a white man or an airplane may one day see an army plane descend from the skies and make a three-point landing and the pilot climb out of the cockpit. Some might suppose that the savage will be unable to perceive the plane and the pilot as anything but unorganized and meaningless, since they are new phenomena to him. But if the concept of man as an organizer of his perceptions so that they have meaning *for him* is correct, the savage will not wait until he has been given formal verbal instruction in a classroom before he organizes his cognitive field into a meaningful perception. He may assign incorrect meaning to his perception, perhaps considering the plane to be a new form of bird and the pilot a god, but he will try to "make sense" of his perceptions, to relate them to himself, to organize them into his understanding.

The significance of this example for the reading teacher is that, regardless of what he tells his students to do, they, too, are not going to hold off on interpretation until they have collected all the facts. The teacher should realize that, as soon as the student experiences *any* facts, they will be organized by him as a perceiver into some sort of meaningful whole.

The reading teacher who is trying to help his students explore the universe through the printed word recognizes that throughout our lives we must act upon our world according to the pictures in our heads and that we need as accurate an estimate of reality as possible; otherwise, our actions will be too much in conflict with our surroundings. We *select* those stimuli in our environment to which we are going to pay attention. We ignore some of the clues brought to us by our senses, and we pay great attention to others. Apparently, our selection is based on two factors, our past experiences and our purpose or need. We pay attention to those clues which have obvious meaning for us, in terms of our experiences, and those which seem likely to forward our purpose or, sometimes, frustrate our purpose.

For example, suppose that two men are at a lunch counter surveying the menu. One is very hungry; the other very thirsty. Both see the same menu, but the first notices the hamburger and the bacon and eggs, and the second skims past these items to focus on the tea, coffee, beer, wine, and so forth. The purposes of these two men differ; so their perceptions differ. The same situation can illustrate how perceptions may differ because of previous experience. An abstainer from alcoholic beverages will not completely miss the fact that beer and wine are available; but if his only experience of beer has been one taste which was bitter and unpalatable, he will quickly skim over this part of the menu and "see" the tea and coffee. The concept under consideration here is selectivity.

THE NATURE OF NEWS

Another major concept should be considered by the reading teacher: *the nature of news*. Wilbur Schramm's description of the nature of news, published in 1949, still seems very useful:

News exists in the minds of men. It is not an event; it is something perceived *after* the event. It is not identical with the event; it is an attempt to reconstruct the essential framework of the event — *essential* being defined against a frame of reference which is calculated to make the event meaningful to the reader. It is an aspect of communication, and has the familiar characteristics of that process. The first news report of an event is put together from a gestalt of eye witness accounts, second-hand accounts, tertiary comments and explanations, and the reporter's own knowledge and predispositions. The report is then coded for transmission, usually by persons who have had no connection with the actual event. It is coded by modifying its length, form, emphasis, and interpretation, to meet the mechanical demands of transmission and presentation, the anticipated needs and preferences of the audience, and the somewhat better known wishes and demands of the buyers of the news. Then the news is trusted to ink or sound waves or light waves, and ultimately comes to an audience, where it competes with the rest of the environment for favor. A typical member of the audience selects from the mass of news offered him perhaps one-fourth of the news in a daily paper, perhaps one-half of the items in a newscast he happens to hear. These items of news are perceived by each individual as a part of another gestalt — his environment and its competing stimuli, the state of his organism at the moment, and his stored information and attitudes. Perception completed, symbol formed, the news then goes into storage with a cluster of related bits of information and attitudes, and becomes the basis for attitude change and action.[2]

Here is a concept of what news is that has very important meaning for the reading teacher. In a democratic society it is *citizens* with votes who are perceiving the world and forming pictures in their heads upon which they base their decisions and actions.

In the classroom, through the process of formal education, teachers try to help their students build bridges between the world of ideas, expressed in oral and written language, and the individual student's daily life. Teachers tend to be people for whom verbal activity is easy and habitual. Students sometimes do not find language easy or even possible as a means to explore their environment. How *can* we expect such students to share our enthusiasm for reading?

READING OTHER LANGUAGES

Ten years ago Paul A. Wagner discussed the relationship of the mass media to reading interests at the annual reading conference and distinguished between reading print and reading "other languages." He said that the teacher has relied mainly, in fact almost completely, on books but that the language of books has always been the province of the elite. Ninety per cent of the people tend to ignore the language of books and rely upon other languages — such as radio, the cartoon, the bold, black condensed Gothic headline, the motion picture, and television.[3]

Wagner was, of course, using the term "language" in a more inclusive way than is usual, but he felt that, so defined, the term had more validity in an educational discussion than the term "mass medium." He stressed the point that only those who understand the language of books are called "readers" but that those who cannot read books may be very adept at "reading" the other languages. Teachers tend to be worshipers of the one language and to teach as they have been taught — with books.

In *Brave New World*, Aldous Huxley presents an unforgettable scene. He describes the incubation in laboratories of babies in bottles, during which technicians add a few drops of this and that to limit the intellectual development of the population according to the needs of society. The workers or drones being created are thus limited in intelligence from before "birth." Two- and three-year-olds are given picture books to look at; but during the process bells ring, loud noises are heard, and electric shocks are felt.[4] These children are being conditioned at an early age to be afraid of books and reading.

[2] Schramm, "The Nature of News," *Journalism Quarterly*, XXVI (September, 1949), 259.

[3] Paul A. Wagner, "Relationship of Mass Media to Reading Interests," in *Developing Permanent Interest in Reading*, edited by Helen M. Robinson ("Supplementary Educational Monographs," No. 84; Chicago: University of Chicago Press, 1956) pp. 90–94.

[4] Huxley, *Brave New World* (New York: Harper & Bros., 1946), chapter i.

In 1966 we have not yet reached the incubator age for human reproduction, nor do we deliberately condition children against books and reading; but as every reading teacher knows, some pupils in the schools *are* conditioned against books and reading. The life of the student outside school is so full of both real-world events — on the playground, in the swimming pool, at the dinner table, and so on — and make-believe events — from movies, radio, and television — that he is forced to become a data-processor. As H. Marshall McLuhan has suggested:

. . . our children today live in a world in which the environment itself is made of electric information. . . . The young person today is a data processor on a very large scale. . . . We haven't really cottoned on to the fact that our children work furiously, processing data in an electrically structured information world; and when these children enter a classroom — elementary school — they encounter a situation that is very bewildering to them. The youngster today, stepping out of his nursery or TV environment, goes to school and encounters a world where the information is scarce but is ordered and structured by fragmented, classified patterns, subjects, schedules. He is utterly bewildered because he comes out of this intricate and complex integral world of electric information and goes into this nineteenth-century world of classified information that still characterizes the educational establishment. The educational establishment is a nineteenth-century world of classified data much like any factory set up with its inventories and assembly lines. The

young today are baffled because of this extraordinary gap between these two worlds.[5]

The single-language approach to the task of exploring the universe is deeply entrenched in our educational system. Along with it goes the division of the universe into fragments, which we call subjects and in which we offer courses and credits — all based upon the language of print, with an overemphasis on the use of textbooks and lectures. The task of the reading teacher, as of all other teachers, is to help students read the clues as to the nature of their universe and to learn what they can do with and to it and what it may do with and to them.

One way for teachers of reading to help students is to recognize the usefulness of the electronic world. The mass media (that is, television, the press, radio, comic books, magazines, and their boards of directors, editors, advertisers, and writers) are in the business of education, too. Hutchins once told newspaper producers that they were teachers, but before they could take his comment as a compliment, he added that he had not said that they were good teachers.

For most people, the mass media provide the means of continuing their education. It is well known that a large majority of our public today does not read books. Reading teachers need to be constantly reminded that the selection of news items and the emphasis given to them by the makers

[5] McLuhan, "Address at Vision 65," *American Scholar*, XXXV (Spring, 1966), 198.

of the media decide for the non-book readers what they will learn.[6]

After successfully teaching students the skill of pronouncing words and inferring meaning from the printing on a page, reading teachers might well give attention to the other languages Wagner spoke of ten years ago. We might note what is going on in communications research, particularly in studies of the process by which signals produce meaning in the mind of the perceiver of the signals.

For example, Sol Worth defines communication broadly as *human interaction through messages*.[7] One of his potentially useful ideas is to consider the motion picture in somewhat the same way that language-arts teachers look at books. He defines visual communication as the *transmission of a signal received primarily through visual receptors, which we treat as a message by inferring meaning from it.*

The diagram Worth uses to illustrate the process of motion picture communication is similar to that of the communication process known to teachers: the encoder, in this case the film-maker, has a "feeling-concern," which may be thought of as a belief that he wants to communicate. He decides to make a film, that is, to organize "image-events" into a story — a film communication. The receiving process occurs in reverse order. The viewer of the film sees the sequence of image-events. In most cases he does not know the film-maker and his personality, or his past experiences, or his purposes. But if he treats the signals on the screen as a message, he infers the "story-organism" from the image-events and becomes aware of the belief system of the film-maker from the images on the screen. If the communication "works," he will be able to infer — to evoke in himself — the feeling-concern of the film-maker.

Selectivity in reporting the news in the newspaper and on television is as important as selectivity in film-making. For example, the late Edward R. Murrow once produced a television show on Senator Joseph McCarthy which portrayed the senator as a giggling psychopath, an irresponsible and unfair man, and a violator of his victims' civil liberties under law. Murrow and his co-producer Fred Friendly selected their scenes from many thousands of feet of film for the purpose of producing a particular feeling-concern in their viewers. Senator McCarthy demanded equal time and shortly after was given it. But the senator did not have available the thousands of feet of film that Murrow had had or the technical know-how or personnel to use the film effectively. Doesn't this example show the desirability of stressing to students the need to be aware of selectivity-for-emphasis upon the part of all film-makers? Doesn't it seem desirable to include in your teaching of reading skills knowledge of the dangers of selectivity?

Probably at the primary levels of

[6] W. H. Ferry, "Masscomm as Educator," *ibid.*, pp. 293–302.

[7] Worth, "Film as a Non-Art," *ibid.*, pp. 322–23.

education the concept of the dangers of selectivity is too complex and sophisticated an idea for inclusion in the curriculum. However, somewhere between kindergarten and grade fourteen, it should be learned.

J. D. McAulay has shown that young children are affected by the mass media of communication and that of these media television seems to have the greatest effect.[8] One authority, in fact, has found that television has four times more influence on a child's social development than have school experiences. McAulay concludes that with proper guidance and direction, third-grade children can begin to handle and understand current national and international events that are discussed on the mass media. He found that when direction was given in the use of mass media, many more children became involved in discussion of current happenings. The topics discussed were of greater importance, vitality, and interest and were more closely related to the national and international scene than the topics discussed by the children who received no direction. As the school year progressed, it was obvious that the mass media had enriched and enlivened the social studies curriculum.

Research in reading and in communications goes on continuously and is reported in a wide variety of scholarly journals; for example, in "What Research Says to the Reading Teacher," a regular feature in the magazine

The Reading Teacher. Reports can be very useful in bridging the gap between *guesses* about the results of particular teaching procedures and knowledge as gained from systematic research on these procedures.

For example, the Himmelweit, Oppenheim, and Vince inquiry, published as *Television and the Child*,[9] is packed with data of particular relevance to educators. In it you can find information about the effects of television on knowledge and school performance, on interests, and on values and about the use teachers are making of this new medium. In another report Himmelweit gives other findings from these studies in Great Britain:

Television viewing undoubtedly takes up more of the child's leisure time than any other activity. On average, a child spends two hours a day viewing. How much a child views depends not on the social level of his home, but primarily on his intelligence. The more intelligent the child, the less time he devotes to television. This is true also of the 10 to 11-year old, even before homework becomes a complicating factor. Within a given intelligence level, how much a child views depends upon a parental example, and the child's range of interests and general adjustment. A child with few hobbies whose parents are inveterate viewers, who in addition is shy, will tend to watch a great deal. Television is not the overwhelming attraction it had been made out to be . . . .

The effect of television on reading proved complex. Reading was at first sub-

8 McAulay, "Mass Media and Third-Grade Social Studies," *Childhood Education*, XLI (November, 1964), 120–22.

9 Hilde T. Himmelweit, A. N. Oppenheim, and Pamela Vince, *Television and the Child* (London: Oxford University Press, 1958).

stantially reduced, but in the majority of cases increased after a time, until for the veteran viewers and their controls no difference was found in the amount of leisure reading. Television affected the type of reading material selected. Fewer comics were read. (The needs they satisfy are better catered for by television.) The taste in books changed: it became more mature, extending over a wider range of topics, including non-fiction. Several libraries commented on the growing demand for non-fiction books.[10]

For the reading teacher who recognizes the challenge of helping students explore the world, the research literature on reading should be fascinating. My selection of concepts and research findings for inclusion in this paper was dictated, of course, by my purposes and my experiences, as well as by what was accessible to me.

TYPES OF LIBRARIES

To help the teacher capitalize on research findings and the concepts presented in this paper, two kinds of libraries are needed. One is the research library, or the professional teacher's library, which provides the journals and books on reading and communications. The second kind of library that is essential to the reading teacher is usually called a "school library." Only if the teacher has library of instructional materials can he effectively open up the universe to his students. It is not my purpose to

10 Hilde T. Himmelweit, "Television, Education and Research," in *Communication Media and the School: The Yearbook of Education, 1960* (Tarrytown-on-Hudson, N.Y.: World Book Co., 1960), pp. 258–59.

suggest *details* of how to teach with instructional materials — this follows in chapter xii — but to suggest that the single-language approach will not reach all students, that the multiple-language approach is necessary, and that the old-fashioned school library with only books and periodicals will not be adequate.

Let us try to create a picture of a modern library, an "instructional materials center" in a "continuous progress school." In the continuous progress plan each student advances as fast as his ability and interest dictate. One student may go through the curriculum of a traditional grade in four months; another student will need fourteen. The plan features individual study stations, where the student keeps his books, progress charts, and other study equipment. When he needs help he consults the teacher and the librarian, or he may be called into "studios" — small groups of five to ten students who happen to need the same lecture or discussion at the same time.

The library — or instructional materials center — is essential to the continuous progress school, since a wide variety of materials are needed by different students at different times. The librarian selects, orders, catalogues, and organizes all materials for use by student and teacher. Anything aiding instruction is instructional material. Circulation of audiovisual material as well as printed material is part of the service. The teacher calls upon the librarian when he has one student or a cluster of students who need material on a given subject. A list of all the books, films, and other materials on the subject is compiled by the librarian and sent to the teacher. Book jackets, charts, pictures, films, and other objects are checked out as often as are books.[11]

I have tried to indicate something of the nature of an ideal school library, but before I go on, I have a pet peeve to dispose of. Some educators talk about a "classroom library." There is no such thing in any classroom that I have ever seen. Five hundred books, a couple of sets of encyclopedias, and a *Who's Who in America* are certainly not a library. A school library consists of several thousand books, films, filmstrips, pictures, recordings, indexes, and reference materials at all levels of difficulty. All these materials are organized for use by a qualified librarian who also integrates them with the school's curriculum. Can we afford this in each and every classroom? The advocates of "classroom libraries" obviously have no understanding of the meaning of the word *library*. Their aim is legitimate — to get books and other materials into the classroom. And of course, there is a way to have our cake and eat it too; we can establish elementary- and secondary-school libraries and then put into the classrooms

11 June Berry, "The IMC in the Continuous Progress School," *Library Journal*, LXXXIX (November, 1964), 4599–4602.

collections of the materials as they are needed.

CONCLUDING STATEMENT

Teachers tend to teach as they were taught. To be maximally effective in providing pupils with the skills necessary for exploring today's universe, the reading teacher needs to extend his perception of his own purposes, methods, and objectives. He simply must open his own mind to the new concepts and research reports that may cause him to rethink and redefine his aims.

If we accept the fact that children today live in a "science fiction" world in which they are bombarded by electronically conveyed stimuli, we as reading teachers must understand the relationship of this world to that of print and the reading of print. Unless the reading teacher is prepared to take advantage of the multiple-language approach to learning, unless he sees the opportunities in the use of television, records, films, and the like, he will fail an important group, the non-verbalists, in his student body; and it may well be that he will fail those who are print- and book-minded as well.

Reading teachers who take advantage of new materials, new approaches to learning, and new concepts will "form new pictures in their heads." They will see their work as including the teaching of the "other languages."

CHAPTER XII

USING AUDIOVISUAL MATERIALS TO STIMULATE INTEREST IN READING

*

IN KINDERGARTEN THROUGH GRADE THREE

DOROTHY WOODS

*

BROADLY SPEAKING, audiovisual materials could include almost every conceivable kind of instructional material. There are, in fact, more than forty different kinds of audiovisual materials in general classroom use today. Almost anything that appeals to the sense of sight may be considered a visual aid. Visual aids, supplemented primarily by the human voice, have long been used as an integral part of the teaching of reading. For this paper, attention will be devoted to some audiovisual teaching materials that make use of the mechanical reproduction of sound and the projection of visual images and to the utilization of these devices, separately and in combination, in the teaching of reading at the primary level.

TAPE RECORDER

The tape recorder can be used in a variety of ways to improve reading instruction. High-quality recorders and portable multiheadphone jacks called "listening centers" are now available at low prices. In combination, these devices should be regular equipment for almost any primary classroom. The tape recorder can be used to awaken interest, even in the earliest grades, since most children respond enthusiastically when they hear their own voices on tape.

Learning to follow simple oral directions can be made fun through the use of the tape recorder. At a designated time, groups of pupils may be assigned a "surprise" activity via a taped message. A multiple-jack headset placed on a table in a corner of the classroom is ideal for this purpose. The "surprise" may be finding and selecting materials for certain art activities or playing games that require following directions.

Teachers of beginning reading classes are likely to find a tape recording of their pupils' oral reading made early in the school year helpful in many ways, especially if similar recordings are made periodically thereafter. The initial recording can serve as a diagnostic tool for the teacher; and later it can be used to determine the effectiveness of the teaching. The child as well as the teacher will be able to recognize the progress he has made over a span of several weeks. To use recordings in this way, the following procedures will be valuable:

(1) Leave a blank space after each pupil's initial recording for the follow-up recordings. A tape recorder equipped with a footage counter will greatly facilitate this calculation. List the beginning and ending footage count with each child's name on the tape container. (2) Have each child give a simple self-introduction, the date, and the name of the story he is reading.

Tape-O-Tec, an innovation for teaching reading skills and listening comprehension, was developed by the writer while teaching in a primary department. The pupils receiving instruction were from ungraded primary first- and second-year classes and had completed the usual first-year work in a basal series. Supplementary reading lessons from a second-year text were tape recorded. The children read silently as the recorded voice of the teacher guided them through a story. Games and other activities were introduced in each of the lessons. Instructions for selected work exercises, for which duplicated pages had been prepared, were next given by the tape. Final instruction for silent re-reading and questions for thought completed the presentation. Space sufficient to accommodate the instructional group was found in the school library. While the majority of the class went about the work of the taped presentation, the writer carried on a reading session with a small group in an adjacent work area.

PROJECTORS AND ACCOMPANYING
MATERIALS

A number of manufacturers offer projectors that are readily convertible to either slides or filmstrips. Excellent ready-made slide and filmstrip materials are available at nominal cost, some on a rental basis. Some commercially prepared transparencies are available for the overhead projector, although this device is, of course, ideally suited to teacher-made materials. The opaque projector will accommodate a great variety of readily accessible materials and is a versatile classroom device. Each of the foregoing aids has its advantages and disadvantages. These need to be weighed by the teacher in the light of her purposes and the materials available.

Slides. Some of the purposes for which the reading teacher might use slides are the following: to introduce or summarize a unit of work, to supplement or add interest to a lesson, to add clarity and understanding to text materials or ideas presented in a lesson, to stimulate discussion, to present pupil-made materials, to provide vicarious experiences, to reinforce learning from other sources, and to provide training in specific reading skills.[1]

Children must be taught to "read" pictures, especially for details in photographs. Primary teachers know that young children grasp relationships and significance but that different levels of ability exist. Well-chosen slides can be helpful for developing

[1] *Audio-Visual Handbook for Teachers* (Trenton, N.J.: State of New Jersey Department of Education, 1954), p. 23.

this phase of reading readiness. Keystone has available a useful series of one hundred colored slides, three and one-fourth by four inches in size, that are effectively designed for developing reading readiness.[2]

High-speed lenses now available on 35 mm. cameras and super-speed film enable pictures to be taken in the classroom without the use of extra light or disturbing flash bulbs. In preparation for "Parent's Night," one teacher made a series of slides of beginning reading activities and showed the slides to parents when they visited her room. Following the slide presentation, the parents were given an opportunity to see the materials used in the classroom.

Polaroid Land transparency film, type 46-L, is now available for "slides in two minutes." Paper or glass mountings may be used, and the resulting slides (three and one-fourth by four inches) projected in any standard lantern slide projector. This type of slide may be used for the same purposes as the 35 mm. slide.[3]

Specially treated glass slides on which the teacher can write with a common lead pencil are available at very low cost. The glass is reusable since the penciled lettering can easily be removed with a rubber eraser. The slides fit any two by two inch projector. A number of word recognition games may be played using hand-lettered slides as a substitute for flash cards.

Filmstrips. During the past decade filmstrips have improved both technically and educationally. "Built in" participation devices and questions and review or application techniques have increased their instructional value at all levels.

Filmstrips offer excellent opportunities for improving reading readiness. The images and type sizes are large and easily visible and are thus capable of holding interest. Elizabeth Alenick has reported the extensive use of filmstrips to complement her reading program with first-year, socially disadvantaged children. The materials she and her teachers used were related to the basal reader series; and the children themselves were taught how to use the projector and the hand and desktop viewers.

During the readiness period, the teachers read stories to the children while pictures of the stories were projected from filmstrips. The children were encouraged to retell the stories in their own words as each frame was reshown. They talked about details in the pictures; concepts with which the children were unfamiliar were explained by the teachers. The stories, as related by the children, were written on the chalkboard by the teachers; and later a book of these stories was prepared and duplicated for each child to take home.

The children's art work was related to the filmstrip stories. The children dramatized the stories, which brought them to life in the classroom. Co-ordinated filmstrips were used to in-

2 Robert Leestma, *Audio-Visual Materials for Teaching Reading* (Ann Arbor, Mich.: Slater's Book Store, Inc., 1954).

3 Florence B. Freedman and Esther L. Berg, *Classroom Teacher's Guide to Audio-Visual Material* (Philadelphia: Chilton Co., 1961).

troduce and reinforce phonics and word-attack skills. Comprehension skills were developed through teachers' questions about the pictures and text on the screen.[4]

Filmstrip stories that have much conversation offer an opportunity for group participation. The teacher or one of the children acts as narrator and reads the descriptive lines; a child represents each character in the story, dubbing in his lines as they appear in the story. The children are required to read only the exact words that appear on the screen.

Text films may be used in games that build sight vocabulary or develop phonics skills. One such game is called "I Can Find." The picture is focused on the chalkboard. The teacher calls upon one child to be "it." "It" goes to the chalkboard; another pupil in the class calls out a word in the text; "it" must find the word, circle it with chalk, and pronounce the word. If "it" is successful, he chooses another in the class to be "it," returns to his seat, and calls a different word to be located in the text film. The game continues until all of the words are circled.

Overhead projector. The overhead projector, which can be operated from the front of the room as the teacher faces the class, uses both slides and other hand-made transparent materials. The making of transparencies

is relatively easy; however, certain pieces of auxiliary equipment and materials are required. Two types of copying machines may be used: the infrared (Thermofax) or white-light (3M) copying machine.

Workbook pages may be transferred onto transparencies and then filed for reuse after the initial presentation. An Oregon teacher found this technique very helpful both for introduction of new units and for review. Working with beginning reading pupils, she made transparencies from workbook pages about rhyming words and projected them on the screen. Attention to single comparisons was achieved through the "revelation" technique: squares of cardboard that had been placed over each of the examples were removed one at a time. As each example was visible on the screen, a pupil was called upon to answer whether the names of the pairs of objects rhymed or not.

The "Stepping Stone" game for word recognition may suggest several adaptations for other reading skills. The teacher prints several sight words on a clear piece of acetate with a colored-ink Flo-Master pen. The words are arranged in a pathlike pattern and encircled with irregularly shaped forms that represent stones. "Water" is added with wavy blue lines around the "stones." The object of the game is for the pupil to pronounce each word correctly. When a word is mispronounced, he "falls into the water" and is out of the game.[5]

Opaque projector. The opaque pro-

[4] Alenick, "The Audio-Visual Approach in Reading," in *Improvement of Reading through Classroom Practice*, International Reading Association Conference Proceeding, edited by J. Allen Figurel (Newark, Del.: International Reading Association, 1964), IX, 129–31.

[5] Morton J. Schultz, *The Teacher and Overhead Projection* (Englewood Cliffs, N.J.: Prentice-Hall, Inc., 1965), pp. 75, 78–79.

jector is particularly well suited for the presentation of reading readiness materials. Picture materials from basal or picture books may readily be projected on a screen, enabling the whole class or a smaller group to see the picture and participate in discussion. With the opaque projector it is possible to place a whole book in the aperture of the projector, which makes available a much greater variety of materials.

The opaque projector is an ideal device for presenting experience stories with the pupils' own illustration. The teacher should type the story out for the children, preferably using a primary typewriter. Illustrations should be kept to the six-by-six-inch size acceptable for full-size projection.

An idea that can increase motivation to read is the making of a paper "film." A series of illustrations made by the children may be pasted to-gether and fashioned into a continuous roll. A story to accompany the film may be typed on the next "frame," which a pupil may read to the class. This kind of project might easily be the outgrowth of a field trip or some other group activity in the reading program.

CONCLUDING REMARKS

A well-balanced use of audiovisual materials, co-ordinated with class work, should sharpen the vividness of impressions from reading and should help simplify the learning process. The main contribution of audiovisual materials is as an additional means of stimulating interest, extending the limits of study, and communicating concepts. The usefulness of audiovisual materials and methods of instruction for improving the teaching of reading is limited only by the imagination and skill of the teacher.

* * *

IN GRADES FOUR THROUGH EIGHT

HENRIETTA KOMAREK

*

PUPILS READ more widely in grade levels four through eight than at any other time in their school careers. By this time most of them have been tasting the satisfactions of independent reading exploration. A lesser number will sustain their interest through high school, and only a few will continue to read widely in adult life. With the increasing pressures and time requirements of stepped-up academic programs and extracurricular activities, even the middle-grade period of wider reading is being threatened. If we are to meet the challenge of the times, we will have to bend all of our efforts to the task of providing increasingly stimulating reading experiences.

Since most basic reading programs begin with training in auditory and visual discrimination, most primary teachers are keenly aware of the necessity of using many kinds of audiovisual materials. They become extremely conscious of the value of these aids and spend a great deal of time making charts, bulletin board displays, pictures, and labels of various kinds. As pupils progress through the grades, however, and the subject matter to be taught increases, their teachers become so intent on covering pages and teaching content that they often fail to realize that the audiovisual techniques of the primary grades are still useful in holding the attention of individuals whose interest is beginning to wane.

Middle- and upper-grade teachers sometimes forget, too, that their pupils need experiential background for the material they are asked to read just as much as the little folk in "headstart" programs. The reading of a story set in Japan will be a much richer experience if preceded by a showing of pictures about life in Japan and maps of the country. To provide such background and stimulation for reading, teachers need to make a greater use of visual and auditory aids. Many teachers lack the confidence in their creative or artistic ability to make charts, bulletin board displays, and other visual aids. A course in the use of audiovisual techniques can do much to help them. Books such as R. E. deKieffer and Lee W. Cochran's *Manual of Audio-Visual Techniques*[1] or George F. Horn's *How To Prepare Visual Materials for School Use*[2] give many practical suggestions with detailed instructions.

USE OF INSTRUMENTS

Some closed-circuit *television* programs are being used successfully in various cities to stimulate reading. In the Philadephia public schools, a series called "Books in Action" dramatizes excerpts from books, plays, and stories on junior-high reading lists. A panel of four pupils and a teacher discuss the plot, author's meaning, and character development in the stories. Another program, for the sixth grade, called "Bookshelf" acquaints its listeners with books.[3] In Dallas, children take part in the dramatization of stories on closed-circuit television.[4] In both Philadelphia and Dallas there is co-operative team-teaching between the television and classroom teachers.

Motion pictures, filmstrips, and re-

[1] Englewood Cliffs, N.J.: Prentice-Hall, 1962.

[2] Worcester, Mass.: Davis Publications, 1963.

[3] Martha A. Gable, "TV Lessons To Stimulate Interest in Reading," in *Improvement of Reading through Classroom Practice*, International Reading Association Conference Proceedings, edited by J. Allen Figurel (Newark, Del.: International Reading Association, 1964), IX, 133–34.

[4] Hazel Horn Carroll, "Magic of Presenting Materials through Television," in *Vistas in Reading*, International Reading Association Conference Proceedings, edited by J. Allen Figurel (Newark, Del.: International Reading Association, 1966), Vol. XI.

cordings are being used today by many teachers to provide enrichment for stories read by their pupils. The very abundance of these materials, however, creates a problem. All too often the materials are not carefully previewed and properly evaluated. Most teachers would never think of having their pupils read a basic text that the teacher had not read; yet they often use motion pictures, filmstrips, and recordings that have not been previewed. Often the only previous contact a teacher has had with the material is the few lines he has read in the publisher's catalogue; sometimes he has seen only the title. If these materials are to be used to their fullest, they must be carefully previewed and evaluated, and their use must be planned for a particular lesson. Filmstrips are the most versatile of the audiovisual materials, since they can be stopped on a frame, turned back, or turned forward with little effort.

As George D. Spache has said, audiovisual devices should not take the place of the teacher or of good discussion.[5] They should be used to provide background experiences and to reinforce teaching. They should be accurate, realistic, appropriate to the lesson, concise, up to date, and well constructed. In his article Spache also lists many sources of audiovisual materials for use in all areas of reading.

The *opaque projector* can be used to show pictures, diagrams, and maps.

[5] Spache, *Toward Better Reading* (Champaign, Ill.: Garrard Publishing Co., 1963), p. 393.

However, whatever the material, it should be well organized ahead of time. Pictures, for example, should be stacked in sequence or attached to shelf paper, accordion fashion, so that they can readily be changed.

The *overhead projector* is being used by more and more teachers today because it is easy to handle and can be used for creative work. Although excellent commercial transparencies are available, teachers and pupils should consider making their own. One sixth-grade teacher has used this technique to stimulate interest in outside reading. She felt that much interest in reading was killed by the requirement of laboriously written book reports that became English lessons. This creative teacher asked her children to give oral book reports and to illustrate them with transparencies that they had made themselves.

The *tape recorder* can be an excellent means of "sparking" the reading period, although all too often its use has degenerated into keeping a record of the old-fashioned "round-the-class" oral reading lesson. When the tape is played back, the poor oral reader cringes when everyone hears his mistakes. As an individual diagnostic tool, however, a tape recording of oral reading can be of some value.

One sixth-grade teacher uses the tape recorder for recording discussions of stories. While he works with one group, another group records their discussion of a story they have read. A pupil leader leads the discussion, using questions provided by the teacher. Later the teacher listens to the tape and makes comments to the group about their discussion.

Another way of utilizing the tape recorder that has been effective is to set up a listening station in one corner of the classroom. The station can be used in several ways. In advance, the teacher can tape appropriate directions or questions for a particular reading lesson. Later small groups can play the tape back and proceed to carry out instructions. Or the story itself can be read orally and taped by a pupil or the teacher and then played back at any time in order to answer questions posed by the teacher. Oral book reports can be taped and listened to for interesting outside-reading ideas. The tape recorder can also be used for dramatization of stories.

A central intercommunication system in a school can also be used effectively for dramatizations of stories, oral book reports, special book reviews, or simulated radio or television book programs.

MATERIALS MADE BY TEACHERS AND PUPILS

There will never be anything that can take the place of the enthusiastic resourceful teacher who is willing to take extra time to prepare or direct the preparation of supplementary materials. The teacher does not necessarily have to have artistic talent; he can generally find a resource person who will be willing to contribute his artistic ability. The teacher can also make use of lettering sets and of the

ideas contained in the many audio-visual-materials manuals that are available in public libraries. He can capitalize on the talents of his pupils, too; many teachers are inclined to underestimate the abilities of their youngsters. With proper direction — and this is important — surprising results can be obtained through the work of pupil committees. At the upper levels, pupils should be taught to operate instruments and also to plan and execute bulletin board displays and other exhibits.

At the primary level, a *picture file* is a "must" for every teacher. It should be a "must" for every upper-grade teacher, too. Properly mounted and displayed, pictures can be of great value in supplying background for a story. Some school libraries and most public libraries have excellent files of well-mounted pictures that are available for teachers' use. Spache, in the article cited before, lists companies from which pictures of various kinds can be obtained.[6] Many good pictures can be accumulated from magazines, Sunday news supplements, publishers' brochures, and the like.

Few teachers use *bulletin boards* and *chalkboards* to their fullest extent. Frequently changed displays of new book jackets can stir interest in independent reading. More important, however, is the use of the bulletin board to display carefully planned materials that are related to the stories being read in class. Three-dimensional objects should be included to lend variety to such displays. A se-

6 *Ibid.*

quence of pictures can be arranged to enrich the reading of a particular selection. Diagrams or maps drawn in colored chalks are also helpful in setting the stage for a story. Too often bulletin boards are used only for notices and a few pictures that remain in place for months.

A common complaint of teachers is that they don't have enough chalk-board or bulletin-board space for "extra" things. There are many devices that can be employed to save space. One is the common window shade, which can be used for chart material and written on with a marker. One ingenious teacher put flannel on a window-shade roller. She sometimes uses this "flannel-shade" as a background for characters dressed in the period of a story. Or she may place cards on it to teach a specific reading skill. When not in use, the shade may be rolled out of the way above the chalkboard.

A *scroll-roll* is another device that can be used to display material to enrich the reading of a story. Pictures, diagrams, or maps can be pasted on a roll of shelf paper, which can be unrolled and temporarily tacked up or used in the opaque projector. The scroll-roll is easily stored when not in use.

A *flip-chart*, composed of a series of poster-board cards that are hinged at the top with rings, is easy to use and easy to store. Also easy to store are display materials on poster-board cards that have been hinged together with bookbinder's tape in an *accordion fold*. George F. Horn lists other

devices that can easily be made by the teacher or her pupils.[7]

Puppets made by pupils can be used in dramatizations of stories to stimulate interest in reading. Information on puppetry can be obtained from the "Book Witch," Victoria Johnson, who has done much to make books come alive for children with her puppets.[8] At upper-grade levels, this device may be more successfully used with some groups than with others.

Dioramas and *models* can also be used successfully to awaken interest. One sixth-grade class enjoyed the background reading they had to do in order to construct dioramas of activities in the various countries they were studying. In one school system a traveling exhibit goes around weekly from school to school. It is made up of dioramas, charts, models, maps, diagrams, and other projects made by students in the intermediate grades in connection with stories in their basic readers. The exhibits are changed frequently.

CONCLUDING STATEMENT

In an age in which audiovisual materials are so skilfully used to capture the attention of human beings, the classroom teacher must double his efforts to use this type of material effectively. Careful planning and evaluation of materials must precede

[7] Horn, *How To Prepare Visual Materials for School Use* (Worcester, Mass.: Davis Publications, 1963).

[8] Victoria Johnson, The United Educators, Inc., Tangley Oaks Educational Center, Lake Bluff, Ill., 60044.

every use of them. Pupil participation in the making and use of materials should be closely directed and supervised. The teacher must be enthusi-astic and confident in his presentation if his use of audiovisual materials is to inspire his students to greater interest in and enjoyment of reading.

* * *

IN GRADES NINE THROUGH FOURTEEN

BONNIE GILLIOM AND JULIA GUMP

*

DEVELOPING STRONG motives for and permanent interest in reading is listed as an objective for nearly every subject taught at the secondary-school or junior-college level today. This objective requires teachers to search conscientiously for new springboards, to try different approaches with different students, and to make use of the technological developments that are so accessible in twentieth-century life.

One approach a teacher can utilize to bring students and reading materials together on the same "wave length" is to capitalize on their interest in non-print devices, since the majority of students find the languages of radio, television, movies, and even comics more intriguing than the language of books. Such devices may range from an amateurish blackboard drawing of Huck Finn's raft to the artistically produced film entitled *Mark Twain's America* — from a picture of the Mississippi River ripped out of *Life* magazine and tacked on a bulletin board to an EDEX Classroom Communicator, which electronically operates filmstrips, films, and slides; gives quizzes; allows questions; stops for homework assignments, individual explanations, and further discussion; and tallies individual student reactions to questions or work assignments.

The scope of available audiovisual materials has expanded almost in direct proportion to the explosion of communication media and with surprisingly little time lag. To keep informed about the kinds of materials that are available, where they may be obtained, and how they may be used, Edgar B. Wesley and Stanley P. Wronsky suggest that teachers do the following:

1. Read a general guide such as the latest edition of Edgar Dale's *Audio-Visual Methods in Teaching* and occasionally a specific guide such as William H. Hartley's leaflet, *How To Use a Motion Picture* (National Council for the Social Studies).

2. Refer to the *Educational Media Index*, a cumulative series of publications listing all types of audiovisual materials. It is compiled by the Educational Media Council and published by McGraw-Hill Book Company . . . .

3. Secure the latest catalogs of audiovisual materials, such as the *National Tape Recording Catalog*, Department of

Audio-Visual Instruction, NEA, Washington, D.C.; *Catalog of NAEB Radio Programs*, NAEB, 1346 Connecticut Avenue, N.W., Washington, D.C.; *Instructional Television Materials: A Guide to Films, Kinescopes, and Videotapes Available for Televised Use*, Instructional Television Library, 10 Columbus Circle, New York; *Programs: A Guide to Programmed Instructional Materials*, U.S. Office of Education, Washington, D.C.

4. Secure information concerning local distributors such as the extension division of a university, the public library, the State Department of Education, or commercial rental agencies.

5. Keep informed of the latest developments by reading the monthly section "Sight and Sound" in *Social Education*.[1]

In addition to keeping abreast of available ready-made audiovisual devices for use in the classroom, the teacher should take advantage of radio and television programs and movies that students see and hear outside the classroom. Public airing of a story boosts, rather than limits, its sales in book form. For example, sales of that musty, old classic *Tom Jones* jumped enormously following the popular film release.

COMMERCIAL AUDIOVISUAL MATERIALS

Two media, motion pictures and instructional television, have the capacity to "hit 'em in the eye and in the ear at the same time," as Percy Foreman describes his own highly successful technique of appealing to juries in criminal law cases. A teacher has at his command more than a half-billion dol-

[1] Wesley and Wronski, *Teaching Social Studies in High Schools* (Boston: D. C. Heath & Co., 1964), p. 270.

lars' worth of educational films that can re-create events that have occurred anywhere and at any time and that can overcome the handicaps of time, size, and distance. In seeking materials to stimulate students to read Mark Twain's works, for example, the teacher can obtain 16 mm. films illustrating Samuel Clemens' life, the background of his works, his contributions as a humorous writer, his personality in an interview (with Twain played by the actor Hal Holbrook), and his work itself, as in the commercially produced *Adventures of Huckleberry Finn*. Three Encyclopaedia Britannica Films on the meaning and the art of *Huckleberry Finn*, narrated by Clifton Fadiman, go beyond the sometimes surface treatment given by educational films and appeal to the more mature reader. Within a short time, the developers of 8 mm. sound films promise to make them the paperbacks of the film field, which should open new vistas for teachers in the use of the medium.

All that films can do, regular in-school instructional television can do, with the added advantages of bringing valuable experiences into the classroom that would be difficult if not impossible to arrange — outstanding guests, the best films at the right time, field trips, microscopic or very small objects for all to see at the same time, experiments for which the school is not equipped — and of having the assistance of a television teacher who is not only a professional educator but also a professional communicator. The disadvantage of instructional television — a lock-step curriculum (content or pacing that does not fit a particular class) — can be overcome by merely turning off the set temporarily or permanently, which should be every classroom teacher's prerogative.

Ready-made visual materials available for use in the classroom include pictures of all shapes and sizes — pictures to be displayed on bulletin boards and felt boards; pictures to be projected, such as slides, film strips, transparencies, opaques, and microfilms; specialized pictures such as cartoons, posters, graphs, charts, and diagrams.

To show how a picture can be used, let us again take Mark Twain and his works as an example. On April 25, 1966, a picture appeared in the *Chicago Sun Times* of California Governor Pat Brown holding a squirming frog named Rough and Ready, which, by a happy coincidence, was also Brown's re-election campaign slogan. What possible avenues to stimulate students to read could this newspaper picture open? There is Twain's story "The Celebrated Jumping Frog of Caliveras County," and there is the story of how Californians annually celebrate the frog jump. On another tack, there are the stories of the California gubernatorial election, of Ronald Reagan's election to a new career, and of the role of entertainers in politics — all of which are thoroughly covered in current periodicals. The possibilities of appeals that teachers can make through just this one picture are limited only by the teachers' and students' imaginations; and with a bit of effort, the picture can be presented in any one of the visual styles previously mentioned.

Recordings of various types and radio broadcasts are another kind of audio material that is available for the classroom. Stanley Solomon has described some of the uses he makes of audio materials. "To kick off a semester in literature, I use recorded blood-and-thunder excerpts from books and plays to be read. I tease students with the bloody stabbing of Caesar heard on MGM's rousing *Julius Caesar* (listen especially for the audible "thump" of the body). . . ."[2] His response to an average English class's sour reaction to poetry is to have the class tape record their reading of *The Cremation of Sam Magee*, throwing in all the extras — a record for background music, twisted cellophane for the essential fire, howling young voices for sled dogs. Another teacher of poetry, J. Irwin Suloway, believes that since "the appeal is so largely to the ear, we should make wider use of recordings by poets or gifted readers. The good teacher of poetry throughout the years has relied on his own voice rather than the printed words to 'sell' a poem to his classes. In one sense a printed version of a poem is as poor a substitute for the heard poem as is a description of a painting for the actual canvas."[3]

For the most part, instructional ra-

2 Solomon, "Disc Tricks," in *Using Mass Media in the Schools*, edited by William D. Boutwell (New York: Appleton-Century-Crofts, 1962), p. 227.

3 Suloway, "Classroom Methods for Developing Reading Interests in Grades Two through Fourteen," in *Developing Permanent Interest in Reading*, edited by Helen M. Robinson ("Supplementary Educational Monographs," No. 84; Chicago: University of Chicago Press, 1956), p. 134.

dio broadcasts have the same advantages and disadvantages as those mentioned for instructional television. Their added advantage is that they are much less expensive to produce, and their added disadvantage, that they appeal to the ear alone. Yet, an appeal to the ear can stir the imagination, the mind's eye, in a most powerful way. Teachers observing students listening to MacLeish's *J.B.* can almost see each student creating his own mental drama. The choice of audio materials on nearly every conceivable subject is so wide that no teacher should lack appropriate materials for her teaching.

CREATED AUDIOVISUAL MATERIALS

Valuable as ready-made materials are, they do not have the advantage of involving students in the development of teaching-learning materials. Active learning experiences that include seeing, handling, smelling, tasting, feeling, and touching are direct and purposeful and have deeper meaning for the learner.

Homemade materials can also fill a void. There has been very little written or produced, for example, about the contemporary author Jesse Stuart. The student exposed to Stuart for the first time may be stymied by the homespun ideas and vocabulary so prevalent in his writing. "Nest Egg," a short story written when he was a high-school sophomore, could be a point of departure. With this brief introduction, students could create instructional materials depicting Appalachia or Stuart's folksy characters and, concurrently, be stimulated to read more of his works. Created materials (individual or class projects) could include the following:

1. Displays (bulletin boards, chalkboards, magnet boards, flannel boards, and exhibits of real things). Students could illustrate legislative procedures to restrict cock fighting, farm settings of rural areas in Kentucky, or Stuart's colorful scenes.

2. Constructions (dioramas, mock-ups, models, sets, and shadow boxes). Students could imitate, adapt, or invent ways to portray the lives of Stuart's mountain people or to contrast Kentuckian folkways with the mores of other parts of the nation.

3. Verbalizations (dramatizations, role-playing, simulations of motion pictures and radio broadcasts, group discussions, debates, buzz sessions, and brainstorming). Students could add realism to their mental picture of Nest Egg, the rooster, by portraying his human traits, by producing an entirely new story about the same personality type in a city setting, or by discussing his influence on the economy of that rural community.

4. Recordings (tape recordings of interviews, guest lectures, student rehearsals, and performances of dramatic or musical productions; and tape recordings of portions of radio or television programs). Students could send Jesse Stuart a blank tape with the request that he read his own work for them; they could make their own recordings of exciting excerpts; or they could tape their own discussions, which could be used to stimulate other classes to read Stuart.

5. Graphics (cartoons, posters, graphs, charts, and diagrams). Students could compete in a cartoon contest illustrating Nest Egg's "personality"; they could co-

operate in lining the walls of the classroom with a time-line depiction of Stuart's life and works up to the present; or they could make acetate overlays to pinpoint the geographic settings of his works.

6. Community resources (people, news departments, libraries, art galleries, museums, and zoos). Students could interview people familiar with Stuart's Appalachia, search old newspapers for information about the author and his work, or take field trips to get firsthand information.

7. Photographs (8 mm. or 16 mm. films, filmstrips, slides, and stills). Students could plan, photograph, develop, edit, use, and evaluate scenes of the unique cultural features of Appalachia.

CONCLUDING STATEMENT

A bifocal look should be taken at the media and the techniques proposed for stimulating student interest in reading. The close-up view calls for judicious selection of educationally sound materials that are appropriate for the objectives of the course and the interests of the students; judicious utilization of the materials (sparingly or abundantly, separately or in various combinations, as points of departure or as culminating activities); and judicious evaluation of the students' responses to the materials.

The long-range view involves a realization of the impact that audiovisual materials can have on stimulating students to read. The combination of the best technological developments with the creative powers of students and teachers can act as a powerful lever for overcoming the resistance of students not previously oriented toward print.

* * *

IN CORRECTIVE AND REMEDIAL CLASSES

MIRIAM JELLINS

*

A USEFUL WAY of thinking about the selection and evaluation of nonprint materials for corrective and remedial instruction is to consider how these materials can function to promote growth toward your stated objectives. Since instructional objectives are formulated from the point of view of specific learner needs, they can serve as an excellent guide for setting up criteria. In this way, activities involving non-print materials will be tailored to your program and purposes, and you will avoid two common pitfalls: (1) the use of entertaining but non-pertinent materials and (2) slavish adherence to one idea about multisensory presentations or, perhaps, to a single commercially prepared product.

Another useful way of thinking

about the selection of non-print materials is to consider them in terms of categories of use. In what parts of the instructional program are these materials most effective? Non-print materials have been reported to be effective in at least three aspects of the program: (1) in stimulating interest, (2) in building concepts, and (3) in reinforcement of previous learning. Other categories of use can be identified. They will be influenced somewhat by an individual's concept of the reading process, by his concept of the learner and the learning process, and, of course, by his concept of the role of the teacher and materials. The discussion in this paper, however, will be confined to the aspects of instruction listed above.

GUIDES TO SELECTION

Start with the objective. Instructional objectives that have been defined operationally—in terms of behavior, content, and area of application — provide a starting point from which decisions can be made as to activities that will have the greatest probability of fostering growth toward these objectives. To illustrate, the objective of stimulation of interest may be stated in the following manner: The learner should find satisfaction in reading books as a regular leisure-time activity. The focus in this objective is on the creation of values. How must the learner behave in order to give evidence of regular reading for pleasure? What can be done to help him select books which may give personal satisfaction? To further this objective, filmed versions of some trade books

may be available for showing, or the bulletin board may be utilized to depict characters or scenes from certain books or stories, or puppets may be used to retell a story or part of a book. These alternatives may also help the learner select books for himself. If he makes his own selection, the probability of positive feelings of satisfaction is greater.

Provide for maximum learner participation. Of course, choices of materials can nullify well-made plans unless the maturity levels, backgrounds, sex, and ages of the learners are carefully taken into consideration. Only if these factors are considered, is it possible to select non-print materials that will be actively utilized by the learner. To develop ability in identifying and interpreting figures of speech, for example, a teacher might very well make a collection of figures of speech and illustrate them by preparing cartoons to project to the whole class. However, it would probably be more educative for learners to prepare their own cartoons based on figures of speech they already know. By collecting his own examples, the learner has an opportunity to identify figures of speech, and in illustrating them, he must exercise some interpretation. For learners at an earlier stage of maturity, collections and displays can also strengthen concepts of texture, hardness, and weight, and thus implement another objective — the extension of the learner's vocabulary of words that give rise to sensory impressions.

Maintain a perspective of the total instructional plan. It is important that the instructional situation be viewed as an integrated whole and in terms of its total impact upon the learner. In corrective and remedial situations, special emphasis must be given to stimulation, reinforcement of skills, and the like; but in many cases, over-emphasis of one kind of material or type of presentation can be as harmful as neglect and may well serve to impede satisfactory progress in reading. When an instructional activity fosters more than one objective, relatively more time should be allotted to it, and conversely, if only a single purpose is served, the time allotted should probably be restricted. Decisions must be made in terms of the use and usefulness of the activity and the materials.

PURPOSEFUL USE OF NON-PRINT MATERIALS

Stimulating interest. One of the more popular uses of still pictures, film recordings, bulletin boards, and displays is to build a background of impressions upon which to base a planned lesson. When used in this manner, the pictures should be ordered by the teacher in such a way that the learner's attention is focused on those concepts that will be important in the lesson that follows. Another helpful, though less structured, use of audiovisual materials is to encourage and promote a permanent interest in reading. In corrective groups, this is often the primary need of the students. For these students, more novel and unusual visual and auditory stimulation will probably be required to capture their attention. Some advantage may be gained by

stressing pupil participation and involvement in the preparation, or presentation, of the materials to be used. For example, a small group of pupils can prepare a short taped dialogue from a book that has been read and enjoyed by two or three of them. Indifferent youngsters have been stimulated to read a particular book by becoming familiar with one or two outstanding characters through recorded excerpts of the book or puppet recreations of one or two interesting scenes. With older groups, short films about popular authors or recordings made by professional artists can serve to arouse interest. Although a variety of media may be used, singly and in combination, it seems important to emphasize that, once aroused, interest must be maintained; teachers need to formulate plans immediately to encourage continued and expanded interest.

Concept building and reinforcement. It is for this aspect of reading instruction that much of the newer electronic equipment can fulfil an important function. Files of transparencies for the overhead projector and still pictures for the opaque projector can be built up for use in clarifying concepts, presenting procedures, introducing new skills with greater effectiveness, and other similar operations. These files are valuable not only because of their immediate availability and their wide range of flexibility in initial presentations but also for reviewing and summarizing material presented before. Although commercially prepared transparencies for the overhead projector may be secured, the usefulness of this instructional aid depends in large measure upon the skill and imagination of the teacher.

For skills practice, short review lessons may be taped or slides may be prepared to guide individual learners or small groups. For example, an individual who needs help in syllabication or auditory-analysis skills may listen for certain sounds or syllables in a recording of multisyllabic words. The memory of another learner who is preparing to read study-type materials may be sharpened by a taped version of one of the preview methods.

When the teaching objective is to encourage the learner to recognize and respond to certain moods as represented in written materials, the film essay — with no narration, only background music — may be used. The viewers should be asked to describe the mood of the filmed episode as they perceive it. This kind of practice should enable learners to read with a more sensitive appreciation of mood. Similarly, the "single-concept" film might be useful for illustrating abstractions such as justice, loyalty, and vengeance, since it could concentrate on a specific concept and thus could provide a deeper and more complete understanding.

The examples given do not pretend to be exhaustive but are suggestive, it is hoped, of ways to develop viable, productive instructional techniques with the aid of non-print materials. As soon as teachers realize the possibilities of non-print visual and auditory presentations, they themselves can become the originators of varied and effective ideas for the use of these media.

GUIDES TO EVALUATION

Although the discussion has focused somewhat more on materials prepared by teachers and students, commercially prepared materials are available and in increasing quantities. The problem of evaluating these materials before purchasing them is made more difficult by their very volume. Commercially prepared materials often have motivational value and may be used to introduce new ideas, concepts, and procedures and to reinforce previous learnings; but they must function in the service of specific instructional aims and objectives. Criteria, therefore, must be established. Generally, to make decisions about commercial materials, teachers ought to know (1) the value of the medium for contributing to desired behavior changes in the learner, (2) its flexibility and adaptability, (3) the provisions made for learner participation, (4) the technical quality (ease of operation or use), and (5) the cost, time required, and availability. Further, teachers should know whether the materials are based on sound pedagogical and psychological principles. Additions to this list of criteria will undoubtedly grow out of instructional needs in different situations; but these are suggested as general guidelines. Ideally, the ultimate aim is to select non-print materials that will aid the teacher in his efforts to promote maximum growth toward maturity in reading.

CHAPTER XIII

PROBLEM READERS

MARY C. AUSTIN

A s RECENTLY as May, 1966, at the Dallas meeting of the International Reading Association, a reading clinic director announced: "The reason 'why' a kid can't read isn't important. . . . We don't worry about who or what is to blame. We just grab a kid and teach him to read."

From time to time we hear similar points of view expressed by persons from varying academic backgrounds. Most educators, however, believe that we can make more rapid and valid diagnoses, and therefore plan better corrective or remedial reading programs, if we have a clear understanding of the causes of reading disabilities. They believe that classroom teachers need to be knowledgeable about such causes and that, certainly, reading specialists need to investigate these causes in some depth in order to help pupils with severe reading problems.

Because learning to read does not depend upon a single ability, we should direct our attention to a constellation of causal factors. Such a constellation was described by this writer at the 1953 reading conference at the University of Chicago.[1] Although the emphasis of concern has shifted somewhat in the present decade, the major areas remain the same. These areas can be discussed in two broad categories: (1) intrinsic factors — those which lie in the child (his intellectual capacity, his personality, his physical constitution) and (2) extrinsic factors — those which stem from the particular conditions of learning in his home, school, and community.

INTRINSIC FACTORS

Intelligence. The fact that intelligence is related to learning ability is so well known that it scarcely requires comment. And just as obviously, mental maturity bears a marked relationship to reading achievement. As a result, the level of intelligence is often used for determining, at least in part, the level of reading achievement to be expected of a child. When reading is defined as thinking, or the ability to deal with abstractions, it is clear that the more intelligent person has a greater capability for the abstract reasoning involved in mature reading. The child with low intelligence brings

[1] Mary C. Austin, "Identifying Readers Who Need Corrective Instruction," in *Corrective Reading in Classroom and Clinic*, edited by Helen M. Robinson ("Supplementary Educational Monographs," No. 79; Chicago: University of Chicago Press, 1953), pp. 19–25.

a low level of concrete thinking to the reading act. He will, therefore, be handicapped when a higher level of abstract reasoning is expected of him. Quantitative scores obtained from tests of mental maturity, however, are not magical predictors of success. They merely suggest levels of expectancy.

Fundamental in our study of problem readers is an assessment by an individual intelligence test. Donald Neville concluded from an examination of 148 fifth-grade children that group intelligence tests, which are highly verbal, tend to underestimate the intellectual potential of poor readers.[2] He suggested the administration of an individual test such as the *Peabody Picture Vocabulary Test* (American Guidance Service, 1959) for a more realistic appraisal.

During the past decade there has been a notable increase in recognition that children with identical scores on the same intelligence test can have quite different patterns of strength. They may also have dissimilar weaknesses. The *Wechsler Intelligence Scale for Children* (Psychological Corporation, 1949) and the revised *Stanford-Binet Intelligence Scale* (Houghton-Mifflin, 1960) serve well as comprehensive intelligence tests for evaluating the abilities and disabilities that children bring to school. The WISC, in particular, permits an appraisal of both verbal and performance abilities. In addition, results of subtests may be analyzed for clues to

impairments that may require further study. If, for example, a child has difficulty in solving perceptual-motor tasks, the psychologist may be asked to examine these abilities further through tests such as the *Marianne Frostig Developmental Test of Visual Perception* (Consulting Psychologists Press, Inc., 1964) or the *Bender-Gestalt* (Grune and Stratton, Inc., 1960).

Benjamin S. Bloom has recently set forth an interesting theory by questioning the constancy of the intelligence quotient.[3] He views intelligence as a developmental concept like height, with the greatest proportion of growth in the earliest years. On the basis of test-retest data and longitudinal studies, Bloom found that the growth of intelligence is marked by uneven acceleration: 20 per cent is developed at age one, 50 per cent at age four, 80 per cent at age eight, 92 per cent at age thirteen, and 100 per cent at age seventeen. Bloom also studied the influence of environment on intelligence. From the data, he identified the extreme environments and labeled them as either deprived or abundant for the development of intelligence. A conservative estimate of the effect of extreme environment, according to his theory, was about twenty points.

Undoubtedly, in the years ahead educators will continue to insist upon the administration of individual intelligence tests to problem readers. They will request both a quantitative and a qualitative analysis of the results of such tests. They will also continue to

2 Neville, "The Relationship between Reading Skills and Intelligence Test Scores," *Reading Teacher*, XVIII (January, 1965), 257–62.

3 Bloom, *Stability and Change in Human Characteristics* (New York: John Wiley & Sons, Inc., 1964).

recognize that intelligence alone does not predict reading achievement with certainty and that numerous other factors may be affecting the current level of reading achievement.

Physical factors. Several physical factors are involved in the process of reading: vision, hearing, speech, physical growth, dominance, and neurological development. All have been the subjects of studies in the period since 1950. Deficits in some of these areas have been more closely identified as contributing factors to reading disabilities than others. In general, the studies conclude that physical factors have been overemphasized as causes of reading failure. When defects of hearing and vision are discovered, for example, we cannot assume that they are the major determinants of the students' reading problems. Yet, it is necessary for classroom teachers and reading specialists to understand the common physical defects which might hinder normal progress in learning to read.

Since visual screening plays an important role in today's schools, visual difficulties should be detected as early as possible — *before* the child experiences learning failure. When failures have occurred and the child has been referred for help in reading, screening will make it possible to detect the child who needs professional visual analysis.

Impaired hearing may contribute to low reading achievement, since reading is affected by language development. The hard-of-hearing student is handicapped in the classroom when the teacher gives oral instructions or uses primarily a phonics approach in teaching reading. Good hearing in the high frequencies is more important when the child is learning to read than hearing in the low and middle frequencies. The amount of loss by decibel, the unit for measuring relative loudness of sound, can be determined by testing on an audiometer and charting the results on an audiogram.

Recent studies have attempted to establish clearer relationships between auditory abilities and reading achievement. Dorothy and Charles Christine obtained data showing that faulty auditory discrimination is a causative factor, at the primary-grade level, in reading retardation as well as in functional articulation problems.[4] Joseph M. Wepman found a close relationship between poor auditory discrimination and the functional articulation deficiencies of certain second-grade children.[5] Positive correlations were indicated among three factors: low reading achievement, functional articulatory defects, and poor auditory discrimination.

Before leaving the consideration of constitutional defects, we should mention four additional factors: (1) childhood diseases or operations which result in prolonged absences from school and the missing of important academic work; (2) chronic conditions that produce lowered vitality — rheumatic fever, asthma, heart trouble,

[4] Christine and Christine, "The Relationship of Auditory Discrimination to Articulatory Defects and Reading Retardation," *Elementary School Journal*, LXV (November, 1964), 97–100.

[5] Wepman, "Auditory Discrimination, Speech and Reading," *Elementary School Journal*, LX (March, 1960), 325–33.

tuberculosis, sinus-tonsil infections, malnutrition, insufficient sleep; (3) glandular disturbances involving endocrine, thyroid, or pituitary glands; and (4) biochemical peculiarities or imbalance.

Schools need to keep accurate, detailed health histories for use by teachers and reading specialists to guide them in interpreting each child's current needs. These histories may shed new light on pupil inattention, apathy, fatigue, short attention span, or other signs of difficulty in the physical realm.

Among the possible physical causes of problem readers, none has received more attention within the present decade than neurological difficulties. Educators, medical people, psychologists, parents — all are intrigued by the renewed emphasis in this area. Research efforts and professional opinions have followed several bents, most of which have been controversial. Some investigators adhere today to a single causation theory. In the latter group, Donald E. P. Smith and Patricia N. Carrigan have proposed a "synaptic transmission model." [6] They hypothesize that all difficulties can be attributed to the balance and level of acetylcholine and cholinesterase at the neurone junctions. Prevention and control by medication are suggested. Carl Delacato has advanced a theory of neurological organization — the integration of the whole individual unilaterally — as the key to language and reading development and language

and reading difficulties. [7] He believes that reading difficulties can be prevented and that such prevention is the responsibility of parents and teachers. One of the values of these exploratory hypotheses is that they spur others to look at old theories and data in new ways and stimulate new directions of thought and discovery.

Although the studies of neurological factors related to reading problems have not provided "final answers," they have produced some important discoveries. Modern surgical techniques, electro-encephalography and electrical stimulation, and new neurophysical techniques have given us insights into the complexities of the brain and the areas involving the language functions. Further investigations need to be made and reported in the literature.

Emotional factors. A third causal factor in learning to read is the child's personality. Research results show repeatedly that failure in reading may pose a continuing block to the normal personality development of boys and girls. Indeed, most problem readers exhibit signs of emotional maladjustment varying from mild to severe. By the time such children are referred to a reading specialist, it is usually too late to assess whether emotion has been a primary cause in their reading difficulties.

Teachers and reading personnel frequently observe the following symptoms of maladjustment: (1) *Low self-*

---

[6] Smith and Carrigan, *The Nature of Reading Disability* (New York: Harcourt, Brace & Co., 1959).

[7] Delacato, *The Treatment and Prevention of Reading Problems: The Neuro-Psychological Approach* (Springfield, Ill.: Charles C Thomas, 1959).

esteem or self-concept. Such a child feels stupid and probably has often been told that he is. He feels he cannot cope with academic work because it is too difficult. He frequently feels that his plight is hopeless. (2) *Excessive desire for the approval of others.* This great desire may permeate interpersonal relationships. Continual rejection by family and friends, accompanied by school failure, culminates too often in dropping out of school or delinquency.

Also observed among problem readers are behavior characteristics such as aggression, expressed in either open fighting, verbal attacks, or counterattacks of mischief-making or buffoonery; withdrawal tendencies, demonstrated by daydreaming and inattention; submissive adjustment, as evidenced by a defeatist attitude toward reading, school, and sometimes life in general; defensiveness, with attendant undue sensitivity; and nervous tension, as exhibited by such outward signs as nail-biting and facial tics. Psychological difficulties can present such a heavy emotional overlay that the reading specialist may need to recommend counseling or some form of psychotherapy before remedial assistance can be undertaken.

EXTRINSIC FACTORS

Environment. The professional literature devoted to the causes of reading difficulties underlines the subtle and pervasive quality of the influences parents can exert on the school performance of their children. Some of these influences result in immediate behavior responses on the part of the child, whereas others only gradually generate a force that the individual resists for a time before succumbing or developing a counteracting immunity. The literature also suggests that generalizations about the effect of environment on learning must be considered in terms of the individual. A detrimental environment for one child may challenge another to attain success in the learning process.

A number of factors in the home environment have been associated with problems in reading. Most important among these appear to be parent-child relationships, sibling relationships, values and attitudes, favorable arrangements for reading, bilingual backgrounds, interrupted school attendance, and extremely limited experiential backgrounds.

Parents often create reading problems for their children, sometimes inadvertently. When children are absent from school, the continuity of their learning experience is broken. An increasing number of pupils enjoy family-approved absences for vacations during the school year. In our highly mobile society frequent moves, sometimes from one geographical area to another, place added burdens on children who must attend several different schools during their early years. Home situations in which children have little or no supervision may also result in absences undetected by parents. Obviously, the attitudes and values of parents have direct effects on their children's behavior.

Parental aspirations for their children should be taken into consideration in working with problem readers.

The Harvard-Newton study, which analyzed data separately for 142 third-grade boys and girls, reported that, in general, parents have higher aspirations for boys than for girls.[8] For boys the results were significant at the 5 per cent level, whereas for girls there was no significant trend. Evidently, high pressure for achievement on the part of parents has a greater tendency to result in the child's being in the high-achievement group, *if he is a boy*. Yet, the evidence also suggested that *very high pressure* does not necessarily make a boy an overachiever. (It should be noted that this study was based on the subjective impressions of teachers of parental pressures; still, the teachers can be presumed to have had many opportunities to gather data for these impressions.)

These findings are in accord with previous research by Geraldine Rickard involving fourth-, fifth-, and sixth-grade boys.[9] After determining the amount of parental demands by means of an interview, she concluded that as achievement demands increased school achievement increased, up to a certain optimum point, but that beyond that optimum point increasing demands were associated with decreasing school achievement.

[8] John B. Carroll and Mary C. Austin, "Underachievement in Reading: A Study of Its Extent and Causes in the Public Schools of Newton, Massachusetts" (Cambridge: Laboratory for Research in Instruction, Graduate School of Education, Harvard University, August, 1957).

[9] Rickard, "The Relationship between Parental Behavior and Children's Achievement Behavior" (unpublished Ed.D. thesis, Graduate School of Education, Harvard University, 1954).

An interesting finding of the Harvard-Newton study concerned the effects of "neatness" of parents and children on achievement. In designing the questionnaire which was to be completed by the parents, the study staff included questions that would reveal any compulsive tendencies of either parents or children on the theory that such compulsive traits, at least on the part of children, might lead to overachievement. The questions were based on the assumption that excessive neatness and "tidiness" — "having a place for everything" — were evidence of compulsive tendencies.

The results were rather surprising and somewhat at variance with the hypothesis. There was a significant trend for *untidiness* to be associated with high achievement in boys, with an opposite but not significant trend for girls.

The "neatness" of the parents showed the most striking correlations. They may be summarized as follows: "Neat" mothers tend to have high-achieving boys but low-achieving girls. "Neat" fathers tend to have low-achieving boys but high-achieving girls. Thus, a child who was in the high group was most likely to have a "neat" parent of the opposite sex and an "un-neat" parent of the same sex. Conversely, a child who was in the low group was most likely to have an "un-neat" parent of the opposite sex and a "neat" parent of the same sex. All of these trends were statistically significant, sometimes below the 1 per cent level (N=152).

Another kind of atmosphere is provided by a different family situation. An interdisciplinary study of family life patterns was initiated in 1962 at the University of Michigan's Children's Psychiatric Hospital. Children chosen for this project were those who had received extensive remedial reading instruction with no tangible results. They had resisted learning to read despite adequate intelligence. Researchers scrutinized the family backgrounds of the subjects, sharing many hours with the family. They also used television cameras to record activities in unguarded moments. A definite family life pattern emerged in which a dominant mother, a passive father, and a manipulative passive-aggressive child were involved. Curiously, if a child's reading began to improve, attention focused upon another member of the family who had become "ill." Transference of mental ill health from one family member to another appeared to keep the structure of this type of family intact and in balance. Within this decade, we are observing with greater frequency the treatment of whole family units by counseling services when one or more members become emotionally disturbed.

The physical facts of housing cannot be overlooked in any discussion of home environment. We are aware of and deplore inner-city ghettos of the metropolis. But even urban renewal enterprises often bring children only a barren day-by-day existence. In one St. Louis project serving hundreds, almost all mothers are working mothers, fathers are either nonexistent or come and go periodically, and the only males with whom boys can identify are sixty-five years of age or older. On too many occasions, children must find their own solutions to the central problems of their lives, often to their personal detriment. The circumstances found in St. Louis are reflected elsewhere. And it is also important to realize that exclusive suburbia represents another kind of ghetto, often with as much isolation and deprivation as in the crowded inner-city slums. The child of wealthy parents, for example, can rattle around in a large house deprived of important companionship. In a not too atypical instance, a seven-year-old boy turned to a warm-hearted, loving maid when his alcoholic mother could not minister to him and found a father image to emulate in an older brother since his executive father was absent from the home for long intervals of time.

Education. Periodically, the schools have been blamed for the failure of a large proportion of the population to achieve success in reading. Laymen have been especially outspoken. Many educators, after thoughtful evaluation of research findings, have concluded that educational factors do play a large part in producing retarded readers. These educational influences appear to be twofold: those that result from inefficient handling of the curriculum, teaching techniques, or materials, and those that result from certain school policies.

The success of a good reading program depends very much upon the competence, know-how, and personality of the teacher. Teachers with widely varying techniques can often teach equally effectively. The most knowledgeable and dedicated teacher, however, is seriously impeded by too large classes, intractable children, heavy curriculum demands, and/or insufficient time for planning. On the other hand, even in the most favorable conditions, poor teaching can and does occur.

Investigations indicate that certain reading difficulties, particularly the milder and more easily corrected ones, are the result of classroom inefficiencies, It is these less seriously retarded readers who are the direct responsibility of the classroom reading teacher. Effective teaching of reading should provide for one or more of the following:

(1) The readiness of the whole child: mental, physical, emotional, experimental, and verbal.

(2) Continuous diagnostic and corrective teaching: guiding each child so that he may achieve according to his various abilities.

(3) Recognition of individual differences: each child progressing at his own rate and according to his needs and abilities.

(4) Systematic and sequential development of basic reading skills, with a proper balance between word skills and comprehension skills.

(5) Use of an adequate variety of reading materials at each level and for each subject area, with a range from simple to challenging to meet all abilities.

(6) Use of a flexible curriculum that may be adapted to the needs and abilities of all children.

(7) Use of materials that are interesting to children and related to their interests.

(8) A stimulating, motivational learning environment, with favorable teacher-pupil, pupil-pupil dynamics.

The co-operation of the school administration is also needed to prevent reading difficulties. School policymakers often contribute to the failure of reading programs by overlooking one or more of the following areas:

(1) Suitable entrance criteria for primary children.

(2) Favorable class size.

(3) Beneficial promotional policies.

(4) Provision of sufficiently varied and pertinent reading materials in the classrooms.

(5) Provision of guidance and assistance in diagnostic testing and corrective and remedial procedures.

(6) Elimination from the classroom of interfering influences such as unreachable, highly disturbed or uncontrollable children.

(7) Professional assistance to teachers that would keep them informed of new research in teaching techniques, testing, and child development.

(8) Provision of clinical services for the physical, psychological, and social needs of children.

The selection and use of materials can be a cause for dismay. In the 1950's, we decried the paucity of materials. Now, with funds available from government sources, we have a greater dilemma — how to make wise selections that will match the needs of the school population being served.

Community. The impact of the community upon children and their ability to read cannot be overestimated, whether that community is rural, urban, or suburban. The community library is a major force for supplementing the school reading program and the opportunities for reading at home. Many children need to be encouraged to use the library. Children with reading problems seldom borrow books, in fact, seldom possess library cards. Parents should have library cards and express pleasure in borrowing books for reading, thus setting an example for their children. When libraries are not within easy walking distance of homes, bookmobiles sometimes bring the library to the community.

Gertrude Whipple has referred to children from low socioeconomic areas as the "children without."[10] For no other group do the intrinsic and extrinsic factors within the causal constellation impinge more upon each other than for the children without. This same interrelationship of factors makes the solution of this group's reading problems a special challenge. Allison Davis, of the University of Chicago, has found that the reading difficulties of both white and Negro children in low socioeconomic areas are related to the following: (1) lack of confidence in their ability and future, based on a deeply ingrained self-contempt that is concealed behind a façade of pseudo-stupidity and resentment; (2) a first learned culture, with its accompanying private dialect; (3) a damaging school curriculum, with its attendant

confusing teacher language; (4) the punitive effect of certain teacher attitudes and relationships; and (5) physical disabilities or lack of medical attention.[11]

Many people claim that these obstacles to learning are insurmountable mountains that educators will never conquer. Others believe that materials more directly related to the needs and interests of the children without and more favorable teacher-pupil attitudes will eventually succeed in this part of the war on poverty.

CONCLUDING STATEMENT

Potential reading difficulties must be discovered as early as possible in the child's school years. The preschool activities of kindergarten children deserve far more attention than is currently being given them. The primary grades should be years during which concerted effort is made to prevent difficulties from developing and careful consideration is given to each pupil's possibilities. Many lives would have been immeasurably altered if informed, alert teachers had recognized clues indicating lack of readiness, immaturity, or physical deficiencies at the beginning of the child's school experiences and then been able to do something about them. Frustrations, damaged self-concepts, and undesirable attitudes toward all learning can be prevented or minimized during these critical years. But if clues are ignored and problems allowed to in-

10 Whipple, "The Special Needs of Children Without," in *Reading for Children Without — Our Disadvantaged Youth*, edited by Gertrude Whipple and Millard H. Black (Reading Aids Series; Newark, Del.: International Reading Association), p. 1.

11 Allison Davis, "Teaching Language and Reading to Disadvantaged Negro Children" (unpublished speech).

crease, the pattern of disability will gain a foothold.

During the past decade, the interdisciplinary study of problem readers has greatly increased. National and local meetings have emphasized the contributions of several fields to a better understanding of the reading process in general and of reading difficulties in particular. In many areas, medical personnel, psychiatrists, psychologists, social workers, and specialists in vision, hearing, and speech have formed close working relationships with school people to make differential diagnoses of seriously handicapped readers.

Fortunately, children have an almost miraculous ability to cope with difficulties without sustaining irreparable damage. Their resilience is often amazing. Sometimes a short period of special help in reading with the full attention of an interested person who uses a variety of materials and approaches to meet instructional needs will be enough. However, sound, effective remedial instruction is not magic. It requires a thorough knowledge and understanding of causal factors, the best possible planning, and the best execution of the plan in accordance with the child's particular capabilities.

CHAPTER XIV

HELPING THE RETARDED READER

*

IN KINDERGARTEN THROUGH GRADE THREE

SOPHIE BLOOM

*

REMEDIAL READING has moved into the regular classroom. In schools with a high proportion of children from disadvantaged backgrounds, the number who are significantly retarded is so great that the usual method of teaching retarded readers individually, or in small groups outside the classroom, is no longer feasible. It is the classroom teacher who must face and handle the problem. We can help the retarded reader in the classroom if we utilize a teaching strategy based on the needs of both the learner and the teacher.

It is true that the home and certain child-rearing practices may not have prepared the child for school adequately. However, placing the blame is not the task of the school; the task of the school is to teach the child. But we can't dismiss the role of the home. We realize more than ever before that the co-operation of the home is imperative for school success, and we must secure as much of this co-operation as possible.

We have all heard the refrain, "If we only had good teachers!" For years we have had dedicated teachers, able teachers, teachers who have wanted nothing more than to have their students learn. Yet many of these dedicated and able teachers who work hard to help the retarded reader, and especially the culturally disadvantaged child, usually end the year in frustration and despair. The children also share in this feeling of frustration and disappointment. The solution lies not in the *teacher* but in the *teaching*.

In this paper, I am going to describe a teaching strategy to aid the retarded reader in the classroom that is being used by one hundred fifty teachers in fourteen schools in Gary, Indiana — the Program in Compensatory Education. The emphasis in this program is on language arts. The teachers are provided with a systematic approach to the detailed problems of language learning and are given systematic training in the implementation of each part.

It has been possible to support this program with a very effective organization within the Gary school system. A co-ordinator was appointed for the entire program, and in each school, a liaison person trained as a reading specialist has given one-third of his

162

time to work with approximately ten teachers in the school.

The training for the teachers consists of large in-service meetings, small grade-level meetings, and meetings of the teachers within each school. The large in-service meetings serve to introduce each area of the program. Major consultants are brought in to give the teachers background and understanding in each of the areas, including the findings of some recent research. They deal with broad aspects of the reading process as well as with specific subskills and their relation to each other. These meetings are followed by small grade-level and individual school meetings, in which teachers meet informally to share materials and techniques and to view demonstration lessons.

The systematic approach used in conjunction with teacher training can be described as following a three-step cycle: *step one*, diagnosis of the needs of children in the subskills of the reading process; *step two*, selection and use of materials and techniques for the teaching of the needed subskills; and *step three*, evaluation of progress by students and teachers to determine whether the skills have been mastered or whether a different approach is needed to lead to mastery. By following the three steps of the cycle for each of the subskills, we expect all the children to succeed, though they may take different lengths of time to master each subskill.

FIRST STEP OF THE CYCLE

The first step of the cycle, the diagnosis, is an attempt to pinpoint the strengths and weaknesses of the children. The diagnosis consists of inventories, some oral and some written, based on sequential development of specific skills. The diagnosis does three things. It breaks down the learning of a skill into such small steps that, with a small amount of effort, each child is sure to learn and feel successful. Second, it assumes that everyone can learn and that the only significant variation will be in terms of *effort* or *time*. In this way, it removes the stigma of judgment of right or wrong — bright or dull. Third, a graphic method of recording results gives visible evidence of achievement and helps the children evaluate their own needs. The inventories operate as a strong incentive to children for learning and give them renewed belief in their own ability to learn.

The inventory itself becomes part of the training. The teacher, aided by the liaison person, obtains two kinds of knowledge from the inventories: knowledge of the children, their strengths and weaknesses, individually and as a class; and knowledge of the reading process. The listing of the subskills gives them a renewed awareness of the subskills and of their sequential development. The liaison person at each school assists the teacher in administering, in scoring, and in charting the diagnostic inventories and is especially helpful in interpreting them.

SECOND STEP OF THE CYCLE

Once the diagnosis is made, the teachers are ready to help individuals and groups of children. The second step is the selection and use of materials and techniques for the teaching of the needed subskills.

The teachers are first given in-service training to orient them to the kinds of materials and techniques that will be most effective. This training includes a scheme for using basic principles of learning.[1] A variety of materials is used, since the program is predicated on the assumption that children learn in many different ways and need repetition with variations. Materials with *cues or powerful stimuli built in,* which will capture the attention of the children, are selected; for example, filmstrips and materials utilizing the opaque projector, overhead projector, and listening centers. Multisensory materials are also used, and care is exercised to see that materials are meaningful in terms of the background of the children.

We know that children do not learn unless each child has *actively participated,* and so we make an effort to stress material that uses every-pupil-response methods and team learning. Many games are played. (The use of games reduces tension, the threat of not learning, and the fear of failure. A child cannot fail at a game — he *can* fail at work.) Special care is taken to see that the learning is *reinforced with rewards* that are meaningful to the children, such as candy and other prizes. In addition, self-correcting materials with built-in reinforcements are used.

[1] See Sophie Bloom, "Israeli Reading Methods for Their Culturally Disadvantaged," *Elementary School Journal,* LXVI (March, 1966), 300–310.

The liaison persons are very resourceful in locating materials; and when materials are not available, the teachers order new materials or use those they have prepared themselves. Again, as in the case of step one, the teachers receive training in the use of materials and techniques at in-service meetings. And at the grade-level and individual school meetings, they discuss and share successful procedures for teaching specific subskills.

The method by which materials are selected and used for word-attack skills will illustrate the second step in the cycle. In the teaching of the sound-to-symbol relationships, for example, the sequence demonstrated by the speech therapist is as follows:

1. Introducing the sound.
2. Listening for the sound.
3. Discriminating between the new sound and other sounds.
4. Producing the correct sound in words.
5. Incorporating the sound into other classroom activities.

The sound is introduced through association with the name of an animal or a familiar object or with both. For example, *F* can be an angry cat sound. A personal reference for each child is a very helpful device; some of the types we use are a notebook-sized phonovisual chart for each child, clue cards illustrating the short vowel sounds, dictionaries made by the children and reference booklets. By having their own references, the children are helped to become more independent learners, even discovering new words for themselves. Many pictures and concrete objects containing the sound are used for practice during the teaching of this word-attack skill.

To help children listen for the sound, they are given practice in context and in isolation. Producing the sound in isolation is important because these children are not able to abstract the sound from a known word until they have heard it first in isolation. They have difficulty in knowing when a sound begins and ends in a word. A variety of games and work sheets can be used, both teacher-made and commercial.

The teachers continue until each child can distinguish the sound when he says it himself, when he listens to himself say it correctly, and when he hears it in context. Only one sound is taught at a time. In each case, the child has to understand what he is trying to do. He has to try it himself. He has to succeed and have objective evidence of his success.

THIRD STEP OF THE CYCLE

After diagnosing the need and getting and using material for the teaching of each skill, whether it be the rudimentary one of recognizing sounds or the advanced one of problem-solving, the teacher must evaluate the progress that is being made. In step three, every effort is made to make clear to the learner the improvement he has achieved. The evaluation differs from the usual in that no grades are given. Evaluation is used only to certify when the child has achieved mastery.

Evaluation also gives the teacher objective evidence of the progress of the child and corrects any misconception he may have that the amount of energy expended in the teaching is equal to the amount of learning taking place. For the evaluation of each subskill, the teacher is provided with a single-sheet test that is easy to administer and easy to score. For example, in the word-attack area, the teachers have single-sheet tests for beginning sounds, ending sounds, short vowels, long vowels, other vowels, syllabication, and each of the word-attack skills. More than one test is available for each subskill since some children may need to take two or more tests before they achieve mastery of the subskill. As the child masters each subskill, a color-coded chart changes from red — the unlearned skill — to blue — the mastered skill.

The teachers need very little training at this stage of the cycle, as the giving of the test is quite simple. Again, the liaison person is there to help in the interpretation of the tests.

CONCLUDING REMARKS

With *all* children it is important to have the co-operation and the support of the parent for the school program. With retarded readers and children of disadvantaged backgrounds, it is even more important to have the parents involved in raising the aspiration levels of their children and in supporting the school program. Our liaison people have planned many excellent parent programs.

In summary, it is clear that we no longer need to tolerate either failure to learn or failure to teach. Research and our experience have shown that retarded readers *can* learn and classroom teachers *can* teach them. A systematic teaching strategy can insure successful achievement and a resulting positive attitude toward reading and learning.

* * *

IN GRADES FOUR THROUGH EIGHT

SISTER MARY EDWIN, S.C.C.

*

GROUPING RETARDED readers can be done on a school-wide basis. The teachers with the help of the principal and the reading consultant can organize the grouping in the following manner. Let us suppose for this example that a school has four fifth-grade classrooms, all of which have students with reading levels ranging from 2^2 through 5 and above. The following combinations could be employed. Room 1, Levels 5 and 4; Room 2, Levels 5 and 3^2; Room 3, Levels 5 and 3^1; Room 4, Levels 5 and 2^2. Each teacher, then, would have a group of good readers and another group of retarded readers. The advantages of such grouping are that the teacher can select materials better suited to the needs and interests of each group. If grouping is not done on a school-wide basis, however, the teacher will have to select materials on the basis of the needs of the majority of retarded readers.

MATERIALS

After deciding who the retarded readers are and on what levels they are reading, the next step is to choose materials. For example, if fifteen students are below grade level and ten of these are on the advanced third level, an advanced third text from a publishing company other than that of the basic series could be assigned. Other materials also are available, such as the *New Practice Readers* (Webster, 1960) and the *Reader's Digest* (Reader's Digest Services, 1960). These materials, however, do not have as well-constructed teacher's manuals as do the basic texts, which outline the skills to be developed and supply additional material for practice.

LESSON PLANNING

When the students have been grouped and appropriate materials selected, the teacher must decide on his plan for working with the two groups. It is important that both groups of readers be allowed adequate amounts of time.

In preparing for a reading lesson with the two groups, the teacher reviews the steps in the lesson plan: preparation, silent guided reading, discussion, oral reading, workbook activities, and development of skills. These steps fall quite naturally into alternating teacher-directed and independent periods. Thus, preparation, discussion, development of skills, and correction of workbooks are teacher-directed tasks, whereas silent guided reading, workbook activities, and skills practice are independent pupil work. The teacher can therefore be working with one group, while the second group is involved in an independent step in the reading lesson. The lesson plan may be similar to the following:

Group One	Group Two
T* Preparation	I Workbook activity
I Silent guided reading	T Development of skills
T Discussion	I Skills practice — preparation for oral reading
I Workbook activity	T Correction of workbook activities and oral reading
T Development of skills	I Enrichment activities
I Skills practice — preparation for oral reading	T Preparation
T Correction of workbook exercises and oral reading	I Silent guided reading
I Enrichment activities	T Discussion

*T = teacher-directed periods; I = independent work.

In most teacher's manuals, these steps are developed in great detail. In grades four to six, each step may take approximately twenty minutes, whereas in grades seven and eight, a half-hour seems to be the amount of time needed for some of the steps. Thus, in the plan given above, a lesson will take approximately three or four days depending on the number of skills to be developed.

DEVELOPMENT OF SKILLS

Although the teacher may know who the retarded readers are, the levels of reading they have attained, the materials to use, and the ways to plan a well-balanced program for them, he may still not succeed unless he determines each individual's strengths and weaknesses. Early in the school year and periodically thereafter, an inventory of word-recognition and compre- hension skills should be taken. Simply testing each student on a list of twenty isolated words from the back of the text will indicate those who need special help in word recognition. Usually, retarded readers will not have mastered the skills of pronouncing unknown words independently. They perceive just the first or last parts of words and guess the rest — often incorrectly. Some of the children will not know the sounds of short vowels or vowel and consonant combinations or how to distinguish word parts — prefixes and suffixes. After taking a word-recognition inventory, the teacher will find that the children are at different levels of development and that he must group them according to their difficulties. During the period of skills development, he will then be working with several small groups on different skills.

To determine weaknesses in comprehension skills, the teacher may use workbook exercises as a diagnostic tool. Can the student follow printed directions, locate an answer, get the main idea, follow a sequence of events, recall details, grasp the author's plan, think critically, and remember what has been read? Specific exercises in the workbook can be used to improve comprehension in each of these areas.

A special technique that can be useful in developing several comprehension skills is a reading guide. A series of factual questions on a selection, for example, may be written on the board or mimeographed on a sheet of paper. The student locates the exact answer and indicates the page, paragraph, and the key word. ("Key words" here should be understood as the first and last words of the sentence or sentences needed for the answer.) A warning may be in order. Students must be guided by the teacher in this kind of exercise *orally* before he can expect them to work independently.

Another helpful technique to aid in the improvement of literal comprehension skills is to direct retarded readers to compare questions using *who, what, when, where, why,* and *how* for certain paragraphs and then to write out the complete answers. This should not be done regularly or the reading lesson becomes a writing task. However — and the point cannot be stressed enough — some form of involvement in writing seems to be important for these retarded readers. Sight and hearing are not enough to reinforce learning. The muscular involvement, which is part of the multisensory approach, will help these chil-

dren retain to a greater degree what they have learned.

Retarded readers must not only be helped to understand the literal meaning of material, however; they must also be helped to evaluate what they have read. This "includes such specific ways of comprehending as differentiating between fancy, fact and opinion; judging the reasonableness and relevancy of ideas presented; sensing implied meanings; establishing cause-and-effect relationships; making comparisons; judging authenticity of materials read; and critically appraising the validity of the author's presentation."[1] Some suggestions for ways to develop these abilities are the following: (1) Have students decide from the title of a story whether it is likely to be real or fanciful. (2) Have them discuss whether a story could have happened and give their reasons for their opinions. (3) Ask such questions as, Why did the character do what he did? How did the character feel? and What would I have done in a similar situation?

TEACHER'S ATTITUDE

No matter how important it is for the teacher to know who needs help, at what levels his students are reading, and how to teach a well-balanced program, the most important factor of all is the teacher's attitude toward the retarded reader. There are still too many teachers who believe that retarded readers are either low in intelligence or lazy. Truly, if the teacher considers

[1] Guy L. Bond and Miles A. Tinker, *Reading Difficulties: Their Diagnosis and Correction* (New York: Appleton-Century-Crofts, Inc., 1957), p. 333.

these individuals dull and incapable of doing better, they will not disappoint him. If he labels this group "his slow group," its members will be convinced they are slow. On the other hand, if he builds up their self-confidence, they will improve. Children want to succeed, and the sooner a teacher gives them a taste of success, the quicker they will improve. Fortunate, indeed, are the children who find a teacher who understands, encourages, and spurs them on to farther horizons.

The question is sometimes asked, Is it psychologically harmful to a child to know on what level he is reading? Definitely no, if the teacher uses this information to understand the child, to help him to experience progress, and to encourage him in each step of improvement. The child knew he was having difficulty before we recognized it. Therefore, let us be honest with him, discuss his problem with him, help him to accept himself as he is, and take every opportunity to help him feel successful.

CONCLUDING REMARKS

In dealing with retarded readers, the teacher should keep the following points in mind: (1) Flexibility must be maintained in grouping; that is, constant evaluation must be made in terms of pupil improvement. When it is quite evident that the child is ready for the next higher level, adjustments should be made. (2) It is important that next year's teacher continue from the point this year's teacher terminated; and therefore, the present teacher should draw up a list of his students' names, the levels on which they are working, and comments about their strengths and weaknesses to pass on to the next teacher. This knowledge is very helpful for new teachers as well as experienced teachers because it gives them a tentative hypothesis from which to work and eliminates much wasted time at the beginning of the year.

Retarded readers must be provided with material that is challenging and yet easy enough for them to experience success. Formal and informal testing should be used to determine the levels of the retarded readers. Once these levels are known, a choice of materials can be made that will fit the needs of the majority of retarded readers. Lesson plans should be arranged in such a way that good readers as well as poor readers get adequate amounts of direction from the teacher. Realization that there are individual differences within both groups will require occasional small-group work, particularly in the areas of word recognition and comprehension. The most important point of all, however, in dealing with retarded readers is for the teacher to have a constructive, honest attitude toward his students. If he is optimistic and confident that they can improve, they assuredly will.

IN GRADES NINE THROUGH FOURTEEN

LYNETTE SAINE GAINES

*

FREQUENTLY, high-school and jun- ior-college students of considerable potential who have been successful in smaller, less demanding schools encounter reading difficulties when they enter more rigorous situations. Others, also of considerable potential, from comprehensive, challenging sec- ondary schools have managed to hold at least average status, in spite of read- ing disabilities, and face each year hoping to maintain their average pace and graduate "on schedule." When these students are referred to reading classes, clinics, or laboratories at high- school or college levels, they bring atti- tudes ranging from appreciation for the privilege of receiving such help from an all-pervasive disdain for any part of such a "degrading experience." Years of experience with the total range of these more promising readers have led this writer to make certain generalizations that characterize a large proportion of them. (1) The ma- jority of these readers respond favor- ably to initial units of work that capi- talize on challenging discussions of such subjects as the nature of the read- ing process or a scheme for thinking and its relationship to higher and lower reading skills. (2) They respond to personalized procedures based on their expressed interests and poten- tials. (3) They require frequent demon- strations of the value of their read- ing experiences in the content areas. (4) Frequently, following systematic help in reading, they make less spec- tacular gains on the more demanding sections of reading tests than on those requiring less thought and purpose- fulness.

The writer will illustrate the first generalization from her experiences with students. Six bright, but consid- erably retarded tenth-grade students returned from a reading session and engaged the whole class in a clear dis- cussion of fundamental reading habits. For them the work in reading had be- come highly self-initiated since they now understood clearly the nature and impact of the reading process. An- other group, from junior college, be- came intrigued with a scheme for thinking, collated by David H. Russell and used in his book, *Children's Thinking*.[1] In that book, the focus is upon materials, processes, and prod- ucts of thinking. Once the students had grasped Russell's idea, it was gratifying to listen to such comments as the fol- lowing: "A lack of concepts is blocking my main ideas." "In this passage, as- sociative thinking could have aided my interpretation." "The conclusion which you have drawn suffers from a faulty process of inductive reasoning."

[1] New York: Ginn & Co., 1956.

This kind of intellectual exercise can go far toward satisfying the requirement that reading be a thinking process, and it can also often elevate a flagging self-concept that may have been induced by the first shock or revelation of reading disabilities.

In connection with personalized procedures (the second generalization) and frequent demonstrations of the values of reading instruction (the third generalization), it may be noted that many teachers of reading at secondary and college levels have lately begun to realize the values of general and diagnostic conferences as an integral part of individualized, student-centered instruction. An effective conference is characterized by (1) a teacher who always has a record of the points to be stressed in such conferences and (2) a student who has learned to engage in wholesome self-analysis of the types of errors he makes in exercises, of his weaknesses in answering certain types of questions, and of the effects of his reading strengths or weaknesses in other areas.

The higher the level of the high-school or junior-college retarded reader, the more difficult it becomes to demonstrate significant and consistent gains in the general spectrum of reading skills (the fourth generalization). Once the reader has made the proper self-appraisal and set certain goals for himself, however, he will not be as concerned about scores or grade equivalents; rather, the value of the instruction for him will be demonstrated in the very attitudes, applications, and aspirations that he brings to the printed page.

HELPING RETARDED READERS OF AVERAGE ABILITIES

With respect to the students with average abilities and obvious retardation in reading and general language levels, three fairly characteristic generalizations may be formulated. (1) These students usually respond favorably to a general developmental program, interspersed with appropriate corrective and re-educative lessons. (2) A large measure of security may be created for these students by specific outlines of the skills to be developed. (3) During the first months of work, mean gains of the group are often spectacular. After that period of rapid growth, the group usually assumes many of the characteristics of the superior group described in the preceding section. Opportunities for this group to receive developmental and corrective training in reading often require considerable administrative arrangements as well as co-operation among teachers. In some high schools a block of time is set aside at least three times weekly for systematic training in reading. In the writer's university, teachers of college Freshmen in the Reading Center have developed a compendium that outlines basic units of work that are necessary to maturity in reading. The presentation and pacing of the units vary with the needs of the students and usually take the form of regular classes for the teaching of skills needed by the whole class and clinic and laboratory periods for individual instruction.

Many students in this average-ability group gain direction and initiative from using the chart of sequential skills developed by Ruth Strang, Constance M. McCullough, and Arthur E. Traxler.[2] This chart organizes the tasks of reading into eleven areas that cover reading development from the preschool years through college. At appropriate places, these authors indicate approximately when instruction should be first introduced in an area, when continued practice and instruction are needed, when an initial degree of mastery may be reached by the "normally progressing" reader, and when only informal incidental experiences will be needed to maintain a particular aspect of reading development. Later in the year — after work on general skills by the class as a whole, after concentration on individual needs, and after some work on transferring skills to content areas — teachers in the Reading Center have found it fruitful to compare the class's achievements with the progression suggested in the chart of sequential skills. The teachers do not abandon flexibility, and they often add items to those listed in the chart; but they have found that this kind of goal-centered approach seems to afford security for the retarded reader who is not severely retarded and who realizes that discipline and enthusiastic effort are all that are necessary for him to succeed.

In spite of specific gains in reading skill, it is not easy to demonstrate to high-school and college students in this group the values of this type of instruction for the content areas since most of the texts in the content areas are

2 Strang, McCullough, and Traxler, *The Improvement of Reading* (3d ed.; New York: McGraw-Hill Book Co., 1961), pp. 101–11.

written at levels far beyond their abilities. The continuous use of such textbooks can only create a frustrating situation. The problem needs much more study. Varied administrative arrangements should be considered. Wider use of multilevel materials would be desirable. A longer school year for students with reading disabilities might be advantageous.

HELPING RETARDED READERS WITH LOW POTENTIAL

Severely retarded readers with below-average intelligence and faulty language usage can present a discouraging picture. Usually, they are the high-school students who are only waiting for the date of legally sanctioned withdrawal from school or the college students who will withdraw before the end of the first year. Sometimes, they manage to survive in high school or college, but at the expense of all that the years were designed to provide in personal fulfilment and liberating influences of a higher academic nature.

Without the support of sufficient research, this writer will only venture to suggest a procedure for training most of these students: an additional year of concentration on skills of communication, utilizing, in most instances, areas and materials in which these students have a chance to succeed. This kind of plan would not relegate the student to any stereotyped level but would give teachers and students a chance to operate under less tension. Many of the points mentioned in other sections of the paper may be applied at this level — encouragement of appraisal by students of their own reading status, personalized procedures, group work on skills of common concern, and some type of goals-centered approach. These points are made, however, in the realization that readers at this level will need much more frequent concrete examples of concepts. These students, who will probably never reach the higher levels of reading skills, can nevertheless be helped to wider reading experiences, for example, comprehension of popular communications media.

With one class of retarded readers with limited potential, this writer planned work that would combine the ideas of paragraph patterns and basic types of writing — narrative, expository, and lyric. Every so often a given idea was presented in several types of materials: materials prepared for a listening station; sketches used in the overhead projector; discussion of the idea as represented in an article of simple phrasing. The groups that had used each material then reassembled, and each had a contribution to make.

Finally, it must be stressed that this group must not be confused with those of average or above-average potential who merely need intensified help in clinical settings to remove their disabilities. These are students, often the most willing of all, who need to learn to do well what they can do well and to be released from the pressures that leave them discouraged and often rebellious.

CONCLUDING REMARKS

For all levels of retarded readers, there seems to be a need for a kind of reordering of the environment. Some retarded readers of high, average, or low potential need to learn to "read" their environment in general before they are ready to learn to read written symbols. For example, they need to learn the right set of adjectives to describe an interesting facial expression on a human being or a painting; they need to be able to see a situation in its entirety before looking for the details; the need to be able to listen in such a way that they know what the speaker said, what he meant, and what he really thought about a particular subject. Each of these non-reading situations illustrates a skill basic to reading: oral language, generalization and summary, and analysis.

IN CORRECTIVE AND REMEDIAL CLASSES

CARITA A. CHAPMAN

*

THE READING teacher, Miss Brown, sat at her desk in the Reading Clinic late one afternoon near the end of the school year, reviewing the annual progress reports of the retarded readers she had helped to achieve reading skills more commensurate with their capacities to learn. Each name brought a recollection of the student's first entry into the clinic. There was Harold, the fifth-grade eleven-year-old non-reader whose mother anxiously inquired, "Miss Brown, do you think he'll ever learn to read?" Robert, the perennial troublemaker and braggart in his home room but the quiet, unassuming diligent worker at the clinic; Shirley, whose frequent day dreaming had inhibited her progress in reading; and Lorraine, the seventh-grade girl who had attended almost as many schools as she had attained grades in school and who, consequently, had not been able to profit from a continuity of learning. These and many other students made very good reading progress, as evidenced by both objective test evaluations and by subjective daily observations by the teacher, in spite of the fact that they had entered the clinic with many deficient reading skills, their own idiosyncrasies, and unsolved emotional problems engendered by poor reading. Miss Brown paused and took a retrospective glance and asked herself, "What were the key techniques employed in helping these retarded readers?"

DIAGNOSING THE RETARDED READER

These students had been referred for special instruction because there was at least a year's discrepancy between their achievement and capacity levels; however, this referral had frequently been based on the results of standardized group tests which often yielded spuriously high scores and were not current. Miss Brown attempted to use the simplest approaches to get the necessary information and to keep testing at a minimum. She administered to each individual the *New Gray Oral Reading Test* (Bobbs-Merrill Co., Inc., 1963) and/or the *Informal Reading Inventory* (Betts Basic Readers, American Book Co., 1964) to identify his instructional level — the highest level at which he could read with teacher supervision and without signs of difficulty (recognition of more than 95 per cent of running words and comprehension of 75 to 80 per cent of the selection). Miss Brown also wanted to determine the independent reading level of each child — the highest level at which he could read with full understanding and with freedom from mechanical difficulties (accurate pronunciation of 99 per cent of the words, with 90 per cent comprehension). These test results were used as a basis for initiating instruction; as the need arose for more diagnostic knowledge of specific difficulties, further formal and/or informal testing was given. To facilitate communication between the home, school, and the clinic, an appropriate form of standardized silent reading test was also administered.

It was not always feasible to administer the *Stanford-Binet Intelligence Scale* (Houghton Mifflin, 1960) or *Wechsler Intelligence Scale For Children* (Psychological Corporation, 1949), which would have yielded more suitable measures of mental ability than the usually administered group intelligence tests; however, all group test scores were accepted with reservations, for they probably underestimated the real ability of the poor reader because of their reading requirements. Sometimes as a quick index to measure potentiality, graded material was read aloud to the student to determine the level on which he could comprehend.

Miss Brown knew there was another dimension to diagnosis, namely, the child's own diagnosis of his reading progress in terms of his interests and attitudes. An interest inventory such as that suggested by Mary C. Austin et al.[1] was adapted to the particular situation. Involvement of the child in an informal discussion, not as a postmortem on his past failures, but as an incentive to gain insight into his pres-

[1] Mary C. Austin, Clifford L. Bush, and Mildred H. Huebner, *Reading Evaluation: Appraisal Techniques for School and Classroom* (New York: Ronald Press Co., 1961), p. 85.

ent reading strengths and weaknesses, was a technique used to promote student-teacher participation in setting long-range instructional goals. These goals could then be based on his present reading level and as much as possible on his current interests and attitudes. In order to provide immediate success and to build confidence in the use of the tools of reading, a series of short-term achievable goals, based on the student's strengths, were established by the teacher.

INSTRUCTING THE RETARDED READER

For students reading at the third-grade level or better who needed help in word attack, Miss Brown taught syllabication principles that would provide a starting point for attacking most words. Those reading below this level received instruction in specific single and blended sounds until they attained a fair degree of mastery, after which they were given syllabication exercises.

Word meanings were taught primarily in conjunction with comprehension exercises instead of through word-study drills. Thus, Miss Brown provided her pupils with opportunities to develop and to extend their vocabularies through the use of contextual and structural clues as well as through the use of the dictionary.

For the majority of the students in the clinic, Miss Brown spent most of the semester developing the receptive or lowest level of comprehension, namely, literal comprehension. She structured group instruction so that the separate reading skills of vocabulary (word attack and word meaning) and of comprehension were woven into a pattern in which each skill reinforced the others and meaning emerged from a successful application of all the skills.

To introduce a particular lesson to the entire group, a novel approach was used to interest the youngsters. For instance, Miss Brown introduced the class to the techniques of finding important details or remembering what they had read by showing a picture of a little-known fruit and questioning the children as to its identity. Finally, the real object, an avocado, was presented to be felt, smelled, and later tasted. Students were encouraged to formulate questions about the strange plant. WHAT was it? WHERE did it grow? WHEN does it grow? WHO grows and eats it? HOW do you eat it? WHY do people like to eat it? A short encyclopedic passage was given to them to read orally; afterward the class's questions were answered, and the class jointly formulated what the passage was mainly about. The six interrogative words were extracted from a particular context and, when put into the following jingle, became quite easy to recall: the person WHO, the place WHERE, the time WHEN, the reason WHY, the way HOW, the event WHAT.

As students read different selections, the appropriate questions were asked to aid the students in finding and remembering important details or facts. This procedure was used for reading conversational or literary selections as well as those from the subject-matter areas of social studies, science, and mathematics.

After the students had gained some skill in reading to answer factual questions, Miss Brown helped them to find the key words in a sentence. She did this by having the students compose a telegram from a sentence she gave them.[2] For example, the sentence "The Los Angeles Dodgers will play in Comiskey Ball Park at eight o'clock on Thursday evening" may be abbreviated as "Los Angeles Dodgers play Comiskey Park eight Thursday evening." A baseball fan would also delete the words "Los Angeles." Exercises similar to this were written out for the class or read to them by the teacher, becoming listening lessons as well. Other single sentences taken from readers, conversations, and content-area materials gave the students additional practice in discovering key words in sentences.

After proficiency was achieved in this area, students were ready to find the key sentence in a paragraph, progressing from the simple to the more complex. Miss Brown started them out with paragraphs in which the main ideas were located in the first or last sentences.

After practice in locating key sentences at the beginnings and ends of paragraphs, additional experiences were provided in which the key sentences were placed elsewhere. The children received much oral group practice and were then given individual opportunities to list the key sentence of selected paragraphs in a column and, from the key sentences, to select the one idea that *best* seemed to sum up the other ideas in the para-

2 Carol Hovious, *Flying the Printways* (Boston: D. C. Heath & Co., 1938), p. 163.

graphs — the main idea. This work was occasionally presented as a mystery game in which the children were detectives working for clues as to the main idea. Finding little commercial material for reading levels four through eight, Miss Brown compiled her own practice paragraphs with key sentences in a variety of positions. The students received much successful practice in working with these paragraphs before being presented with paragraphs in which there was no directly stated main idea.

Commercially designed tests, workbooks, and the like, present the reader with four or five possible alternative expressions of the main idea of a selection. Miss Brown found it extremely helpful to teach the children to weigh each alternative in terms of their own ideas and to decide whether it was TB (Too Broad — includes too much), TN (Too Narrow — doesn't include enough), ND (Not Discussed in the story), NA (Not Accurate according to the story), or obviously, C (Correct). A few practice exercises with this terminology and the students were on their way.

When the students had learned to find the important details and main ideas of a selection, the stage was set for developing two other important skills, namely, following a sequence of ideas and predicting outcomes. Since the paragraph had been stripped of all superfluousness, the main parts stood in relief, and it was easier to apply these new skills. Simple outlining was also a natural consequence of locating main ideas and details in longer passages. The students easily saw that Roman numeraled headings in outlines are the main ideas and capital-letter headings are important details. If time and student progress permitted, Miss Brown moved from the receptive (literal) level of comprehension to the more advanced levels, critical and creative reading.

READING FOR PLEASURE

Miss Brown developed reading skills in class by using mostly study-type materials. The work in class necessarily required a slower rate of reading than pleasure or recreational reading. Therefore, the youngsters were encouraged to read independently outside of class some of the easy, readable, and accessible books from the clinic library. The children were helped to select those books with subjects of universal appeal for children of their ages or those that would fit a particular child's unique personality and interest. The small clinic collection of books served only to whet the appetite for further reading. Specific instruction was given to the students to help them read these books at a slightly faster pace, since they were easier than those used for instructional purposes. Special assistance was also given in the rapid reading skills of scanning and skimming.

In summarizing her reflective thinking, Miss Brown was pleased that she had helped these retarded readers increase their insights into the reading process, and, thus, to come closer to satisfying the challenge set forth by King Solomon in the tenth century B.C.: ". . . with all thy getting get understanding."

CHAPTER XV

THE ROLE OF TESTING IN READING INSTRUCTION

*

FREDERICK B. DAVIS

*

IN PAPERS presented at previous reading conferences, Arthur E. Traxler discussed various aspects of the role of tests in the measurement of ability to read. In 1951, he provided a critical survey of tests for identifying difficulties in intepreting what is read.[1]

In 1958, he discussed the values and limitations of standardized reading tests.[2] His main point was one with which this writer heartily concurs; namely, that the process of reading is so complex that tests of ability to read must be carefully constructed on the basis of a thorough and systematic analysis of the process and of the outcomes desired. This point will be elaborated later, using Traxler's excellent paper as a point of departure.

Broadly speaking, testing plays three major roles in reading instruction. Tests are used to (1) assess an individual's performance in reading at a given point in time, (2) assess changes over a period of time in the reading of individuals or groups, and (3) estimate the degree to which individual or group potential for reading has been realized.

READING MECHANICS

Although the fundamental objective of reading is comprehension, this objective cannot be attained efficiently (or even at all) unless the reader is able to convert symbols, which we may call graphemes, into meaningful concepts. This conversion is an associative and reasoning process that can profitably be separated into two stages: first, the mechanics of recognizing the symbols; and, second, the evocation of associations and the weaving together of these associations to recreate the ideas that the author had in mind.

Although effective silent reading should not involve vocalization or even perceptible subvocalization of phonemes (combinations of graphemes), an analysis of reading skill may often profitably require that tests of oral reading of graphemes, words, sentences, and so on, be made. If an individual can convert graphemes into

[1] Traxler, "Critical Survey of Tests for Identifying Difficulties in Interpreting What Is Read," in *Promoting Growth toward Maturity in Interpreting What Is Read*, edited by William S. Gray ("Supplementary Educational Monographs," No. 74; Chicago: University of Chicago Press, 1951), pp. 195–200.

[2] Traxler, "Values and Limitations of Standardized Reading Tests," in *Evaluation in Reading*, edited by Helen M. Robinson ("Supplementary Educational Monographs," No. 88; Chicago: University of Chicago Press, 1958), pp. 111–17.

phonemes and blend phonemes into words with a high degree of skill and fluency, any difficulty he has in comprehending what he is reading must lie in his lack of experiential associations or his inability to weave these together through reasoning.

The mechanics of reading involve eye movements, perceptual accuracy, the association of graphemes with the corresponding phonemes, the blending of phonemes to form words, and word recognition. A number of elaborate diagnostic tests are now available to measure various components of the mechanics of reading. The *Gates-McKillop Reading Diagnostic Tests* (Bureau of Publications, Teachers College, Columbia University, 1962), the *Durrell Analysis of Reading Difficulty* (Harcourt, Brace & World, Inc., 1955), George D. Spache's *Diagnostic Reading Scales* (California Test Bureau, 1963), and the *Diagnostic Reading Tests* (Committee on Diagnostic Reading Tests, Inc., 1963) come readily to mind.

The diagnosis of difficulty in reading is a clinical problem and should be carried on by specialists. All of the tests mentioned above should be used only by such specialists since these tests are sometimes difficult to administer and yield scores that can be unreliable and tricky to interpret, partly because differences among the scores are even less reliable than the scores taken one by one.

RATE OF COVERING MATERIAL

To the layman, the measurement of rate of reading sounds like a simple undertaking, requiring only that the number of words covered per minute be determined. Unfortunately, careful consideration of the problem quickly reveals that a count of the number of words covered per minute may be a meaningless figure.

It is apparent on a moment's thought that any reader's rate is greatly affected by his purpose in reading. How greatly is illustrated by some data reported by Frank Laycock.[3] The average rate of 391 applicants for admission to college when they were asked to read a passage at their normal rate was 220.4 words per minute. When they were given a similar passage and were asked to read as fast as possible without missing important points on which they would be tested, they averaged 308.1 words per minute. Another request for them to increase their speed of reading without sacrificing comprehension resulted in an immediate 40 per cent average gain in rate. Three important implications for the measurement of rate of reading may be derived from these data:

1. Rate of reading must be measured under conditions that unambiguously define the purpose for which the reading is to be done and that provide assurance that this purpose is being fulfilled by the reader.

2. Evaluation of the results of training programs for increasing speed of reading should always exclude any increase in speed that a reader could have made before the training began by simply

3 Laycock, "Significant Characteristics of College Students with Varying Flexibility in Reading Rate: I. Eye-Movements in Reading Prose," *Journal of Experimental Education,* XXIII (June, 1955), 311–30.

stepping up his speed of reading without appreciable loss of comprehension.

3. Very different tests are required for measuring the rate at which material is covered for different purposes.

Rate of reading is also greatly influenced by the complexity or difficulty of the material that an individual is seeking to understand. Data published by John C. Flanagan provide an illustration.[4] He administered three equivalent reading scales of twenty items each to 317 twelfth-grade students in such a way that they worked at different predetermined rates on each of the three scales. The average score of the group was 10.5 in eighteen minutes of working time, 9.7 in twelve minutes of working time, and 7.0 in six minutes of working time. Thus, with a clearly defined purpose (that of responding correctly to test items of a familiar kind at predetermined rates), these students sustained a loss of comprehension when their working time was cut by one-third and then by two-thirds.

Analysis of the data showed that the percentages of loss of comprehension between the twelve-minute and six-minute working times were nearly the same for students whose scores in the eighteen-minute working time were in the highest, middle, and lowest thirds of the group. This result suggests that, with the purpose of the

reader and the complexity of the material held constant, there is a fairly uniform *inverse* relationship throughout the range of ability between *rate* of reading and *level* of comprehension. It may be noted in passing that the students could refer back to the reading passages as they responded to the comprehension questions; hence, memory played no appreciable part in determining the results of this experiment.

The inverse relationship between *rate* of reading and *level* of comprehension under the conditions of Flanagan's experiment makes such good sense that one wonders why anyone has ever thought the relationship to be otherwise. The reason is, doubtless, that the correlation coefficient between rate of reading (indicated by the number of test items read during a time limit) and level of comprehension (indicated by the number of items answered correctly when every student has had time to consider every item) has been found to be positive. As a matter of fact, Flanagan found it to be .17 in his group of 317 students. In a classic experiment Paul Blommers and E. F. Lindquist found it to be .30 in a sample of 672 students in grades eleven and twelve.[5]

Procedures used to check comprehension in reading at the same time that rate is being measured have usually been inadequate in at least one of the following ways:

4 Flanagan, "A Study of the Effect of Comprehension of Varying Speeds of Reading," in *Research on the Foundations of American Education*, Official Report of the American Educational Research Association (Washington, D.C.: American Educational Association, 1939), pp. 47–50.

5 Blommers and Lindquist, "Rate of Comprehension of Reading: Its Measurement and Its Relation to Comprehension," *Journal of Educational Psychology*, XXXV (November, 1944), 449–73.

1. The tests commonly include a fairly large percentage of items that can be answered by many examinees before they have been shown the passages on which the items are based.

2. The tests are often administered with such short time limits that every examinee does not have time to try every item, and scores are not corrected for chance success. In these circumstances, an examinee who is tested at the beginning and at the end of a reading-training course may read the test material so rapidly on the second testing that his comprehension is markedly lower than on the first testing. Yet, he can obtain a higher comprehension-test score on the second testing than on the first simply by marking answers to more items — at random, if necessary. With no correction for guessing, he is likely to answer a fraction of the items correctly by chance alone. His test scores will then give the false impression that he has greatly increased his rate of reading while maintaining or even improving upon his original level of comprehension. The most effective remedy for this situation is to use the conventional correction for chance success, especially if every examinee does not have time to consider every item within the time limit. Naturally, a test designed to measure speed cannot permit chance to effect results.

3. Estimates of individual and group gains during reading-training courses have often been based on a direct comparison of scores on equivalent forms of a test properly administered before and after the course without taking into account the fact that the training received during the course may have so altered the purposes of the examinees that the initial and final scores are not equivalent. In other words, tests that measure equivalent mental functions when they are administered to randomly determined parts of a group of examinees at one sitting may not measure the same mental functions when they are administered to the same group of examinees before and after a period of training.

At the sacrifice of established norms, the mental functions measured by tests given before and after a training period can usually be made more nearly equivalent by instructing the examinees before the initial testing that they should read as rapidly as possible while still getting the information needed to answer questions about the material. This, either explicitly or implicitly, is a principal effect of most remedial or other training courses in reading.

4. Estimates of individual and group changes produced by training courses in reading have rarely taken into account possible regression to population means. Still more rarely have estimates of changes been compared with the appropriate standard errors of measurement (or standard errors) to determine whether they are statistically significant. (I shall discuss this point further in a later section of this paper.)

5. The tests are given after the material on which they are based has been removed from sight. As a consequence, they measure a combination of comprehension and memory of the facts and understandings presented in the material.

To avoid some of the problems involved in measuring rate of reading, tests of rate of comprehension have become increasingly popular. The scores from these tests measure the rate at which the examinees are able to read material and respond correctly to questions about it while the material remains in front of them for reference. The best-known tests of this type are probably the *Cooperative English Test: Reading Comprehension* (Cooperative Test Division, 1960), the *Davis Reading Tests* (Psychological Corporation, 1962), the *Nelson-Denny Reading Tests* (Houghton Mifflin Co., 1960), and parts of the *Iowa Silent Reading Tests* (Harcourt, Brace & World, Inc., 1956).

Any speed-of-comprehension score should be corrected for chance success. Of the tests mentioned that yield speed-of-comprehension scores, only the *Davis Reading Tests* (Psychological Corporation, 1962) yield scores that are so corrected. It has been suggested that, instead of correcting for guessing, all students be instructed to mark answers to all items even if they have not read some of them. This procedure introduces chance elements into the scores, and the more conscientious students find it hard to carry out.

LEVEL OF COMPREHENSION

As Traxler and others have indicated, any test of comprehension in reading, whether also a test of speed or not, should be carefully planned and constructed to measure the most important elements or skills involved. This is particularly true of level-of-comprehension tests, which are so constructed that few, if any, examinees are not able to consider every item within the time limit. Such tests should include passages and items that cover a wide range of difficulty, with a few items near the end so penetrating that only a few exam-inees can be expected to answer them correctly.

Of the tests now available, the new *Cooperative English Test: Reading Comprehension* (Cooperative Test Division, 1960) and the *Davis Reading Test* (Psychological Corporation, 1962) were designed to provide level-of-comprehension scores by making both halves of their tests complete level-of-comprehension tests. The effect of this arrangement is that the score on the complete test becomes a speed-of-comprehension score and that on the first half a level-of-comprehension score, because all, or almost all, examinees have time to consider every item in the first half in the time limit. This procedure leads to efficiency in testing because the more rapid readers are kept busy providing data during the entire time limit. It also tends to make the purpose of all examinees uniform in taking the test; almost no one has time to go back and double-check his responses to the items in the first half (that yield his level-of-comprehension score). In other types of relatively unspeeded tests in comprehension, the faster readers are, in effect, given a second chance at the items yielding their level-of-comprehension score. Their greater speed provides time in which they can check their work and to some extent causes a spurious inflation of their comprehension scores.

Relatively unspeeded tests of comprehension in reading of the conventional type include the paragraph-reading sections of the *California Achievement Test* (California Test

Bureau, 1957), the Survey Section of the *Diagnostic Reading Test* (Committee on Diagnostic Reading Tests, Inc., 1963), the *Iowa Tests of Basic Skills* (Houghton Mifflin, 1956), the *Iowa Tests of Educational Development* (Science Research Associates, Inc., 1963), the *Metropolitan Achievement Test* (Harcourt, Brace & World, Inc., 1962), the *Sequential Tests of Educational Progress* (Cooperative Test Division, 1963), and the *Stanford Achievement Test* (Harcourt, Brace & World, Inc., 1964).

Now let me consider which skills of comprehension in reading should be measured. When the *Cooperative English Tests: Reading Comprehension* were first designed in 1939, a search of the literature was made to find which skills had been suggested as important by authorities in the field. As soon as these were put in a single list, it was found that they overlapped very greatly. By eliminating overlap and skills that seemed impossible to measure by objective items that could be easily scored, the list was reduced to nine operational skills:

(1) Remembering word meanings
(2) Deducing the meaning of words from context
(3) Following the organization of a passage, as in identfying antecedents and references
(4) Identifying the main thought of a passage
(5) Answering questions for which explicit or paraphrased answers are given
(6) Weaving together the ideas in a passage
(7) Drawing inferences about the content of a passage

(8) Recognizing literary devices and identifying an author's tone and mood
(9) Drawing inferences about an author's purpose and point of view

These constituted the basic framework on which the original tests were constructed.

To determine whether each of these skills is, at least to some extent, unique in the list of nine, an analysis of their variances and covariances was made. The identities of the resulting uncorrelated factors were adduced from a knowledge of the nine skills that had determined them. These fundamental abilities in comprehension are the following:

I. Remembering word meanings
II. Reasoning with verbal materials
VII. Following the organization of a passage
VIII. Recognizing literary devices and identifying the author's tone and mood
III. Focusing on the implied meanings of a passage
IV. Drawing inferences about an author's intent, purpose, or point of view
VI. Finding correct answers to questions to which explicit or paraphrased answers are given
V. Deducing word meanings from context.
IX. Identifying the main thought of a passage

You will note that the Roman numerals attached to these fundamental abilities are not in numerical order. This is because they are arranged in order of their reliability coefficients. The first ability, "Remembering word meanings," had a reliability coefficient of .94, which can be regarded as very high. This ability is basically memory of meaningful material — namely, words. The data show that, as might be expected, it is the most important ability that underlies comprehension in reading.

The second ability, "Reasoning with verbal materials," is of next greatest importance in reading comprehension. It involves weaving verbal ideas together. In one study, reasoning in verbal materials had a correlation with arithmetic reasoning of —.32 and with figure analogies (a non-verbal test) of —.12. With syllogistic reasoning (expressed in verbal form), reasoning in verbal materials correlated only to the extent of +.05. These data point to the conclusion that this fundamental ability is not a general reasoning skill; it is instead specific. If it is to be developed, the training will probably have to be done by means of practice exercises based on passages like those in typical reading tests. Longer stories may also be used. But the responses made by readers should always be discussed and correct answers to questions identified and explained. By comparison with the first two abilities, the others are much less influential in determining a reader's level of comprehension. In fact, the last three on the list (VI, V, and IX) were not firmly established by the study from which these data have been taken.[6] This may be only because they were unreliably meas-

[6] Frederick B. Davis, "Fundamental Factors of Comprehension in Reading," *Psychometrika*, IX (September, 1944), 185–97.

ured in the original study. To explore this possibility, the writer is now engaged in a study of the more subtle skills in comprehension that will utilize the relatively new technique of cross-validated uniqueness analysis.

Although the abilities III–IX are not of as fundamental an importance as abilities I and II, they may be of great consequence in certain types of reading. For example, the comprehension of literature (which involves the recognition and understanding of such literary devices as allusion, metaphor, and simile) depends greatly on ability VIII. The understanding of editorials and political tracts depends heavily on ability IV. The social consequences of increasing by only a small amount the ability of American citizens to evaluate propaganda and advertising appeals are obviously of great importance in a democratic society. These may be only tiny aspects of comprehension in reading, but they may be potentially very important.

In constructing the *Davis Reading Tests* (both Series 1 for grades eleven and twelve and for college freshmen and Series 2 for grades eight through eleven), certain of the nine skills were grouped and skill 1, "Remembering word meanings," was omitted. As already mentioned, this skill is inevitably measured in the process of measuring the others because they are all expressed in words. In assembling the tests, about 25 per cent of the items were selected to measure skill 5; 25 per cent to measure skills 4 and 6 combined; 25 per cent to measure skills 2, 7, and 9 combined; 12.5 per cent to measure skill 8; and 12.5 per cent to measure skill 3. Regardless whether one agrees with this assignment of percentages, one at least knows the basis of the decision.

The use of comprehension tests in reading is increasing most rapidly for programed instruction and for informal purposes in the classroom. In programed instruction, testing is an integral part of the teaching-learning process to an extent rarely attained in conventional teaching procedures. After a sequence of learning exercises has been presented and covered by the pupil at a rate appropriate for him, a check test is given. This often consists of a single question. If the pupil answers correctly, he is shown the next sequence of learning exercises; if he answers incorrectly, he repeats the sequence, or some suitable remedial exercises are provided. Thus, programed instruction is a melding of teaching, testing, reteaching, testing, and teaching. Instant diagnosis of failure to learn a step in the programed sequence and immediate confirmation of successful learning are provided by check tests.

The danger in this procedure is the astonishing degree of unreliability tolerated in the check tests. A single question may be found to have a reliability coefficient of the order of .15 to .20. For an item of 50 per cent difficulty that is scored *one* if answered correctly and *zero* if answered incorrectly, a standard error of measurement of about .46 results. Inaccuracy of this relative magnitude would be regarded as intolerable in an ordinary reading test. In programed instruction, it must lead to a good deal of inefficiency in learning, because pupils who fail a check item when their true score is "pass" have to repeat sequences unnecessarily; conversely, pupils who pass a check item when their true score is "fail" are moved on to subsequent learning exercises for which they may lack some foundation element.

Even more serious is the risk of low content validity in a single check item; that is, the question may measure only one (or, in general, fewer than all) of the elements in the material that has just been taught. This danger argues for the very frequent use of single check items immediately after each element of the material has been covered.

The same problems beset the use of informal teacher-made tests in reading instruction. In addition, such tests rarely have adequate norms or norms expressed in meaningful units, such as percentile ranks in defined groups at specified stages of instruction.

There is little doubt that check tests in programed instruction and informal tests for classroom use will increase more rapidly than any other types of tests. Their shortcomings and dangers must be kept in mind if their efficiency and accuracy are to be increased.

ASSESSMENT OF CHANGE IN READING PERFORMANCE

Since the primary purpose of teaching is to produce learning — that is, change — in students, the estimation of the amount of change is of paramount importance in education. Yet, surprisingly enough, until recently there has been a decided lack of information about the best techniques for accomplishing the assessment of change. Some of the most important considerations are discussed at this point.

Test validity. The first requirement in selecting a testing instrument is to be sure that it measures the learnings that the teaching is intended to produce. It is sometimes difficult to find standardized tests that have two or more equivalent forms available that meet this requirement. In addition to test content, the directions for administering the tests and scoring them affect validity. If a student learns over a period of instruction to mark answers at random on all items he has not had time to consider carefully, his final score can differ greatly from his initial score. Yet the change will not reflect any actual improvement in his ability to read accurately with comprehension. Therefore, it is especially important that speeded tests yield scores that have been corrected for chance success.

Test reliability. Other things being equal, the higher the reliability coefficient of a reading test the better. Because, as Traxler pointed out in 1958, a reading-comprehension item takes a great deal of examinee time (in contrast with a recognition-vocabulary item, for example), the reliability of reading tests is usually low per unit of time. Since publishers encounter resistance to long tests, most tests of a reader's level of comprehension yield scores of only moderate reliability — say, about .80. For this reason,

it is often good practice to use two equivalent forms of a reading test and average the examinee's scores. It should be noted that, if this practice is followed, norms cannot be based on the administration of a single form to each examinee.

Range of ability measured. Tests used to measure change should cover a wide enough range of ability that no examinee will get an initial score equal to that which would be yielded by chance selection of answers and no examinee will get a final score that is perfect. Otherwise, we cannot tell how much higher or lower these students might have scored, and the resulting gain or loss scores will be underestimates of true change.

Units of measurement of scores. It is too much to hope that increments of ability represented by one score point will be the same at all levels of scores. Nonetheless, if scores from a reading test are expressed in score units like Flanagan's Scaled Scores, Gardner's K Scores, stanines, or some other kinds of normalized standard scores, there is a tendency for the increment of ability represented by one score point to be more nearly the same throughout the range of scores than if raw scores are used.

Estimates of change. The simplest way to estimate the amount of change made by an individual pupil is to administer equivalent forms of a test at the beginning and at the end of a training period. The initial score is subtracted from the final score, and the resulting difference is used as a crude estimate of change. This estimate is shown on the first line of

TABLE 1

THE ASSESSMENT OF CHANGE

Crude Estimate of Change	*Smallest Change Worthy of Serious Consideration*

Individual:

$$C = B - A$$

$$\frac{3}{2}\sqrt{s_{\text{meas B}}^2 + s_{\text{meas A}}^2} \qquad (1)$$

Group:

$$\overline{Cs} = \overline{Bs} - \overline{As}$$

$$\frac{3}{2}\sqrt{\frac{s_{\text{meas B}}^2 + s_{\text{meas A}}^2}{Ns}} \qquad (2)$$

Refined Estimate of Change

Individual:

$$\hat{C} = W_B B + W_A A + K$$

$$\frac{3}{2}\sqrt{W_B^2 s_{\text{meas B}}^2 + W_A^2 s_{\text{meas A}}^2} \qquad (3)$$

Group:

$$\hat{\overline{Cs}} = W_B \overline{B} + W_A \overline{A} + K$$

$$\frac{3}{2}\sqrt{\frac{W_B^2 s_{\text{meas B}}^2 + W_A^2 s_{\text{meas A}}^2}{Ns}} \qquad (4)$$

Key:

A = individual score on Test A (initial test)
B = individual score on Test B (final test)
C = crude estimate of individual change
$\hat{C}$ = refined estimate of individual change
$\overline{Cs}$ = crude estimate of mean change in subsample s
$\hat{\overline{Cs}}$ = refined estimate of mean change in subsample s
$\overline{A}$ = mean score on Test A in a single age or grade group
$\overline{B}$ = mean score on Test B in a single age or grade group
$\overline{As}$ = mean score on Test A in subsample s
$\overline{Bs}$ = mean score on Test B in subsample s
N = number of cases in a single age or grade group
Ns = number of cases in subsample s
s_A, s_B, r_{AA}, r_{BB}, $s_{\text{meas A}}$, and $s_{\text{meas B}}$ = familiar statistics computed in a single age or grade group

$$W_A = \frac{r_{AB}\, s_B(1 - r_{BB}) - s_A (r_{AA} - r_{AB})}{s_A(1 - r_{AB}^2)}$$

$$W_B = \frac{s_B (r_{BB} - r_{AB}^2) - r_{AB}\, s_A(1 - r_{AA})}{s_B(1 - r_{AB}^2)}$$

$$K = \overline{B} - \overline{A} - W_B\overline{B} - W_A\overline{A}$$

equations on the left-hand side of Table 1. The smallest difference worth paying serious attention to is shown on the same line to the right. The second line of equations in Table 1 shows how to make a crude estimate of the average change made by a group and how to judge whether it is large enough to warrant serious attention.

These procedures should not be used to compare changes made by students or groups with widely different initial scores; neither should they be used to estimate changes made by students or groups selected for training on the basis of the initial test scores. For such purposes, refined estimates must be employed. The equations in line three of Table 1 should be used to make and evaluate refined estimates of changes for individuals, and those in line four for groups. Again, the smallest difference that is worth paying attention to is given on the right-hand side of each of these lines.

ESTIMATING POTENTIAL FOR PERFORMANCE IN READING

Teachers of reading at every grade level, especially teachers of remedial reading, constantly feel the need for estimating the potential performance level in reading of individuals or groups. Usually, this is done by administering individual tests of mental ability that require little or no reading or by so-called non-verbal group tests. The scores from such tests are compared with scores, such as age- or grade-equivalent scores, from reading

tests in some common scale. The differences between an individual's scores on the mental-ability, non-verbal, test and the common scale are then used to decide whether he is falling short of his potential.

To be effective, this procedure demands that three basic conditions be satisfied:

1. The test used to measure performance in reading must be a valid measure of the particular skills involved.

2. The test used to estimate potential must measure an ability (or cluster of abilities) that is crucial for learning the particular skills measured by the reading test. The best information we have regarding the nature of human abilities indicates that many of them are only loosely correlated with one another. Thus, it is possible that ability in spatial visualization is not at all important in the comprehension of stories that a student is required to read in English classes. Scores on a non-verbal figure-analogies test may have little or no relevance to an estimate of a child's potential for pronouncing words. Such tests would also have little or no value for measuring the realization of potential for performance in reading.

The measurement and statistical techniques required for testing potential have been worked out in detail by the writer presented in *Educational Measurements and Their Interpretations.* [7]

3. Any differences between the measures of potential and actual reading performance must be evaluated to determine whether they could easily be explained as a chance deviation from a true difference of zero.

[7] Frederick B. Davis, *Educational Measurements and Their Interpretation* (Belmont, Calif.: Wadsworth Publishing Co., 1964), chapter xi.

The first and third conditions can usually be satisfied reasonably well if due care is exercised, but not the second condition. Unfortunately, it is always difficult and often impossible to find a test of abilities that are crucial to the performance of reading skills that does not demand the use of these skills. In short, it is usually not possible to measure potential for reading satisfactorily, and as a result, it is also not usually possible to estimate the extent to which an individual or group has realized its potential. Perhaps the best approach to an estimate can be made by a skilled clinical psychologist. But even this approach must be employed with more caution than is usually displayed. Performance in various aspects of reading is not primarily dependent on *non-verbal* abilities but on a cluster of *verbal* abilities. Yet clinicians often use differences between non-verbal test scores and reading-test scores as one basis for diagnosing disability in reading.

CHAPTER XVI

WHAT IS EVALUATION?

*

RALPH W. TYLER

*

THE TERM *evaluation* arose when educators became dissatisfied with appraisals of educational achievement that were based on a sampling of the content of teaching materials rather than on a systematic analysis of general educational values to which good schools were dedicated. Reading tests in the 1920's and 1930's were constructed as detailed studies of vocabulary and of the percentages of pupils who could answer the questions correctly; they did not include any comprehensive examination of the major educational values that teachers of reading sought to develop in their students. Most test items required "plain sense" comprehension of material, and provided little or no evidence of the degree to which pupils were acquiring such other values as interpretative skills, interest in a wide variety of informative and literary materials, responsive and disciplined appreciation of literary works, and habits of reading for information and enjoyment. The recognition by many experienced teachers and other students of education of the inadequacies of the appraisals of that time led to an emphasis upon evaluation, that is, a procedure for appraising the educational values actually developing in an educational program.

The acceptance of this idea led further to the formulation of certain new techniques for appraisal and to some redefinition of older criteria of sound measurement. Evaluation begins with the identification of a school's goals; that is, educational objectives must first be identified and defined before their degree of attainment can be assessed. Identifying all of the major objectives of a reading program and defining them clearly were difficult steps in the early days of evaluation. Today these objectives — such as skill in comprehending prose material, skill in interpreting general expository materials in science and social studies, interest in reading, and skill in evaluating the authenticity of materials — are fairly well defined. But difficulty is still encountered in defining satisfactorily other kinds of objectives for various stages of maturity; for example, skills in interpreting poetry, drama, and novels; ability to judge the quality of various types of literary works; and experience in appreciating stories, poetry, and other complex literary works. Yet these kinds of objectives are attempted by thoughtful and experienced teachers. What they involve should be clearly enough understood so that the progress of students toward them can be appraised. Further efforts are obviously needed to identify and define important educational objectives in reading.

In 1958, I pointed out:

. . . Twenty-five years ago the prevailing conception of educational tests was a paper-and-pencil device, usually consisting of true-false or multiple-choice items. These devices could provide evidence of the amount of information the student could recall, and could indicate, too . . . his ability to comprehend reading passages. But they were not relevant to some other important objectives. They did not provide evidence of habits, attitudes, interests, and appreciations. Few exercises required depth of understanding or of interpretation. As we sought to develop means for evaluation, it became clear that we must broaden the concept of an educational test. We now think of an educational test as a series of situations which call forth from the student the kind of behavior defined in the objective and permit a record to be made of the student's actual behavior. A test of reading interpretation could consist of a series of situations in which the student is stimulated to read and to interpret what he is reading and in which a record can be made of the student's interpretations. A test of reading interests should consist of a series of situations in which the student is free to choose activities and a record can be made of the extent to which he freely chooses to read.

This conception of an educational test makes possible the use of a variety of testing devices; not only can paper-and-pencil exercises be used, but also such procedures as observation, interview, questionnaire, samples of products made, and records obtained in other connections may serve as evaluation devices.[1]

During the past eight years the soundness of the notion of a broader test has become very widely recognized. In reading and in other fields, however, the use of devices other than paper-and-pencil tests is still very limited, even though better tests (multiple-response tests) are now available for measuring interpretative skills. Except for diagnostic work performed by teachers in the readiness and primary stages of reading, the appraisal of achievement in reading is largely restricted to paper-and-pencil tests of the skills of comprehension and interpretation. But the need for evaluating new curriculums, new materials of instruction, and new teaching devices has given rise very recently to questionnaires seeking information about reading interests and habits; observations of speech behavior, particularly as it reveals knowledge of vocabulary and linguistic structure; and interviews with parents about early language experiences.

In 1958, I stated that the accepted criteria for judging measurement devices, namely, validity, objectivity, and reliability, were not abandoned in evaluation but were redefined in terms appropriate to this broader conception of educational measurement.

[1] Ralph W. Tyler, "The Essential Aspects of Evaluation," in *Evaluation of Reading*, compiled and edited by Helen M. Robinson ("Supplementary Educational Monographs," No. 88; Chicago: University of Chicago Press, 1959), p. 6.

The most important criterion, validity, was redefined to require that an appraisal device obtain as a response a sample of the kind of behavior it purports to measure, or at least, a sample of highly correlated behavior. This conception of validity is central to evaluation and is quite different from the earlier coefficients of validity, which indicated the internal homogeneity of items.

In spite of the basic importance of the redefined conception of validity, many of the new instruments of evaluation are not constructed to meet this criterion. The most common practice is to assemble exercises which test reading comprehension and/or interpretation and to try them out at the grade levels for which they are intended. The criteria for retaining, modifying, or eliminating exercises are (1) coefficients of correlation between the pupils' performance on an item and on the total set of items and (2) the progressive increase, from the lower to the higher grades, in per cent of pupils who answer an exercise correctly. These criteria indicate that the exercises are homogeneous and that certain skills are learned during a particular grade span; but they do not indicate whether the test measures the skills which they were constructed to measure. As a result, there is less demand for a careful definition of objectives and for an appraisal of achievement in terms of these objectives than would be the case if the newer concept of validity were more widely used in constructing evaluation instruments.

Although the other two appraisal criteria, objectivity and reliability, have also been redefined in terms of evaluation, they have not yet been widely applied, because the variety of appraisal instruments has not been greatly extended. With the wider use of questionnaires, interviews, observations, and performance tests, new operational procedures to determine the degree of objectivity of these instruments will have to be developed.

The conception of evaluation that has developed over the years since 1933 recognizes that the educational effects of different instructional procedures, materials, teaching personalities, and the like, are influenced by a number of characteristics of students. In the Eight Year Study, for example, it was found that a free reading program that greatly influenced reading interests in one school seemed to have had much less effect on reading interests in another school. Yet, the appraisal of mental ability revealed no appreciable difference in distribution between the two schools. The characteristics of the learners that may have affected the results of this study were, in addition to age, sex, and intelligence, social class, educational and occupational goals, cultural level of the home, parents' attitude toward the importance of education, interests, types of motivations, social acceptance by peers, physical growth, and work experience.

Since 1958 there have been further demonstrations that characteristics of students may influence the direction and extent of learning. Studies of children from low socioeconomic backgrounds indicate that the following characteristics are most important for progress in reading: confidence that they can learn, a belief that human efforts can make a difference in the world and in their own lives, a broad oral vocabulary, and speech habits that parallel conventional language patterns. Recognition of these characteristics is helpful in planning reading programs for disadvantaged children and in interpreting results. Increasingly, the relevant characteristics of the learners will be taken into account in appraisals of educational programs.

A final point made in my 1958 presentation was that evaluation was coming to include an assessment of the conditions of learning in an educational program as well as the characteristics of the pupils and the skills that they learned. I stated then:

When the Eight-Year Study began, it was commonly assumed that curricular plans, teaching methods, and instructional materials were in themselves clearly defined factors which could be assessed in terms of their effectiveness in producing desired learning in the students. Educational experiments had been conducted comparing the "laboratory method" of science instruction with the "lecture-demonstration method," comparing "large-class instruction" with "small-class instruction," comparing the "reading method" of language instruction with the "grammar translation method," and so on. Often several investigations of the same "methods" yielded quite different results. In the Eight-Year Study, several schools explored such innovations as "pupil-teacher planning" and the "core curriculum." As we observed the developments in different schools of what was thought to be the same innovation, and as we talked with teachers about them, we began to realize that a phrase like "pupil-teacher planning" takes on concrete meaning in terms of the way in which such innovation is conceived, developed, and actually carried on by the teacher. We sometimes found as much variability in results obtained among classes purportedly using the same "method" as we found among several different "methods."[2]

Recognition of the need to examine the conditions of learning in connection with the evaluation of learning is currently evident in studies for new courses and curriculums that are being developed with the assistance of funds from the federal government. In my visits to a number of classrooms in which new curriculums are being used, I have found a wide variation both in what is being done and in the ideas of students and teachers about the new courses. Similar observations have been made by others who are interested in these new curriculums.

An illustration of variations in learning conditions is provided by the ways in which a new beginning reading program based on linguistic principles is being applied in different schools. In some cases, the teachers have gained an understanding of the theory of teaching reading as linguistic development and are using the materials very much as the builders recommend. In other cases, teachers use the new materials as though they were primers and preprimers that followed the phonics approach; and in

2 *Ibid.*, p. 8.

still others, teachers are treating the materials as if they were supplementary readers appropriate to the "look-say" approach. These variations probably result in part from the differences in attitude or special training of the teachers. Whatever the reason, however, the different conditions of learning are fully as important in influencing learning as the materials themselves or the theory on which they are constructed. Hence, a study of these conditions is in many cases essential to an evaluation of a program.

NEW EMPHASES IN EVALUATION

Since 1958 the evaluation of new courses, instructional materials, and technology has become increasingly important. Because these new courses are focused on different objectives, they require new evaluation instruments. In many cases appropriate instruments are not available and must be constructed following the general guidelines established earlier in such investigations as the Eight-Year Study.

Some of the new courses are based on theories of learning that either did not exist or were not well known when older courses were constructed. For example, many of them are planned in terms of "learning by discovery," which is a kind of inductive learning. The materials are designed to help the pupil develop concepts and see relationships through observing phenomena and reflecting upon what he has observed. This is in contrast to an earlier approach of naming and defining concepts and generalizations first, then asking the learner to verify them or to find illustrations. Programs involving new theories of learning are likely to have initial difficulty in being carried out in a way that properly reflects the basic theory. Hence, it is important in evaluating them to ascertain the extent to which they actually represent the teaching-learning process.

A number of the new curriculums are attempts to devise a more defensible sequence of learning units than has been characteristic of earlier curriculums. An appropriate evaluation of a new sequence requires instruments that can measure the progress of students toward the objectives of the sequence, determine the extent to which the sequence and organization are actually being followed in classes using the new materials, and provide evidence of the sequential development of the students. Heretofore, little evaluation of this sort has been undertaken.

Today, the largest new educational efforts are being directed toward programs for disadvantaged children. The most crucial educational task for these children is to learn to read. Hence, more than half of the funds expended under Title I of the National Defense Education Act in 1965–66 went for programs to strengthen reading. The act required that school districts evaluate their new efforts to educate disadvantaged children, and this proved to be very difficult, since the existing tests and other evaluation devices focused on the average pupil. More than half of the first groups of disadvantaged children to take these tests showed a zero score.

This does not mean that the children had learned nothing but that the tests had too few exercises at the initial levels of learning, where they could have made a showing. Recent studies have provided further evidence of the inadequacies of the available evaluative instruments.

Because of pressure to keep testing time within a class period, test-makers have eliminated items that most pupils can answer and those that few can answer. If the purpose of testing is to establish reliable means for class groups, or to rank individuals, this kind of test is a proper way of increasing the efficient use of testing time. But if the purpose is to measure the progress of those students who would fall in the top or bottom quarters of the group, this procedure defeats the purpose. Hence, there is a pressing need to devise evaluation instruments that can appraise the progress of those who begin at a low level and proceed at a relatively slow pace.

The difficulty of evaluating the progress of disadvantaged children has suggested an entirely different conception of the problem of teaching children to read. It could now be stated as follows.

Children coming from homes where conventional language is used, where books are found, where other learning experiences have been provided, and where learning has been encouraged will learn to read one way or another. In fact, at least three-fourths of American children learn to read well enough to meet the demands of their situations. For them, the question of which of the good reading programs is best is relatively unimportant.

Learning to read is a problem for only a fraction of our children. For many of them an effective approach has not yet been found. Research, development, and experimentation need to be centered on the children who have not been making regular progress in reading. Evaluation of their progress should be specially designed. Tests of achievement, pupil characteristics, and conditions of learning should all be relevant to and focused on the special learning problems of these children. This approach can be extended to other critical problems in reading intruction, such as developing mature reading interests, attitudes, habits, and skills in those adolescents whose reading patterns appear to be frozen at the stage of comic books and plain-sense comprehension of simple prose.

NEW PURPOSES OF EVALUATION

Since 1958, the introduction of high-speed computers that are increasingly economical to purchase and operate has made it possible to scan, score, analyze, and record the responses to a variety of test forms, questionnaires, and check lists in a very short time and at a fraction of the cost of manual operations. This new technique has increased interest among educators and research workers in developing means of diagnosing learning problems of students, identifying learning programs relevant to their needs, and monitoring progress made by the students. The possibility of individualized instruction within the framework of classes and schools of conventional sizes now seems real and capable of demonstration within a relatively short time. However, in order to develop an appropriate individualized instructional program for the learner, evaluation instruments that can sample adequately the behavior involved in each step of the program are required. This is a new requirement for evaluation, and its incorporation into the over-all conception of evaluation is only now beginning to take place. Initial efforts to construct diagnostic evaluation instruments of this sort are just getting under way.

Another new purpose for educational evaluation is to provide the public with information about the educational levels of important sectors of our nation and the progress being made in raising these levels. This could be called a national assessment of the progress of education. For this assessment we need the kind of data we now have about other matters of public concern, such as population growth and its rate of increase, the extent of internal migration, the income levels of our people, and the incidence of disease. This type of information about education is needed to keep the people informed about the progress and problems of our country so that they will have a sounder basis for their opinions and actions. Since we do not now have sound or adequate information on education, personal views, distorted reports, and journalistic impressions are the sources of public opinion, and the schools are frequently attacked and frequently defended without the necessary evidence. This situation can only

be corrected by a careful, consistent effort to obtain valid data.

In 1964, the recognition of this need, the Carnegie Corporation of New York, a private foundation, appointed an exploratory committee on assessing the progress of education. I was asked to serve as chairman. The committee is charged with the development and trial of evaluation instruments and procedures for assessing the progress of education in the United States. Recently the Fund for the Advancement of Education added its support to the project.

The project has involved scholars, teachers, and reading specialists in formulating statements of the contributions that reading instruction can make to the development of children and youth and the objectives that the schools are seriously seeking to attain. For each of the major objectives, prototype exercises have been constructed which, it is believed, will give pupils an opportunity to demonstrate the behavior required by the objective. The list of objectives, along with the prototype exercises, has been reviewed by a series of panels of public-spirited citizens living in various parts of the country in cities, towns, and villages. Each panel reviewed the material and made a judgment about each objective in terms of the questions, Is this something important for people to learn today? and, Is this something I would like to have my children learn? This procedure, which resulted in very little revision of the original list, was designed to assure that every objective was (1) considered important by scholars and specialists, (2) accepted as an educational task by the school, and (3) deemed desirable by leading lay citizens. The committee wished to forestall criticism from these three groups.

The national assessment will provide census-type data for population groups larger than a classroom, a school, a school system, or even a state. The present plan is to assess a probability sample of 192 populations that represent all possible combinations of the following five categories: boys and girls; four geographic regions; four age groups (nine, thirteen, seventeen, and adult); urban, suburban, and rural areas; and two socioeconomic levels.

The fact that populations are to be assessed and not individuals also makes it possible to extend the sampling of exercises far beyond the kinds contained in a typical individual test. Thus, with a population of ten thousand, each person might take only one-twentieth of the exercises and still contribute to a sample of five hundred for each exercise. Furthermore, because the participants do not have to be in classes, the exercises to be used are not limited to the usual test items. Interviews and observational procedures may also be employed to furnish information about reading interests, attitudes, and habits.

To summarize the educational attainments of the several populations, the following sorts of things, rather than test scores, will be reported:

In the sample of seventeen-year old boys of higher socioeconomic status from rural and small town areas of the Midwest, it was found that 93 per cent could read a typical newspaper paragraph like the following . . . ; 76 per cent could

recognize the unsupported assertions in the following selection . . . ; 52 per cent spent at least two hours a week in reading material that was not part of their assigned work; and 24 per cent reported that they enjoyed poetry like the following . . . .

The need for dependable data on the progress of American education is increasingly recognized. An assessment such as the Carnegie Corporation committee is helping to make should at least be a constructive beginning.

EVALUATING LEARNING INFLUENCES OUTSIDE THE CLASSROOM

There are important factors influencing student learning that cannot be directly controlled by the classroom teacher but that can be affected by group action. As these are gradually being identified, efforts to evaluate them are also being made. The institutional expectations as perceived by the pupil, the peer groups to which the pupil belongs or whose members he respects, and the attractive personalities with whom he identifies are found to exert an influence on the direction and amount of learning. Most schools, particularly high schools and colleges, impress upon the student the kinds of persons valued by them and the kinds of achievements expected by them. In some places intellectual achievements are highly valued; in others, athletic prowess, social skills, or friendliness. In general, it can be said that the institutional emphasis, as it is perceived by the students, affects the nature and extent of their efforts, either positively or negatively.

In most schools, the friendship

groups are varied in their composition and openly or tacitly endorse different standards. Some may support the educational purposes of the school. Some may emphasize social activity or other behavior that is largely irrelevant to education. These groups are sometimes in rebellion against the school or members of the staff. It is clear that the attitudes of friends can substantially affect one's actions, materially facilitating or impeding learning.

As children grow up they commonly find persons in their environment to whom they are attracted and frequently attempt to emulate their behavior. This process of identification can exert a significant influence on learning and is particularly potent in helping the student develop new attitudes and attempt new activities.

These extra-classroom factors are obviously important influences on learning. They must be further identified, and techniques for their evaluation must be explored. The appraisal of these extra-classroom factors is likely to become part of the total concept of educational evaluation.

CONCLUDING STATEMENT

In concluding my presentation eight years ago, I said:

In the light of the history of the past quarter of a century, evaluation is seen as a growing conception; used as a term to cover the process of appraising the results of learning, it has developed into a process involving educational objectives, educational tests and measurements, the appraisal of characteristics of the learner, and the assessment of learning conditions. I believe that the conception will continue to grow as we identify other important areas which must be described or assessed if we are to understand education more fully, and more wisely guide the learning of our students.[3]

In reviewing developments in evaluation since 1958, it seems clear that the conception is still continuing to grow. The broad areas that were emerging then are more obvious now. Some of the important factors in these areas that were not recognized earlier have now been identified. The tasks involved in the evaluation of courses, materials, and methods of instruction are being reformulated. New purposes are gaining attention, and initial efforts are being made to evaluate extra-classroom influences on learning. It is possible to say with greater confidence than before that evaluation is a vital and growing conception.

3 *Ibid.*, p. 9.

CHAPTER XVII

ADMINISTRATIVE PROCEDURES FOR HELPING TEACHERS
IMPROVE READING INSTRUCTION

*

DEVELOPING OBJECTIVES FOR A SCHOOL-WIDE READING PROGRAM

GEORGE E. KEEM

*

ELEMENTARY AND secondary-school administrators, consultants, and supervisors are today faced with a myriad of innovative and, at times, perplexing attempts to adjust to our society as it is and as it is becoming. The twin explosions — knowledge and population — coupled with pressure for unprecedented rapidity of change, necessitate knowledgeable decisions with respect to new ways of doing things. Programed instruction and teaching machines, computerized scheduling, instant retrieval systems, closed-circuit television, team teaching, non-graded schools, and increased specialization are among the new procedures accorded considerable publicity. Comparable attention is being given to improvement of the quality as well as the quantity of instruction in reading — from kindergarten through high school.

School-wide improvement in the teaching of reading demands, as does any curricular area, an organized approach if it is to be significant. Ralph W. Tyler has indicated the first fundamental question that must be answered in developing any curriculum and plan of instruction: What educational purposes should the school seek to attain?[1] And J. Roy Newton has summarized guideposts for administrators endeavoring to establish purposes (objectives) for instruction in reading as follows:

1. The recognition of need for reading improvement should come from teachers, parents, and students, as well as from the administration. The situation in which change is dictated from above should be avoided.

2. Once a faculty, or a substantial part of it, has indicated a realization of the need for improvement, the administrator should give enthusiastic support in terms of time, money, and personal effort.

3. Avoid the feeling that individuals and divisions of the school are being criticized. Concentrate on the parts of the program that are effective and build on these.

4. Change just for the sake of change is not desirable. An effective program is the result of careful and deliberate organization, based on a realized need.

5. Make use of the combined resources of the teaching staff and the community. Educate by involvement.

[1] Tyler, *Basic Principles of Curriculum and Instruction* (Chicago: University of Chicago Press, 1955), p. 1.

6. When the time comes to hire a reading specialist, make sure he is fitted for the job by personality as well as training. Give him a free hand in organizing remedial and special-class reading. Do not expect miracles overnight.

7. Make sure reading materials are adequate. To provide staff, schedule classes, and then to fail in supporting the program with materials is false economy.

8. Give tangible support to the Reading Improvement Committee. A professional library, consultant services, and in-service training courses are evidences of real support.

9. Provide time. At first regularly scheduled meetings may be devoted to consideration of reading problems. Special meetings help, but when a faculty really grapples with the reading question, released time every school day for a year is not too much.

10. Schedule work in reading within the school day. It is neither fair nor realistic to expect boys and girls or teachers to become enthusiastic about a program that the administration obviously regards as an extra.

11. Avoid embarrassing girls and boys. Sell them on the self-improvement aspect rather than the compulsory you're-so-bad-you-have-to approach. Select names for classes that are simple statements of fact without implications.

12. Remember the individual. Any reorganization should improve his reading as a learning tool, make him independent, free him to explore new fields and respond to new ideas, and enable him to understand the world around him as well as to understand himself.

13. Avoid slavishly copying a reading program reported as successful in another school system. Be eclectic; select parts of several programs and incorporate special features to meet individual situations.

14. Share know-how in professional meetings, reporting successful practices, arranging visitation, or inviting demonstration.[2]

PROCEDURE

More specifically, a direct approach to developing objectives involves several discrete, although related, sequential and procedural steps.

1. A point of departure that is often found to be functional is the establishment of need for improvement. One of the more common methods for documenting need is analysis of standardized tests or informal reading inventories or both. Pertinent standardized tests with appropriate grade levels (elementary and secondary) are described and evaluated in various editions of the *Mental Measurements Yearbook*.[3] Procedures for preparing and scoring informal inventories may be found in a recent publication by Marjorie Seddon Johnson and Roy A. Kress.[4] Further assistance in developing inventories, including examples, is provided in works by Mary C. Austin, Clifford L. Bush, and Mildred H. Huebner,[5] Emmett A. Betts,[6] Nila Banton Smith,[7]

2 Newton, *Reading in Your School* (New York: McGraw-Hill Book Co., 1960), pp. 251–52.

3 Oscar K. Buros, *The Mental Measurements Yearbook* (Highland Park, N. J.: Gryphon Press, 1953 (4th ed.), 1959 (5th ed.), 1965 (6th ed.).

4 Johnson and Kress, *Informal Reading Inventories*, edited by Ira E. Aaron ("Reading Aids Series"; Newark, Del.: International Reading Association, 1965).

5 Austin, Bush, and Huebner, *Reading Evaluation* (New York: Ronald Press Co., 1961), pp. 3–94.

6 Emmett A. Betts, *Handbook on Corrective Reading for the American Adventure Series* (Chicago: Wheeler, 1956), pp. 8–42.

and George D. Spache.[8] For secondary teachers, a chapter in one of the Kansas Studies in Education, "Reading Skills and Methods of Teaching Them," contains an extensive identification of reading skills as they relate to the several academic areas, which might be used in developing an informal inventory for each content field.[9]

2. Need for improvement having been established by the analysis of standardized tests and informal inventories — supplemented, perhaps, by opinion questionnaires — an *ad hoc* committee should be selected. Appointed or elected, the committee should be comprised of one representative from each secondary-school content field, a reading specialist, and one secondary school administrator. The committee's assigned task will be to define, in behavioral terms, the reading skills, abilities, knowledge, and appreciation that are desirable for all pupils who receive a high-school diploma to possess. Assistance in defining objectives in behavioral terms may be obtained from works by William H. Burton[10] or Ralph W. Tyler.[11]

3. A school-wide reading improve-

ment committee should then be activated. Regardless of method of selection, its membership should be representative of each grade level in the elementary school, each content field in the secondary school, each of the special services, and the administrative staff. Chaired by a reading specialist or consultant, the committee should be charged with establishing a set of terminal objectives for the program in developmental reading. These objectives, stated in behavioral terms, are to be based on a consensus of objectives recommended by (1) the *ad hoc* committee, (2) authors and publishers of basal series in developmental reading, (3) the writings of specialists, and (4) members of the school-wide reading improvement committee. A random sampling of relevant suggestions from pupils, parents, and leaders of the community may also be enlightening and helpful.

4. At this stage, refinement and definition of terminal objectives — for the kindergarten through twelfth-grade developmental reading program — become the responsibility of building principals. Each building will function as a separate entity and will establish, also in behavioral terms, subobjectives for each terminal objective. The subobjectives should then be placed in a vertical sequence in terms of each grade or reading level and articulated horizontally in terms of content fields.

The school-wide reading improvement committee should be responsible for providing each building with requested materials, consultant services, in-service orientation or training, and the like.

[7] Smith, *Graded Selections for Informal Reading Diagnosis* (New York: New York University Press, 1959 [Grades 1–3]; 1963 [Grades 4–6]).

[8] Spache, *Reading in the Elementary School* (Boston: Allyn & Bacon, 1964), pp. 242–59.

[9] "Reading Skills and Methods of Teaching Them," in *Reading in the Secondary Schools*, edited by M. Jerry Weiss ("Kansas Studies in Education"; New York: Odyssey Press Inc., 1961), pp. 237–68.

[10] Burton, *Guidance of Learning Activities* (New York: Appleton-Century-Crofts, 1952), pp. 414–58.

[11] Tyler, *op. cit.*, pp. 28–40.

5. Progress reports should be presented by principals at intervals prescribed by the school-wide committee. These reports will provide an opportunity for co-ordination and articulation of objectives among elementary, junior-high, and senior-high buildings.

6. The terminal objectives — for example, ability to grasp the main ideas and all major supporting ideas in twelfth-grade history materials — each with its hierarchy of articulated and ordered subobjectives, should then be presented to consulting authorities for acceptance.

7. As the objectives are accepted, they will become mandatory cornerstones upon which the entire developmental reading program will be built.

As a final suggestion, the establishment of need for improvement in reading may advantageously be assigned to the school-wide reading improvement committee suggested in No. 3. This arrangement may, in the long run, conserve time and effort.

MATERIALS

Several materials other than those heretofore mentioned may prove helpful. *Organizing Schools for Effective Education*, by Daniel E. Griffith and others, provides insights for administrators.[12] *Fundamentals of Curriculum Development* contains an excellent discussion of action-research as a technique for curriculum development; it also suggests a method for inducing and controlling curriculum change.[13] A valuable resource for help in organizing a staff for group problem-solving is Franklyn S. Haiman's *Group Leadership and Democratic Action*.[14] The twenty-eighth yearbook of the American Association of School Administrators, *Public Relations for America's Schools*, contains a discussion of media and techniques useful in curriculum change.[15] Basic competencies in content and skill fields are identified in *Measurement and Evaluation in the Modern School*.[16] Finally, *Reading in the Secondary Schools* contains extensive, and inclusive, bibliographies for college as well as secondary-school levels.[17]

[12] Danville, Ill.: Interstate Printers and Publishers, 1962.

[13] B. Othanel Smith, William O. Stanley, and J. Harlan Shores, *Fundamentals of Curriculum Development* (New York: World Book Co., 1957), pp. 445–49, 499–526.

[14] Haiman, *Group Leadership and Democratic Action* (Boston: Houghton Mifflin, 1951).

[15] Washington, D. C.: National Education Association, 1950.

[16] J. Raymond Gerberich, Harry A. Greene, and Albert N. Jorgenson, *Measurement and Evaluation in the Modern School* (New York: David McKay, 1962), pp. 347–590.

[17] *Reading in the Secondary Schools*, edited by M. Jerry Weiss (New York: Odyssey Press, Inc., 1961).

HELPING TEACHERS MEET THE OBJECTIVES OF A READING PROGRAM

MARGARETHE F. LIVESAY

TEACHER PREPARATION in the field of reading instruction is, in most cases, far from adequate.[1] Elementary teachers on the job, sincerely desirous of teaching well, ask many questions that reveal a need for help. Why are some students unable to read? How can their problems be diagnosed? How can the necessary help be provided? Secondary teachers ask the same questions and more; they have difficulty accepting the existence of under-achievement in reading and frequently are little prepared to know what to do about it. At the same time, they have the responsibility to continue their regular instructional program for the average and superior achievers.

The need for in-service education of staff and leadership in improving instruction is becoming more and more obvious. A consultant with time to devote to meeting teacher needs seems an imperative adjunct to the organization of any school system. The devices used for in-service training are many, and in each of them, the consultant provides the leadership and knowledge that special training and experience have made possible.

At the beginning of the school year it is well to plan time for teachers to

become oriented to the needs of the students they will teach. Everyone realizes that new teachers need orientation; but even experienced teachers need to be made aware of the problems particular students will meet as they approach the reading tasks in a particular grade or subject. This is the time to review objectives, go over cumulative records, study and interpret test results, and decide what further testing, if any, is needed. The consultant can help teachers plan for both group and individual instruction, and can make suggestions about the instructional aids and materials to use.

OBSERVATION OF OTHER TEACHERS

One well-established technique for meeting individual needs at the primary level is classroom grouping. The problem that arises here is that of providing for individual differences in growth rate as well as for initial differences in ability. Groups must be kept flexible so that students can move from one to another as change is evident. The skill required to keep groups flexible does not come easily to all teachers. It may be helpful to provide time for those having trouble to observe others who are particularly skillful in grouping. When they have observed other teachers in action, they will begin to realize the advantages of

[1] See, for example, Mary C. Austin *et al.*, *The Torch Lighters: Tomorrow's Teachers of Reading* (Cambridge, Mass.: Harvard University Press, 1961).

grouping across grade and classroom boundaries in order to teach specific skills. Conferences following these periods of observation not only provide for the answers to questions but lead to joint planning. A team approach may develop, and all teachers will become stronger as a result.

When textbooks in content areas are introduced in the middle grades, other problems arise. The amount of time that can be spent on reading instruction is reduced by the pressures to teach many other things. Teachers need to be informed that they can still, in effect, teach reading all day long with books and materials designed to present subject matter. Reading is, after all, very important, since success in high school, as well as in college and vocational training, depends to a great extent on the ability of students to read textbooks and related content-area materials.

DEMONSTRATION LESSONS

The time to teach reading skills is when this type of book is first presented in the middle grades. To realize the efficiency of a technique such as SQ3R, for example, the student needs to use it repeatedly until the procedure becomes a habit.[2] Once it has been introduced to students, teachers must continue to demonstrate its effectiveness for the completion of assignments.

Teachers need help in learning different kinds of questions to ask. Students need to establish the habit of

2 Francis P. Robinson, *Effective Study* (rev. ed.; New York: Harper & Bros., 1961), chapter ii.

reading inquisitively. Teachers who ask only factual questions are not developing their students' abilities to the full. Teachers must set an example with good questioning. This may be done by guiding students through an adequate study plan such as SQ3R. It may also be done by helping students realize that once they have determined the main idea of a paragraph or an article they can go on to ask more significant questions such as "Why?" and "How?"

Secondary teachers are frequently helped by a demonstration of the results that can be obtained by the introduction of vocabulary and new concepts at the beginning of a lesson. The presentation of words in context by using sentences from the text and the appropriate word-attack skills helps students not only learn the new words but also reinforce their knowledge of word-attack skills.

The use of textual material in teaching reading skills is a good basis for demonstration lessons. The consultant or demonstrating teacher will want to use material from the unit being studied by the class. Time should be taken beforehand to acquaint the demonstrator with the students, and afterward, for conferences between the demonstrator and classroom teacher to allow for questions and explanation of technique.

CONSULTANT VISITATION

There is much value in seeing ourselves as others see us. This is the idea behind classroom visitation by a consultant. Too often, however, the teacher develops feelings of insecurity as a result of such visits. We need to do much to dispel the idea that the consultant is there to criticize. The purpose of such visits is to help the teacher, to strengthen instruction by allowing the teacher to see missed opportunities for teaching or reinforcing reading skills. Particularly in the content areas in secondary school teachers are unaware of the extent to which they could effectively teach reading. The consultant sees opportunities in the most common classroom occurrences for skill development. It may be a student's excitement in telling of an experience that the consultant can use to encourage further research and the practice of reference skills. It may be a student's stumbling over the pronunciation of a word that provides an opportunity to demonstrate syllabication and the sounding-attack skill. It may be the regular classroom teacher's giving of an assignment without setting a purpose or guiding the students in the proper approach to reading the material.

Secondary teachers, although sincerely concerned about the wide range of differences in students' reading abilities in their classrooms, often fail to use the opportunities for overcoming these differences to be found in grouping, multilevel texts, and differentiated assignments. One reason is the complexity of planning. Another is their lack of experience.

Teachers spend many hours selecting textbooks only to find that a portion of each class cannot read them. Three solutions to the problem are possible: (1) Have more than one text available. (2) Use no text at all

but provide a reference list for reading to solve stated problems. (3) Use one text but differentiate assignments according to the reading abilities of the pupils. Those at the lowest level of ability can read for factual information, to find specific answers to specific questions, some perhaps in illustrations rather than in the printed word. Others with higher ability can read to relate details to main ideas, to understand the sequence of events, to draw conclusions. Those on the highest level can read to relate what is being read to previous reading or, through additional research, to relate it to the problem or topic at hand.

There is a real need to break down the widely accepted notion that to have equal education all must do the same thing, read the same text, respond to the same questions. This is so well established that students themselves may at first complain if they have to do more than some of their classmates. Gifted students are prone to want to do no more than the average or the minimum required so as not to risk being different. However, if a challenging teacher indicates that he expects each to contribute to the whole lesson by doing what he can do best, and if he employs a little creativity and much flexibility in making assignments, students soon accept the procedure as a natural one. Once busy at constructive pursuits, they seldom complain about differences they know exist.

STAFF MEETINGS

Grade or department meetings offer time-saving means for the development of better instructional methods. In such meetings, the reading skills needed in the various subject areas can be identified and plans made for teaching them within the framework of the planned sequence of topics.

Teachers need to exchange information on the needs of students — their strengths and weaknesses in skills in each area. A poor reader is not only likely to have difficulty with reading his text but also to suffer handicaps in written expression. He may have learned to compensate for these inadequacies through a greater development of listening skills, and he may be able to express his ideas quite well verbally. By using each student's skill strengths, their learning can be made more efficient.

There needs, then, to be effective staff communication, both about the skills needed in general in the subject areas and about the skills needed by individual students. Interdepartmental planning sessions several times a year can provide opportunities for such communication. The correlation of activities from one class to another can also make teaching more effective and can be accomplished with cooperative planning. For example, if outlining skills are needed in history, the English teacher could simultaneously teach ways to identify main ideas and to relate details within a paragraph. It is the isolation of skills, not the disturbance of a predetermined sequence in the curriculum, that makes teaching ineffective.

WORKSHOPS

Faculty workshops can be a most effective way of providing inservice training. They are most meaningful when planned to integrate theory with practice and most successful when teachers themselves have had a part in planning them. Several sessions after school may provide this kind of training, although teachers often feel their energy exhausted at the end of a teaching day. Schools are beginning to grant released time for in-service training or to reimburse teachers for Saturday sessions. If after-school sessions are held, they should be limited in number and length, for too many over too long a period will tend to exhaust interest in the topic under discussion.

The workshop may be either the lecture-discussion type or the work type during which materials and actual lessons are planned. For both types, it is well to gather professional books and materials into a centrally located place to facilitate their use. Teachers are eager to find time for professional reading and frequently have difficulty locating good professional resources. Allowing time for reading followed by discussion and sharing is a profitable workshop technique. It is important that the working groups be small enough for the free flow of ideas and that teachers from several subject areas be included in each group. In this way, an awareness that problems are arising in several areas for the same students can be reached and measures taken to help them.

The continuing workshop has proven successful. In this type of workshop a problem is posed and studied in a general way in one or two sessions.

Teachers then use their own classrooms for observation and work with the problem with their own students, returning for workshop sessions several times during the school year. Classroom research is stimulated in this way, and the sharing of results encourages those who feel less competent in teaching certain skills to try methods other teachers are using.

CONCLUDING REMARKS

It should be apparent that, whether the device for improving instruction in reading is a preschool orientation program, in-service education such as demonstration lessons, classroom visitations, staff meetings, and workshops, or individual teacher conferences, the role of the consultant is an important one — in leadership, in sharing know-how, in doing those things for which teachers find it difficult to find time. Left to their own resources, most teachers will try to do a better job. But if reading is as important to the educational process as we say it is, and if the teaching of reading skills is everyone's responsibility, then all teachers ought to be given the help of a full-time consultant who will make it possible for them to do not only a better job but an excellent one. In this way all our objectives will be met.

AN ALL-SCHOOL EFFORT TO IMPROVE INSTRUCTION IN CRITICAL AND CREATIVE READING

RUTH ROBBINS

*

As the world changes so must reading instruction change."[1] During the colonial period of our country, reading instruction was characterized by the memorization of religious passages; our forefathers wanted to instil moral and spiritual values in their youngsters. The revolutionary years saw children deep in the rules of elocution in an effort to stamp out regional dialects. The young country then moved to an emphasis on literature in order to compete with culturally superior Europe.[2] And so the changing purposes for reading instruction have reflected the changing needs of our country right up to the present space age.

Reading instruction in the space age faces real challenges. The best of all previous periods still needs to be taught; and in addition, there are demands on reading from a pluralistic society that is trying to maintain a position of world leadership. John Q. Public must be able to read beyond the level of literal understanding and interpretation; he must be a critical

[1] Nila Banton Smith, *Reading Instruction for Today's Children* (Englewood Cliffs, N.J.: Prentice Hall, 1963), p. 10.

[2] *Ibid.*, pp. 3–7.

and creative reader. He must be selective and flexible as the world parades its activities before him in the mass communication media.

When the purpose of learning to read was to be able to memorize phrases or selections of literature, the reading act was limited to the mechanical calling of words. As more materials became available and students were expected to understand what they read, the skills of literal understanding and interpretation were added.

Today there is still entirely too much instruction limited to literal understanding, not only in reading classes, but in many content areas as well. A. Sterl Artley has stated that unless critical reading is taught we can expect to make little progress toward the resolution of our national and international problems.[3] And yet, in a survey of reading practices in our country's public schools, as Mary C. Austin and Coleman Morrison have reported, "It was rare indeed that members of the study staff heard teachers trying to help children . . . develop critical reading skills."[4]

Why is there this discrepancy between what we know should be done and what we actually do?

Perhaps, first of all, it is because reading has only recently "come of age." The concepts of critical and creative reading put in brief first appearances some twenty years ago. In the past ten years interest and research

[3] Artley, "Critical Reading in the Content Areas," *Elementary English*, XXXXI (February, 1959), 122.

[4] Austin and Morrison, *The First R* (New York: MacMillan Co., 1963), p. 40.

have increased; but interest, research, and actual teaching have not kept pace with each other. Interest and need are very high at present, but research and teaching are still dragging far behind.

Thus, teachers are not prepared to teach critical and creative reading. Basal readers frequently do not present material that lends itself to critical evaluation and creative activity. Schools are still saddled with a curriculum that leaves no time for thinking — a curriculum that is content-oriented but does not recognize the advantages in a natural integration of many subject areas.

Second, a rapidly changing society hesitates to cut the secure traditional ties to old educational institutions. And a dearth of evaluation instruments makes it difficult to judge the new techniques and materials for teaching the higher level skills.

INHIBITING FACTORS

There are at least six factors which inhibit the teaching of critical and creative reading in our schools. The first, and perhaps one of the most important, is the lack of understanding and consensus as to what critical reading and creative reading actually are. So that we can meet on some common ground of understanding, the writer would like to propose two definitions: *Critical reading* is judging the truthfulness, significance, or worth of written material on the basis of criteria developed through experience. *Creative reading* is generating new ideas and attitudes from the interaction of the experience of the reader and that of the author.

Teachers themselves represent the second inhibiting factor. Most teachers have been trained in schools that did not explore the teaching of critical or creative reading. Many teachers do not know how to teach these dimensions of the reading act because they don't know how to read critically or creatively themselves. To help these teachers involves, at the least, in-service education. However, it is not enough to stand in front of the faculty at 4:00 P.M. and complacently state that they must teach critical and creative reading. The teachers must be actually taught how to read critically and creatively before they can teach their students. Teachers should be encouraged to do for themselves what they recommend parents do for their children. The ability to read critically and creatively depends to a great extent on experience and not on still another course in the teaching of reading. It would be more profitable and certainly more fun to tear apart a recent best-seller than to spend another faculty meeting listening to the principal practice his oral reading skills.

And this brings us to a third inhibiting factor, the administrator. How can a teacher have the time to think, the desire to read, or the energy to teach if the better part of the day is spent on such trivialities as collecting money, filling out forms, bandaging the recess casualties, redoing the register, or patrolling the lunch room? It is the obligation of any administrator to minimize the clerical work and baby-sitting duties of his faculty. Any after-school meetings should be called only when absolutely necessary to impart information that could be given in no other way. Since teaching the higher skills of the reading process is much more difficult and demanding than teaching the basic skills, teachers must be given the time to prepare and the time to teach. Their energy should not be sapped by doing physically exhausting non-teaching activities.

A fourth factor inhibiting the teaching of critical and creative reading can be the community. The school is a social institution and reflects the needs and aspirations of the community it serves. There are many communities in our country that are not aware of the rapid changes taking place in education today. These communities want the school to feed their young a prepackaged body of content. Controversial issues — which are the breeding ground for critical and creative reading — are thus frequently taboo. Supervisors and administrators have the obligation of educating the community to the need and importance of freedom in book selection, freedom in reading habits, and freedom in thinking. Our children will learn how to handle controversial issues by working with them and learning to spot their weak and strong points. Incidentally, we rarely tap our community resources as much as we should. One way of gaining community understanding and support of needed curriculum changes is to have community leaders on curriculum writing projects.

A fifth inhibiting factor is the written and unwritten curriculum guides.

If we are going to have the time and the know-how to teach critical and creative reading, some aspects of current curriculums are going to need major overhauling. Content-oriented curriculums are committed to the memorization and regurgitation of a traditional body of material that will guarantee the transference of our culture to the next generation. This kind of curriculum seems to be dedicated to the process of dissecting a naturally integrated discipline. The area of language arts is a case in point.

Sputnik shook up many science curriculums. People were awed at the rapid rate of increase of knowledge in the areas of science, and were generally agreed that no school child could be expected to master the content of science. He must first be taught basic concepts and not specialize until grade ten or so.

The area of social studies is not so fortunate. Textbook publishers are meeting the demands for changing curriculums by offering "fused," "integrated," and "co-ordinated" social studies texts. A close look at some of these reveals that they are geographically or historically oriented. Many of those who influence curriculum development are not really convinced that there is a knowledge explosion in social studies as well as in science. There is a long, time-honored tradition in the scope and sequence of social studies. It will still be many years before all of the upper intermediate teachers will be willing to forego that good old sterile approach involving place geography and the memorization of names, dates, and

places. And yet where is critical reading needed more than in the area of social studies? Our survival as a democracy may well depend upon the ability of our citizens to critically analyze the social world in which they live.

Reading specialists have a special responsibility in all efforts to revise curriculums. Without reading skills, the teaching of any major content area cannot be successful. Whenever a curriculum in a content area is being rewritten, the reading specialist should help to insure the integration of the pertinent reading skills. Reading consultants or supervisors, or in their absence, administrators, must facilitate implementation of the teaching of reading skills in content areas. It is in these special disciplines that help is particularly needed and where it bears final fruit.

Finally, the sixth inhibiting factor is weakness in, and often lack of, evaluation instruments. Teachers will begin to teach critical and creative reading seriously when satisfactory measurement devices are available. And such devices are most difficult to construct, especially since our concepts of critical and creative reading are so hazy and, indeed, since the nature of the processes themselves have not been clearly defined. Certainly, teachers cannot devise instruments to evaluate progress, even informally, in areas they don't understand. Without means of evaluation, however, these dimensions of the reading process will continue to be neglected. Since critical and creative reading are elusive and intangible forces, we must, at this point, assist teachers to measure underlying skills that appear to be essential to them while we wait impatiently for more satisfactory evaluation tools and more successful teaching procedures.

CONCLUDING STATEMENT

This paper has identified six inhibiting factors in the teaching of critical and creative reading, but no doubt there are six times six more. If administrators, consultants, and supervisors are to have school programs that integrate the teaching of these skills in all areas, they must be aware of the reasons why the skills have been neglected. From this base, movement toward concrete implementation may be possible.

There are specific activities we can now engage in. We can set up in-service meetings to bring the faculty up to date on what we do know about methods and materials for teaching and evaluating creative and critical reading. We can provide the time for teaching these dimensions of the reading process by revising curriculum guides and by seeing to it that the classroom teacher is a teacher and not a combined baby-sitter and office clerk. We can provide multiple texts and other materials and tap our community resources.

There is no time to sit back and consider the situation. This is an area where educational practice must for once keep pace with the needs of society. There are too many demanding forces at play in our society to permit this area to lay fallow for any period of time.

* * *

AN IN-SERVICE PROGRAM DIRECTED TOWARD HELPING TEACHERS MOTIVATE RELUCTANT READERS

EDITH JANES

*

THE Gary Reading Council of the International Reading Association sponsored study groups to provide in-service education in reading. Members of the council were asked to suggest topics they would like to explore. The list of topics was circulated so that teachers who wished to participate could select a study group that interested them. Each group met once a month for five months. The culminating activity was a summary of the work of each group presented by its chairman at the annual spring dinner of the Gary Reading Council.

PLANS

The value of these study groups was reflected in classrooms during the year and, in many instances, over an extended period of time. One of the especially successful groups was made up of twenty teachers from grades one through ten who decided to become familiar with books that might be used to change student attitudes and behavior. At the first meeting the leader reported on an interesting new book and told how she had used it successfully to help a boy solve a problem he was experiencing. Then the group planned together the programs for the next four meetings. The second meeting was to be a panel discussion of difficulties encountered in motivating students to read and ways of overcoming them. And the three following meetings were to be taken up with individual reports by committee members on books they had used successfully to help a specific child relieve tensions or overcome problems and fears. The group set the following tasks for themselves:

1. Each teacher would select students from his classes who had serious problems. He would search for appropriate books, find a way of getting the students to read them, and report the results to the group.

2. Each teacher would read some of the resource books listed on the bibliography distributed by the leader and would share any additional materials he found.

3. The group would prepare a list of books that might be used to help students overcome or become reconciled to their own problems.

4. Each teacher would try to read twenty books with which he was not familiar so that this list of books would be accurately classified and be useful to teachers.

ACTIVITIES

At the second meeting, as planned, a panel discussed problems of motivating reluctant readers and arrived at the following conclusions:

1. Parents must be informed of the necessity for encouraging their children to read and must be informed of ways they can help.

2. The school day is becoming shorter. It is becoming increasingly difficult for the classroom teacher to find time to read aloud to students or for students to do recreational reading in the classroom.

3. Many teachers are not familiar with enough books to be able to make recommendations that are appropriate in subject matter, interest level, and reading level.

4. Efforts must be directed toward helping poor readers improve in comprehension so they can enjoy what they read. They need to be guided to compelling stories that will hold their interest, since it is likely that they have never read an entire book.

5. The supply of interesting materials at all reading levels is increasingly abundant. With school libraries, public libraries, extension services, delivery services, and bookmobiles, a student's reading is limited only by his own initiative or by his teacher's failure to help him find the right books.

The three meetings that followed were intensely interesting for everyone because the entire group was eager to share its experiences in motivating reading. One could fill a book with the interesting case histories of the students that were helped by reading a book or several books. The teachers felt much more secure in recommending books after this intensive project and were inspired to continue the drive to motivate reluctant readers. Some of the individual projects are described below.

One ninth-grade English teacher was determined to make a special effort to motivate her two lowest classes to read more books. The forty-four students in these two classes had records of delinquency, absenteeism, and non-achievement. Many had repeated one or two grades and were potential dropouts. Most of them had never read an entire book. After conferring with the principal and the reading teacher, the teacher initiated the following program.

The *Gates Reading Survey* (Bureau of Publications, Teachers College, Columbia University, 1960) was administered just prior to the beginning of the second semester. The test scores ranged in grade equivalents from 3.1 to 10.5, with about one-fourth of the pupils scoring from third to fifth grade, one-half scoring in fifth or sixth grade, and one-fourth scoring from seventh to tenth grade. Reading instruction was planned to help students improve their reading skills, since it was not expected that they would enjoy reading until they acquired sufficient facility.

The teacher was able to order an adequate supply of interesting paperback books ranging in reading levels from very easy to rather difficult. Rapid reading techniques were demonstrated to the class, and efforts were made to help each student improve his rate. The teacher felt that if the students could see their progress from day to day they would be inspired to greater efforts. This proved effective. Students were given their first speed test at their current reading rates, which ranged from 78 to 384 words per minute. Each day, as their rates increased gradually, they became more interested in improving them.

Students were encouraged to check out paperback books, and it was soon apparent that these books had great appeal. Parents were informed of the project and were asked to co-operate by providing a quiet time and study space for students to read each evening. Six of the students read twenty books at home, and only two did not finish a book at home. About one-third read less than five books, one-third read from five to nine books, and one-third read from ten to twenty books.

In similar projects at other schools in grades six through twelve, a rate improvement campaign also appeared to be a fine motivating device. Although the teacher knows that the over-all goals are to improve reading skills, to develop an interest in reading, and to get reluctant readers to learn the joy of finishing a good book, the focus on rate improvement provides daily opportunities for students to see small gains and to practice reading with interest and concentration.

A librarian and reading teacher started a project with five sixth-grade teachers in a school to develop work-study skills. It was decided that Mexico would be the subject for study. The librarian and the reading teacher took the lead in developing co-operatively with the classroom teachers the lessons and study guides to be used by the teachers and the work sheets to be used by the students. The lesson included library skills, reference skills, and outside reading experiences, as well as textbook assignments. Scores of the *SRA Work-Study Skills Tests* (Science Research Associates, Inc., 1964), given before and after the project, showed that the students did improve their study skills. It was also felt that the entire participating staff profited from this experience.

This same librarian had a list of the reading levels of all students with which she came in contact. When a teacher asked for a booklist on a certain subject for her class, the librarian prepared a list to fit the needs of that class. A pamphlet, *A Search for Values*, was prepared for a slow eighth-grade class. It contained some pertinent information for students, an annotated list of books, and a suggested form for reporting the values emphasized in each book.

One seventh-grade social studies teacher who had a fair knowledge of materials made a concentrated effort to get every student to read more. She selected books that would be appropriate for each class and used various methods of getting students to ask for them. Descriptions of some of these techniques follow:

1. She would display the book, relate it to the topic of the day, and describe an incident or two in the book.
2. She would read an excerpt from the book, stopping at an interesting place.
3. She would read the blurb from the book jacket.
4. She would occasionally provide time

for students to report briefly and interestingly on books that could be recommended to other members of the class.
5. She would find time to make recommendations of specific books to reluctant readers.

One teacher became very interested in preparing for a humanities fair, an exhibit of artifacts related to history, art, law, literature, or other activity of mankind. She enlisted the co-operation of her principal and the entire faculty in preparing a very fine experience for students. The faculty decided that the project would continue for one month and culminate in an exhibit at the regular P.T.A. meeting.

The teacher who had started the fair brought to school a collection of artifacts she had accumulated during journeys abroad. She placed them on a mobile table and rolled them to each room in grades three through six. She explained to each class the purpose of the humanities fair, told them about her artifacts, and explained how students could enter similar articles for exhibit. There were to be no prizes for the exhibits, and all children were encouraged to participate. The response was amazing — one hundred and thirty-five children turned in entries.

Each exhibitor selected an interesting artifact from home and wrote about it. Many sources of information, including encyclopedias, textbooks, and periodicals, were consulted. "Former" reluctant readers read avidly to find answers. Parents contributed information about each item. In some instances, letters had to be written to relatives overseas to get the needed facts. Research became vital as it was carried on for a purpose.

At the regular P.T.A. meeting, the children of Greek, Hungarian, and Mexican parentage wore the costumes of their countries. They did extensive research in books and among their relatives in order to write accurate information about their costumes. Each stood or sat beside his description during the exhibit.

One boy discovered that his father had been awarded a medal for his services in World War II. He collected facts from his father and prepared a very fine paper using this data.

This project also provided many contacts between school and home. Teachers went to homes to help bring items to school, and parents made extra trips to school to bring in items and to offer help. There was an interesting side effect; one Mexican mother told her child's reading teacher during a visit to the home, "This is a fine project. For the first time since my daughter started to school, she is not ashamed to be from Mexico."

CONCLUDING STATEMENT

Helping students to move from skills-oriented stories in basal readers to genuine interest in books at each level of development is a worthwhile goal for each teacher. Some students can move into good literature at once. Others will need to be guided through a transitional type of simpler book before enjoying the classics. Teachers need a broad knowledge of books that are available so that they can make appropriate choices for reading aloud to their classes, for instruction, and for solving specific problems.

In-service programs to help teachers motivate reluctant readers may vary from a structured program in which each class follows the same procedures to an inspirational program in which each teacher uses his own ideas and devises his own activities. The structure of the program will depend on its goals. Important facts to remember in any program are the following:

1. The teachers' knowledge of appropriate books and materials usually needs to be extended.

2. Teachers should be helped to understand any new techniques that are to be introduced.

3. The best in-service programs guide teachers in the particular project and stimulate ideas for new projects.

4. The best means of evaluating a program to motivate reluctant readers is to observe whether they are absorbed in books.

EVALUATION OF A TOTAL READING PROGRAM

ELEANOR M. LADD

*

I N ORDER to evaluate a total reading program, one must first identify the goals of the program, both immediate and long-term. Once the goals have been identified, one can measure the achievement of the reading program against these goals.

Examples of immediate goals are the common ones of establishing basic reading skills and increasing and extending recreational reading. A long-term goal is adult enjoyment of reading different types of materials with a variety of skills. We need to avoid thinking that the chief goal of a reading program is to produce students who are able to stay at or above grade level on standardized reading achievement tests every year of their school lives.

Evaluation implies more than looking at test results. It includes analyzing carefully the results of several kinds of testing, comparing these results, and noting discrepancies. It is to be hoped that it will include a scrutiny of all aspects of the life of the child, including personal and social adjustment and physical and mental growth. Test scores take on meaning when compared with these other factors.

Administrators have responsibility for decision-making in many areas that directly affect reading programs. Any total evaluation would include objective answers to the following questions:

1. How competent are my teachers?
2. How good is the reading readiness program?
3. How close to the lives of the children is the curriculum?
4. Is more than one method of unlocking new words being taught?
5. How large are classes?
6. Are good materials adequately supplied?
7. How good is the in-service education program in reading?
8. How much supervisory help in reading is available to teachers?
9. Is the supervisory staff keeping up with research?
10. How adequate are the library facilities?
11. Is reading taught beyond the elementary grades?
12. Are the content-area subjects being taught from the point of view of reading skills?
13. Are the school's graduates reading?
14. How extensive are special services?

For two reasons it makes good sense to support the beginning reading program with everything we have. First, correction and remediation are expensive in terms of money and the mental health of children (and their families); and second, if sufficient help with reading is not forthcoming by the end of the sixth grade, the child has probably lost all chance of academic success.

There are a number of types of evaluation plans available to fill the needs of various kinds of communities. As situations change, a school system may conceivably wish to engage in more than one type. It is the writer's opinion that if the philosophy of a school system includes the belief that basic skills development should be only one part of a balanced reading program, then it is important to be consistent and evaluate all parts of the program. Let us take a brief look at the ways in which each part of the program may be evaluated.

TYPES OF EVALUATION

Evaluating the degree of success in developing skills is a part of the ordinary routine in most school systems. The information revealed by this type of evaluation is of value in planning the entire instructional program. The principal failing in most school systems is that not enough use is made of the results. The relationship of the subtest scores to each other and to the verbal and non-verbal intelligence test scores can reveal information that is very valuable for planning, as long as the subtests are reliable. As the years go by and scores accumulate, a great deal is revealed about each individual. If these tests are group tests, however, they are more valuable, on the whole, for providing an overview of a program, so that it may be compared with previous years

and with programs throughout the nation, than for evaluating specific individual performances. The choice of appropriate measuring instruments, the timing of the testing during the school year, the training of the teachers, the statistical procedures to be used in interpreting the data, and the planning to implement the information revealed by the testing all involve important decisions and require the co-operative efforts of everyone involved.

More and more classroom teachers are not scoring standardized tests themselves and are therefore having to wait several weeks or a month before test results are returned. Unless steps are taken, such as an item analysis, before the tests go to the central processing department, much diagnostic value will be lost.

As is well known, study and reference skills are necessary for success in the content areas. Students must learn to change gears in going from literature to chemistry. These skills are very hard to evaluate, however, since there are so few suitable tests presently on the market and those that are in existence do not provide a sufficient number of items to give much direction to instruction. Locally made tests may suit a teacher's purposes much better than the commercial ones currently available.

An evaluation should also be made of recreational reading to determine whether the skills program is producing people who read. It is vital to know if young people are reading a variety of types of materials, if the kinds of books they need are available, if the atmosphere in the library is inviting, if the students are able to use the card catalogue and reference works, and if everyone in a school has access to the library. A study of recreational reading would not be complete without data also from the public libraries.

At times specific information about the abilities of students may be required; for example, the phonic knowledge of primary children, the study skills of older children, or certain skills of the college bound. To provide information of this type, research studies focus on testing just one aspect of reading. In fact, this past year there were twenty-one separate studies of the various methods of teaching first grade reading in progress at one time. Such special studies help answer explicit queries about improving reading instruction.

Efforts to improve instruction in reading often focus on the primary-grade reading program. It is heartening to feel the impact of the Headstart Program and to see the progress in early-childhood education these past few years. However, the advantages of beginning-reading methods of instruction cannot be definitely ascertained until the children reach grade six or grade seven, since the long-term effects of the methods on more mature reading must also be observed. This is not to imply that initial success is not important. The psychological value alone weights the scales in the direction of any method that gives an initial impetus and that does not adversely affect comprehension.

A discussion of evaluation would not be complete without mentioning the possibility that more diagnostic testing than most group tests provide may sometimes be necessary. In the ordinary course of events, 10 to 25 per cent of the students in a school system will reveal deficiencies on a group test. In order to give adequate help to such children, however, further diagnostic tests are necessary.

Another type of evaluation that may be employed is a survey of the reading program and of pupil progress conducted by a professional team. Such a survey has the value of being objective and, thus of being more acceptable to the critics of the school. The administrator will often find it possible to make more changes and to take more concrete action than usual with the results of a survey by a professional team to lend support.

IMMEDIATE ITEM ANALYSIS

There are two techniques that can help teachers get more information from standardized tests. One is a classroom item analysis done immediately upon completion of achievement tests, and the other is "the reading reinforced technique," a method of getting three scores denoting different skills from the same test.

The first requires an analysis of each item and the drawing up of a form on which items are placed in different columns denoting separate categories of skills. For instance, items 3, 7, 12, 14, 18, and 20 might test understandings about phonics. These items would all be placed in column one, the phonics column, so that a child can mark each one as the teacher reads the correct answer. In this manner, the child and teacher can ascertain the specific "rights and wrongs" for items pertaining to a particular reading skill.

Mr. Roe Martin, of Polk County, Florida, has had considerable success in distributing achievement tests immediately after administering them to another class for item analysis. Using the form made for a particular test, classes from grade three through grade twelve have provided this information for several years. The teacher can determine immediately by looking at each column whether a student has a pattern of deficiency in a particular area. The achievement tests are then sent to the central processing department for scoring. Until these results are known, the teacher has the interim information provided by the item analysis with which to plan his program of instruction.

The second technique, labeled by Dr. Walter N. Durost "the reading reinforced technique," is used immediately at the conclusion of any standard testing period. Pupils who have not finished are allowed to proceed at their own pace as long as they can, using a red (or any other color) pencil. This technique yields an untimed score, which will disclose whether speed was a factor.

For children in classroom situations from grades two through four, and for all corrective or remedial students, the reinforced technique may be used to obtain a listening score that can be compared with reading achievement. The teacher reads aloud an item and the possible answers while the student reads silently. The teacher then waits for the pupils to mark their answers before proceeding to the next item. The reason for not suggesting the reinforced technique for classroom groups above grade four is that by that grade most children can read faster silently than the teacher can read orally. The voice gets in their way, and the results are less useful.

CONCLUDING STATEMENT

In summation, the process of evaluation can help us keep track of the progress of individuals and of the school system as a whole. Any information that is elicited can be used in planning in-service education programs and in making curricular changes. The results of evaluative studies keep the community appraised of the progress of its schools and give objective evidence that may be used for many purposes.

HELPING TEACHERS MEET THE NEEDS OF UNDERACHIEVERS IN READING

LAWRENCE G. MOBURG

∗

UNDERACHIEVEMENT is a term of fairly recent vintage. Yet teachers and administrators have long been concerned with the problem of underachievement, and the literature of the past forty years has dealt extensively with remedial reading programs and techniques for teaching the retarded reader. "The Underachiever in Reading" was selected as the central theme of the 1962 Reading Conference; the reader is referred to the proceedings of that conference for an exhaustive discussion of the problem.

Five distinct types of underachieving readers have been described by Helen M. Robinson (1) The *slow learner* is a pupil whose intelligence quotient ranges from 70 to 90 and whose rate of learning is slower than average in all school subjects; the slow learner is an underachiever when his reading achievement lags behind his general rate of learning and behind his estimated capacity to read. (2) The *retarded reader* is a pupil whose intelligence quotient falls within the average range (from 90 to 110) but whose achievement in reading is substantially below the normal range for students of his age and grade. (3) The *bright underachiever* has an intelligence quotient above 110; he may be reading at or above the norm for his age or grade but substantially below his capacity. (4) The *reluctant reader* is a pupil whose reading achievement scores are in harmony with his capacity to read but who does not read voluntarily for his personal pleasure or satisfaction. (5) The *culturally or socially deprived pupil* is the product of an environment which has not supplied him with the cultural and language experiences so vital to success in school and in life.[1]

In general, then, the underachiever in reading is a pupil whose reading achievement is substantially lower than his estimated capacity to read. The purpose of this paper is to suggest methods by which reading consultants, supervisors, and administrators may help teachers provide for such students within the classroom. Three areas will be considered here: identification, diagnosis, and instruction.

IDENTIFICATION OF THE UNDERACHIEVER

The process of identification involves the use of formal and informal means of screening each student in a

[1] Helen M. Robinson, "Characteristics of the Underachiever," in *The Underachiever in Reading*, edited by H. Alan Robinson ("Supplementary Educational Monographs," No. 92; Chicago: University of Chicago Press, 1962), pp. 10–14.

classroom to determine the presence of a reading difficulty. Teachers should understand that identification must precede diagnosis; identification is a process by which students are selected for diagnosis and correction of reading difficulties.

Teachers must be acquainted with the problems involved in identification. An essential procedure in identification is the comparison of a student's capacity to read, as indicated by an intelligence test, with his actual reading achievement, as indicated by a reading survey or achievement test. It is not completely satisfactory to compare the scores of these tests since group intelligence tests require reading, which penalizes the poor reader, and both kinds of tests have often not been standardized on comparable populations. Therefore, any comparison of capacity and achievement must be looked upon only as a rough indicator. Other means of identification must also be used.

Teachers must be provided with a definite procedure to follow in the identification of underachievers. It is the responsibility of the consultant to help teachers develop a variety of specific techniques and materials to use with their students. He might do this by conducting a series of in-service sessions — workshops, grade-level or subject-level meetings, classroom demonstrations, and informal conferences.

The first step in any identification procedure is to decide upon a method of comparing capacity and achievement. A study by Carol K. Winkley compared seven methods of identi-fying underachieving readers.[2] She found that two of the methods — the Bond and Tinker Formula[3] and the *Expected Achievement Grade Placement Tables*[4] — identified the highest percentage of the total number of underachievers. Both of these methods are particularly well suited for classroom use since they consist of tables that may be compiled in advance.

A second step in identification should be an investigation of the student's past and present academic progress, particularly in the area of arithmetic. Average to good performance in a subject that does not depend heavily upon reading ability is a further indicator of a poor reader's potential. If the student's grades in other content areas seem to be higher than his poor reading ability would lead one to expect, there is a possibility that he has developed good listening skills to compensate for his poor reading skills. The results of a listening test, such as the *Durrell-Sullivan Reading Capacity Test* (Harcourt, Brace & World, Inc., 1945), the *Sequential Tests of Educational Progress: Listening* (Cooperative Test Di-

[2] Winkley, "Building Staff Competence in Identifying Underachievers," in *The Underachiever in Reading*, edited by H. Alan Robinson ("Supplementary Educational Monographs," No. 92; Chicago: University of Chicago Press, 1962), pp. 155–62.

[3] Guy L. Bond and Miles A. Tinker, *Reading Difficulties: Their Diagnosis and Correction* (New York: Appleton-Century-Crofts, Inc., 1957), pp. 76–81.

[4] Los Angeles City School Districts, *Expected Achievement Grade Placement Tables, for Ages Six Years to Sixteen Years Six Months* (rev. ed.; Los Angeles, Calif.: Evaluation and Research Section, Los Angeles City School Districts, 1955).

vision, Educational Testing Service, 1957), or the *Diagnostic Reading Tests: Listening Comprehension* (Committee on Diagnostic Reading Tests, Inc., 1963), would thus provide still another estimation of the pupil's capacity to read.

Another means of identifying the underachiever consists of a careful examination of each student's cumulative folder. Teachers should be particularly attentive to any information dealing with the student's social, physical, and emotional history. Such varied factors as immaturity in the first grade, a culturally deprived or sterile home environment, speech or hearing handicaps, and emotional problems, may help to confirm the teacher's identification of the student as an underachiever.

A fourth method of identification is informal observation by the teacher. Subjective judgments of trained, experienced teachers may be invaluable additions to identification, particularly in the case of the reluctant reader. Informal means may take the form of daily classroom observations of a student's reading, individual pupil conferences, informal reading inventories, and directed reading activities.

DIAGNOSIS OF THE UNDERACHIEVER

Once the teacher has identified the underachieving readers in his classroom, he must determine the specific areas of difficulty for each student. Again, it is the duty of the consultant to establish a definite diagnostic procedure which teachers may follow. In-service meetings concerned with class-

room diagnosis should follow those devoted to identification procedures. Workshops, classroom demonstrations, and teacher conferences should continue; in addition, the reading specialist may wish to use a practicum or case-study approach to help teachers become familiar with the methods and materials of diagnosis. In the case-study approach, each teacher works with the records of a student who has already been identified as an underachieving reader. The in-service sessions are devoted to the application of specific diagnostic techniques of the teachers, with the reading consultant acting as instructor and advisor.

The consultant should help teachers develop both formal and informal techniques of diagnosis. A wide variety of commercially prepared tests for groups and individuals are available, and teachers should have access to these tests and be familiar with the uses which may be made of them.

The first phase of diagnosis should be designed to reveal the student's general word-attack ability. As an in-service education leader, the reading consultant must see that every teacher is able to listen to a sample of a pupil's oral reading and determine the presence or absence of problems in word recognition. A standardized measure of oral reading, such as the *Gray Oral Reading Test* (Bobbs-Merrill Company, Inc., 1963), will help the teacher identify word-attack difficulties and will suggest areas for further investigation. If an analysis of the student's oral reading does indicate word-attack problems, more specific information can be attained from such tests as the Dolch *Picture Word Cards* (Garrard Press, 1941) and *Basic Sight Cards* (Garrard Press, 1952), the Wepman *Auditory Discrimination Test* (Language Research Associates, 1958), the Huelsman *Word Discrimination Test* (Miami University Alumni Association, 1958), the *McCullough Word Analysis Test* (Ginn & Company, 1963), and portions of the *Gates-McKillop Reading Diagnostic Tests* (Bureau of Publications, Teachers College, Columbia University, 1962).

Standardized tests may also be used to diagnose reading difficulties in the areas of vocabulary, comprehension, and rate. The reading specialist should help teachers extract diagnostic information from any achievement or survey test the student has already taken, as well as administer and interpret specific diagnostic tools like the following: the O'Rourke *Survey Test of Vocabulary* (Psychological Institute, 1940), the *Michigan Vocabulary Profile Test* (World Book Company, 1949), the *Van Wagenen Analytical Reading Scales* (M. J. Van Wagenen, 1953), and the *Van Wagenen Rate of Comprehension Scale* (M. J. Van Wagenen, 1953).

The use of standardized diagnostic tests must not be the sole means of classroom diagnosis, however. The supervisor or consultant should also introduce teachers to a variety of informal diagnostic techniques: informal reading inventories, teacher-devised tests focused on specific reading skills, student interest and attitude inventories, school and medical records, and student and parental interviews.

INSTRUCTION OF THE UNDERACHIEVER

Although diagnosis must precede instruction, diagnosis must continue throughout the instructional period, too. Formal and informal diagnostic measures should be used in order to keep instruction aimed at specific reading needs. In helping teachers plan instruction, the reading specialist must stress the need for specific, limited objectives. For example, "to recognize known whole words in compound words" is a much more realistic instructional goal than "to improve word-attack skills."

As a result of the identification and diagnostic procedures carried out in the classroom, the teacher may discover that some students are severely retarded readers and should receive daily instruction in special classes conducted by teachers trained in remedial techniques. Other students may be able to benefit from corrective instruction provided by the regular classroom teacher. The reading consultant must point out that teachers are responsible for helping all the underachievers in their classrooms, even though some of them may receive specialized remedial instruction from other teachers. The fact remains that even severely disabled readers will spend most of their time within the regular classroom, and teachers cannot ignore them because of their severe reading problems.

The reading consultant, then, must provide teachers with specific instructional methods that may be used with all underachieving readers within the classroom. An area of instruction that should benefit all students — not just underachievers — is the area of study skills. The consultant may help teachers develop plans for teaching methods to organize study that will meet the needs of students representing a wide range of ability and achievement. The basis for this plan might be Francis P. Robinson's SQ3R method,[5] Ralph C. Preston and Morton Botel's *How to Study*,[6] or some other published materials in this area. Teachers should make extensive use of the textbooks that are currently in use, so that students may have direct experience in applying the study methods they have learned.

The consultant may also help teachers meet the needs of underachievers in other ways. He may provide supplementary books and materials written at a lower level of difficulty than the regular textbooks in the classroom. Through conferences and demonstra-

[5] Robinson, *Effective Study* (rev. ed., New York: Harper & Bros., 1961).

[6] Preston and Botel, *How To Study* (Chicago: Science Research Associates, 1956).

tions, he may help the teacher integrate these supplementary materials into the regular course of study. He may also assist the teacher in the areas of classroom organization and flexible grouping procedures, so that the teacher may set aside a definite portion of time for the instruction of underachieving readers. Where special remedial classes are offered, the consultant must co-ordinate the scheduling of students for these classes and see that the remedial teacher and classroom teacher work in harmony toward common goals.

CONCLUDING STATEMENT

In all phases of his work with underachievers, the teacher must be aware of the value of continuous evaluation. The consultant's job is to help teachers utilize informal and formal means of evaluation so that the identification and diagnostic procedures may be constantly strengthened and the instruction of underachieving readers made steadily more effective.

CHAPTER XVIII

NOTEWORTHY BOOKS PUBLISHED
SINCE THE 1965 READING CONFERENCE

*

FOR ELEMENTARY-SCHOOL PUPILS

SARA INNIS FENWICK

*

PROGRESS IN reading during the last seventy-five years has been accompanied by progress in producing the books children read. The preparation of an annual list of noteworthy books brings into focus several steps in the progress of writing, illustrating, and publishing trade books.

The first development that is quickly apparent is the increase in numbers of books published for children. Last year this total was 2,895 books; in 1891 it was 460. For more than thirty years, critics have been suggesting that perhaps too many books were being published for children, and it is obvious that the great increase in numbers had not been matched by a similar increase in books of outstanding quality. Nevertheless, the years have brought some valuable additions to our bookshelves: more beauty in picture books, new inventiveness in easy-to-read materials for beginning readers, and a wealth of informational books on subjects that are new in the field of children's literature.

Evidence of the increase in both volume and quality of informational books is provided by the variety of interests represented at several grade levels in the following selection of books from last year's publication lists. Today's children are sometimes described as too fact-oriented because the reading of informational as compared with fictional literature has risen dramatically in recent years. A more likely explanation of this change, however, may be found in the greatly increased availability of interesting, attractive informational books on timely subjects written in a straightforward style that represents a considerable advance over the didactic, fictionalized presentation of factual material in the last century and the early decades of the present one. Children's interests have not changed; children have always had an absorbing curiosity in the world about them. It is a happy development that we have found some ways to satisfy these interests in books that at their best are written with clarity and accuracy, are logically organized to provide helps to ordering the knowledge in a field, and stimulate and challenge the reader to further investigation.

In the field of children's fiction

there has been a similar development. The changes have not occurred to any significant degree in the reading interests of children but, rather, in the materials available to them for reading. Studies of the early 1900's list preferences for adventure, fantasy, home life, school, war, romance — depending for priority on sex and age — and these same interests are found in any inventory of preferences by today's readers. The adventure may be taking place in a different scene, but the appeal of the action is the same.

It is both a comfort and a surprise to many adult critics who decry the great increase in attention to informational books that there has been a corresponding growth in the number of retellings of material from the reservoir of traditional literature — the hero tales, myths, folk tales, and fables, many of which were previously almost unknown to American readers. The book list in this volume includes only a few titles from a large number that have enriched our resources in this area of literature.

The list that follows is not in any sense a list of the best books published since the 1965 reading conference; it is a selection of approximately one hundred good books published during the past year. Further guidance in selecting books to satisfy individual interests and needs may be found in the *Children's Catalog*, from H. W. Wilson Company; in the *Elementary School Library Collection*, by Mary V. Gaver, from Bro-dart, Newark, New Jersey; and in current reviews of the *Booklist and Subscription Books Bulletin*, from the American Library Association (Chicago), the *Bulletin of the Center for Children's Books* (University of Chicago), and *Horn Book*, from Horn Book, Boston.

FOR KINDERGARTEN THROUGH PRIMARY GRADES

AIKEN, CONRAD. *Cats and Bats and Things with Wings*. Atheneum, 1965 (poetry for younger children in a handsome picture book).

ALAN, SANDY. *The Plaid Peacock*. Pantheon, 1965 (amazing tale of a peacock chick who grew a plaid tail; a read-aloud book).

ALDIS, DOROTHY. *Dumb Stupid David*. Putnam, 1965 (read-aloud verse tells the tale of adjustment to a new baby brother).

ANNIXTER, PAUL. *The Cat That Clumped*. Holiday, 1966 (a read-aloud story about Herbert, a cat who wanted to make a big, important noise).

BRIGHT, ROBERT. *Georgie and the Magician*. Doubleday, 1966 (another amusing picture book about the friendly little ghost, Georgie).

DUVOISIN, ROGER. *Petunia, I Love You*. Knopf, 1965 (more adventures of popular Petunia, the Goose, in a picture book).

GRIFALCONI, ANN. *City Rhythms*. Bobbs, 1966 (picture book, with special uses among inner-city children).

HOLMAN, FELICE. *Elizabeth and the Marsh Mystery*. Macmillan, 1966 (a story in delightful style of the identification of a mysterious bird; good science and good story).

JOSLIN, SESYLE. *There Is A Bull on My Balcony (Hay un Toro en Mi*

Balcon): *And Other Useful Phrases in Spanish and English for Young Ladies and Gentlemen Going Abroad or Staying at Home*. Harcourt, 1966.

KANE, HENRY B. *Wings, Legs or Fins*. Knopf, 1966 (brief text and good photographs tell how some animals travel).

KEATS, EZRA JACK. *Jennie's Hat*. Harper, 1966. (gay picture story of an old hat newly trimmed by Jennie's friends, the birds).

KUSKIN, KARLA. *Sand and Snow*. Harper, 1965 (verses comparing the joys of summer and winter).

LAFONTAINE, JEAN DE. *The Rich Man and the Shoe-Maker*. Watt, 1966 retelling of a fable, with beautiful illustrations by Brian Wildsmith).

LEODHAS, SORCHE NIC. *Always Room for One More*. Holt, 1965 (folk tale in rhyme; illustrated by Nonny Hogrogian; received the Caldecott Medal).

LIFTON, BETTY JEAN. *The Rice-Cake Rabbit*. Norton, 1966 (retelling of a Japanese folk tale in a picture book).

LINDGREN, ASTRID. *Springtime in Noisy Village*. Viking, 1966 (translation of an attractive picture book from Denmark).

LORD, BEMAN. *The Perfect Pitch*. Walck, 1965 (an easy-to-read baseball story with an element of fantasy).

McGOVERN, ANN. *If You Lived in Colonial Times*. Four Winds, 1966 (a brief, illustrated description of colonial life).

MATTHIESEN, THOMAS. *ABC, An Alphabet Book*. Platt, 1966.

MERRIAM, EVE. *Catch a Little Rhyme*. Atheneum, 1966 (delightful rhymes, with some especially for city children).

——. *The Story of Ben Franklin*. Four Winds, 1965 (a short, simply written biography).

PALMER, CANDIDA. *A Ride on High*. Lippincott, 1966 (inner-city adventures of two boys who lost their pass for the elevated train).

RASKIN, ELLEN. *Nothing Ever Happens on My Block*. Atheneum, 1966 (a picture book of the interesting events taking place on Chester's street).

REY, MARGARET E. *Curious George Goes to the Hospital*. Houghton, 1966 (another adventure of a favorite picture-book character).

ROCKWELL, ANNE. *Sally's Caterpillar*. Parents Press, 1966 (the life cycle of the monarch butterfly in a picture-book format).

SELSAM, MILLICENT. *Benny's Animals: And How He Put Them in Order*. Harper, 1966 (easy-to-read introduction to classification of animals).

——. *How To Be a Nature Detective*. Harper, 1966 (simple ways to discover animal tracks in an easy-to-read book).

SKAAR, GRACE. *Nothing but Cats, and All About Dogs. Two Very Young Stories*. Wm. Scott, 1966 (republication in one volume of two older titles issued separately; minimum text, good concepts of size).

SLOBODKIN, LOUIS. *Yasu and the Strangers*. Macmillan, 1965 (amusing picturebook tale of a Japanese boy's school-bus trip).

TITUS, EVE. *Anatole and the Poodle*.

Whittlesey, 1965 (amusing picture-book story of the adventures of that brave and dashing French mouse Anatole).

TRESSELT, ALVIN R. *Hide and Seek Fog*. Lothrop, 1965 (read-aloud story in simple text and lovely illustrations of a three-day fog at Cape Cod).

VOGEL, ILSE-MARGRET. *Hello Henry*. Parents Magazine, 1965 (read-aloud picture book about two Henrys lost in a supermarket; one is white and one is Negro, but this is incidental to a realistic, simple story).

WABER, BERNARD. *Lyle, Lyle, Crocodile*. Houghton, 1965 (an amusing read-aloud story about an amiable crocodile who rescues her neighbors from their burning house).

ZEMACH, HARVE. *Salt; A Russian Tale*. Follett, 1965 (folk tale retold in picture-book format, with delightful watercolor illustrations).

ZION, EUGENE. *Harry by the Sea*. Harper, 1965 (everyone's favorite picture-book dog has an adventure at the seaside).

ZOLOTOW, CHARLOTTE. *If It Weren't for You*. Harper, 1966 ("I'd be the only child," but there would be some disadvantages, too; kindergarten picture-book story).

FOR MIDDLE ELEMENTARY GRADES

ANDERSON, HANS CHRISTIAN. *The Ugly Duckling*. Scribner, 1965 (a picture-book version; illustrated by Adrienne Adams).

BEHN, HARRY. *Poems and Pictures*. Harcourt, 1966 (poems about the out-of-doors).

BOND, MICHAEL. *Paddington Marches On*. Houghton, 1965 (more amusing adventures of the London Brown family's adopted bear, an animal who invites trouble).

BRINK, CAROL R. *Andy Buckram's Tin Man*. Viking, 1966 (robots built out of Campbell Soup cans share the action of this story with their inventor, twelve-year-old Andy).

BULLA, CLYDE R. *Lincoln's Birthday*. Crowell, 1966 (simply written, useful biography).

BURCHARDT, NELLIE. *Project Cat*. Watts, 1966 (although the housing project did not allow cats, a small group of girls took care of this one).

CARLSON, NATALIE S. *The Empty Schoolhouse*. Harper, 1965 (realistic story of the Louisiana schoolhouse that was integrated and then closed because of adult bigotry).

CAUDILL, REBECCA. *A Certain Small Shepherd*. Holt, 1965 (a Christmas miracle in Appalachia).

CLEARY, BEVERLY. *The Mouse and the Motorcycle*. Morrow, 1965 (a humorous tale of a boy and a mouse combining fantasy and reality).

DAUGHERTY, CHARLES M. *Benjamin Franklin; Scientist-Diplomat*. Macmillan, 1965 (simple biography stressing scientific and practical inventions).

DUBOIS, WM. PENE. *Alligator Case*. Harper, 1965 (humorous tall-tale adventure of a crime in a circus solved by a boy detective and a real alligator).

FLANDERS, MICHAEL. *Creatures Great and Small*. Holt, 1965 (beautifully illustrated book of humorous and sophisticated verses that are about animals).

FLEISCHMAN, SID. *McBroom Tells the*

Truth. Norton, 1966 (tall-tale about an unusually productive farm).

FRIIS, BABBIS. *Kristy's Courage.* Harcourt, 1965 (realistic story of a small girl with a scarred face who is helped to adjust to many problems connected with her handicap).

GAGE, WILSON. *Ghost of Five Owl Farm.* World, 1966 (a well-developed mystery about a haunted house).

GREEN, KATHLEEN. *Philip and the Pooka and Other Irish Fairy Tales.* Lippincott, 1966.

GREEN, ROGER L. *Tales from Shakespeare, Retold.* Atheneum, 1966 (modern retelling of eighteen plays).

——. *Tales of the Muses Told: Ancient Greek Myths.* Walck, 1965.

HAVILAND, VIRGINIA. *Favorite Fairy Tales Told in Italy.* Little, 1965.

HUTCHINS, CARLEEN M. *Moon Moth.* Coward, 1965 (description of the life cycle of the luna moth).

JARRELL, RANDALL. *The Animal Family.* Pantheon, 1965 (gentle humor and beauty in a story of a lonely hunter and a mermaid who together make a home for a bear, a lynx, and a boy; an unusual book for the perceptive reader).

JOSLIN, SESYLE. *Spaghetti for Breakfast (Spaghetti per Prima Colazione): and English for Young Ladies and And Other Useful Phrases in Italian and English for Young Ladies and Gentlemen Going Abroad or Staying Home.* Harcourt, 1965.

LARRICK, NANCY (compiler). *Piper, Pipe that Song Again!* Random, 1965 (anthology of poems for boys and girls in the middle grades).

LEODHAS, SORCHE N. *Ghosts Go Haunt-*

ing. Holt, 1965 (a collection of ghost tales).

McCORD, DAVID. *Take Sky, More Rhymes of the Never Was and Always Is.* Little, 1966.

MANNING-SANDERS, RUTH. *Peter and the Piskies; Cornish Folk and Fairy Tales.* Roy, 1966.

PRICE, CHRISTINE. *The Valiant Chattee-Maker: A Folktale of India.* Warne, 1965.

ROBERTSON, KEITH. *Henry Reed's Baby-Sitting Service.* Viking, 1966 (the amusing adventures of Henry in his summer project to make money).

SAUNDERS, F. W. *Building Brooklyn Bridge.* Little, 1965 (a good description of the planning and building of a large bridge).

SOMMERFELT, AIMÉE. *My Name is Pablo.* Criterion, 1966 (a story of a Mexican peasant boy and his friend, a Norwegian boy).

STOLZ, MARY S. *The Noonday Friends.* Harper, 1965 (a realistic story of the family relationships and school life of a little girl in a lower middle-class urban family).

THOMPSON, VIVIAN L. *Hawaiian Myths of Earth, Sea, and Sky.* Holiday, 1966.

TURKLE, BRINTON. *Obadiah the Bold.* Viking, 1965 (a short, well-illustrated tale of a Quaker of the early 1800's who has ambitions to be a pirate; a read-aloud story for younger children).

WRIGHTSON, PATRICIA. *Down to Earth.* Harcourt, 1965 (a science-fiction tale of a Martian boy's sojourn in Sydney, Australia; for older readers in the middle grades).

FOR UPPER ELEMENTARY AND
JUNIOR-HIGH GRADES

ALEXANDER, LLOYD. *The Black Cauldron*. Holt, 1965 (high adventure and good writing in a fantasy that is a sequel to *The Book of Three*; for older readers).

ASIMOV, ISAAC. *The Greeks: A Great Adventure*. Houghton, 1965 (a history of ancient Greece, informally written).

BONHAM, FRANK. *Durango Street*. Dutton, 1965 (realistic story of the violence of the teen-age gang struggles).

BOTHWELL, JEAN. *Lady of Roanoke*. Holt, 1965 (a fictionalized account of the "Lost Colony" of Roanoke, Virginia).

BOWEN, ELIZABETH. *The Struggle Within: Race Relations in the United States*. Norton, 1965 (a good treatment of historical, political, social, and economic problems of race relations).

BRINSMEAD, HESBA T. *Pastures of the Blue Crane*. Coward, 1966 (a junior novel with a setting in Australia and an unusual handling of the interracial problem).

BRONOWSKI, J., and SELSAM, MILLICENT E. *Biography of an Atom*. Harper, 1965 (an explanation of the carbon atom).

BROWN, IVOR. *Dr. Johnson and His World*. Walck, 1966 (a lively description of England in the days of Dr. Johnson; full of interesting detail).

BROWN, MARCIA. *Backbone of the King; The Story of Pakaá and His Son Ku*. Scribner's, 1966 (traditional hero tale from Hawaii).

COOLIDGE, OLIVIA E. *People in Palestine*. Hougton, 1965 (seven stories describe political and religious life in Palestine between the time of Jesus' birth and A.D. 66).

DOWNEY, GLANVILLE (ed.). *Stories from Herodotus: A Panorama of Events and Peoples of the Ancient World*. Dutton, 1965 (stories of the wars between the Greeks and Persians).

DUGGAN, ALFRED. *Growing Up with the Norman Conquest*. Pantheon, 1966 (interesting social history told through the lives of five children of different economic levels).

EMERY, ANNE. *A Spy in Old West Point*. Rand, 1965 (a historical tale of the Revolutionary War).

FISHER, ARLEEN. *The Dickinsons: The Life of Emily Dickinson as Seen Through the Eyes of Her Brother Austin*. Atheneum, 1965.

FITZHUGH, LOUISE. *The Long Secret*. Harper, 1965 (the sequel to *Harriet the Spy*, with the same searching characterization of a pre-adolescent girl).

FLEISCHMAN, SID. *Ghost in the Noonday Sun*. Little, 1965 (buried treasure and mutiny in a tongue-in-cheek pirate story).

FOSTER, G. ALLEN. *Communication: From Primitive Tom-Toms to Telestar*. Criterion, 1966 (the history of different media and the factors that influence development).

GLUBOK, SHIRLEY. *The Art of Africa*. Harper, 1965 (excellent photographs of art objects accompany a simply written, informational text).

HARNUM, SARA, and REED, GWENDOLYN. *Lean Out the Window: An Anthology of Modern Poetry*. Illustrated by RAGNA TISCHLER. Atheneum, 1966.

HENTOFF, NAT. *Jazz Country*. Harper, 1965 (the experiences of a white teen-age musician who wants to break into the Negro jazz world).

HOLM, ANNE. *North to Freedom*. Harcourt, 1965 (the story of a twelve-year-old boy's escape from a prison in Eastern Europe and his travels across the continent in search of his mother).

MEAD, MARGARET. *Anthropologists and What They Do*. Watts, 1965 (interesting profiles of the varied careers in anthropology).

MELTZER, MILTON (ed.). *In Their Own Words: A History of the American Negro, 1865–1916*. Crowell, 1965 (the sequel to a volume of the same title covering the years 1619–1865).

POOLE, LYNN and GRAY. *Fireflies in Nature and the Laboratory*. Crowell, 1965.

The Quest of Columbus: An Exact Account of the Discovery of America, Being the History Written by Ferdinand Columbus. Edited and adapted by ROBERT MEREDITH and E. BROOKS SMITH. Little, 1966.

ROLLINS, CHARLEMAE H. *Famous American Negro Poets*. Dodd, 1965 (twelve Negro poets in a collective biography, together with some of their poems).

SALISBURY, HARRISON E. *Russia*. Macmillan, 1965 (informative and lively writing by the Moscow correspondent of the *New York Times*).

SCHECHTER, BETTY. *The Dreyfus Affair: A National Scandal*. Houghton, 1965.

SHIPTON, EVE. *Mountain Conquest: A Horizon Caravel Book*. Harper, 1966 (the history of the conquest of most of the leading mountains of the world).

SILVERBERG, ROBERT. *Scientists and Scoundrels: A Book of Hoaxes*. Crowell, 1965 (thirteen hoaxes, most of them from scientific fields).

STERNE, EMMA G. *I Have a Dream*. Knopf, 1965 (an account of the civil rights movement, with a focus on the people who are the leaders).

STEVENSON, WILLIAM. *The Bushbabies*. Houghton, 1965 (adventures of a game warden's daughter who walked with a Swahili tribesman on a long journey to return her pet bushbaby to its home).

SUTCLIFF, ROSEMARY. *Heroes and History*. Putnam, 1966 (heroes of Britain discussed in the framework of their places in history).

THOMPSON, PHILIP D., O'BRIEN, ROBERT, and the EDITORS OF LIFE MAGAZINE. *Weather*. Time, 1965 (one of the *Life* science series, with many excellent photographs and diagrams).

TREVINO, ELIZABETH B. DE. *I, Juan de Pareja*. Farrar, 1965 (account of the life of an artist-slave of the Spanish painter Velázquez; received the Newbery Award for 1965).

FOR HIGH-SCHOOL AND JUNIOR-COLLEGE STUDENTS

SUSAN SAX

*

YOUNG PEOPLE during very early adolescence are self-absorbed and occupied with fantasies about growing older. Books about young romance, junior proms, sports cars, and high-school sports events are written particularly for this age group.

Young adults of high-school and junior-college age do not need to read projections of teen-age life. They already know what to expect at this age level, and their interests are broadening and maturing. For this group of readers no special literature exists. They select adult books, and their choices are greatly influenced by current national interests.

This year, social service and the problems of poverty seem to be dominant themes. There are several books about the Peace Corps, one about the problems of migrant workers, and one by a civil rights volunteer in the South. Examinations of the life of the poor can be found in both fiction and nonfiction books. *Two Blocks Apart*, by Charlotte Meyerson, contrasts the views and problems of two New York boys, one from a slum area and one from the middle class. *Kate and Emma*, by Monica Dickens, is a novel that deals with a similar contrast between two London girls of different social backgrounds. Ruth Wolff's *A Crack in the Sidewalk* is about a young girl growing up in a tenement and struggling for a different life.

Not all of the books are of a sociological nature. There are the usual suspense and mystery novels, studies of unusual animals, and narratives about travel and exploration. Such reading matter is absorbing and informative, although of a fleeting nature. Books that deal with social service and the problems of poverty, on the other hand, may build compassion and understanding, giving new insights that will affect the course of a life.

BADER, A. L. (ed.). *To the Young Writer.* University of Michigan Press, 1965 (a group of established authors, poets, and critics analyze writing techniques and personal approaches to the craft).

BEARD, PETER HILL. *The End of the Game.* Viking, 1965 (lavishly illustrated account of game animals, hunting, and adventure in Africa).

BELFRAGE, SALLY. *Freedom Summer.* Viking, 1965 (young author tells of her summer working as a civil rights volunteer in Mississippi).

BENNETT, JACK. *Mister Fisherman.* Little, Brown, 1965 (a wealthy teen-age boy and a South African fisherman share an adventure at sea and gain mutual understanding).

BERNSTEIN, JEREMY. *Ascent: Of the*

Invention of Mountain Climbing and Its Practice. Random, 1965 (Yale physics professor writes of mountain climbing and the exploits of some famous climbers and guides).

BOULLE, PIERRE. *Garden on the Moon.* Vanguard, 1965 (fictionalized account of the development of space flight, culminating in a moon race between the major powers).

BRODRICK, JAMES. *Galileo: The Man, His Work, His Misfortunes.* Harper, 1965 (a study of Galileo's accomplishments, his personality, and his conflicts with the church).

BROOKS, EARLE and RHODA. *Barrios of Manta.* New American Library, 1965 (the experiences of two Peace Corps volunteers in Ecuador).

BUEHR, WALTER. *Home Sweet Home in the Nineteenth Century.* Crowell, 1965 (amusing study of the home conveniences and gadgetry of the nineteenth century: bottle warmers, vacuum cleaners, devices for heat and light, the first watches, and so on).

BURGER, DINOYS. *Sphereland: A Fantasy about Curved Spaces and an Expanding Universe.* Crowell, 1965 (a mathematical fantasy intended as a sequel to Abbott's *Flatland,* an 1890 classic about the experiences of a square in a two-dimensional space).

CARRIGHAR, SALLY. *Wild Heritage.* Houghton, 1965 (a study of animal behavior, with correlations drawn to human behavior).

COUSTEAU, JACQUES-YVES. *World without Sun.* Harper, 1965 (pictures and text convey the experiences of five men who lived for a month in an underwater colony in the Red Sea).

CROW, JOHN A. *Italy: A Journey through Time.* Harper, 1965 (a popular history of Italy, with special emphasis on the Renaissance).

CURRY, PAUL. *Magician's Magic.* Watts, 1965 (descriptions of famous magicians and some of their outstanding tricks).

DAVID, JANINA. *A Square of the Sky.* Norton, 1965 (autobiographical fragment describing the author's early years in a Polish ghetto).

DAVIS, BURKE. *The Summer Land.* Random House, 1965 (authentic period novel set in North Carolina at the turn of the century).

DAY, J. EDWARD. *My Appointed Round: 929 Days as Postmaster General.* Holt, 1965 (former postmaster general presents amusing observations about his work and contacts).

DEAL, BORDEN. *A Long Way To Go.* Doubleday, 1965 (adventure novel about the cross-country trek of three children in search of their parents).

DEFORE, PENNY. *With All My Love.* Prentice-Hall, 1965 (a young girl tells of the insights she gained while working as a volunteer in a Korean orphanage).

DICKENS, MONICA. *Kate and Emma.* Coward McCann, 1965 (a novel about two young London girls of different social backgrounds who are both trying to cope with severe personal problems).

DICKSON, MORA. *A World Elsewhere: Voluntary Service Overseas.* Rand McNally, 1965 (selected letters from young people working for Voluntary

Service Overseas, the British version of the Peace Corps).

DOROZYNSKI, ALEXANDER. *The Man They Wouldn't Let Die*. Macmillan, 1965 (chronicle of the remarkable physical rehabilitation of the Russian physicist Lev Landau, whose life was seriously jeopardized after an automobile accident).

DRÖSCHER, VITUS B. *The Mysterious Senses of Animals*. Dutton, 1965 (recent studies of animal behavior entertainingly presented for the lay reader).

DUNLOP, RICHARD. *Doctors of the American Frontier*. Doubleday, 1965 (a colorful history of doctors and medicine in the nineteenth century).

DURHAM, PHILIP, and JONES, EVERETT L. *The Negro Cowboys*. Dodd, Mead, 1965 (an accurate and readable account of the most picturesque of the Negro cowboys).

EBY, OMAR. *Sense and Incense*. Herald Press, 1965 (young missionary writes of his three years of teaching English in Somalia).

EZICKSON, AARON J. (ed.). *The Peace Corps: A Pictorial History*. Hill and Wang, 1965 (photographs and sketches of the varied aspects of Peace Corps work, supplemented by excerpts from informal reports by the volunteers).

FARR, FINIS. *Margaret Mitchell of Atlanta: The Author of "Gone with the Wind."* Morrow, 1965 (biography of the author of the famous best seller).

FEIFFER, JULES. *The Great Comic Book Heroes*. Dial, 1965 (witty analysis of comic books).

FITZGERALD, FRANCIS SCOTT KEY. *Scott Fitzgerald: Letters to His Daughter*. Scribner, 1965 (insights into Fitzgerald's concerns and motivations as a writer from his letters to his daughter).

FITZGIBBON, CONSTANTINE. *The Life of Dylan Thomas*. Little, Brown, 1965 (compassionate biography of the Welsh poet).

FRENZ, HORST (ed.). *American Playwrights on Drama*. Hill and Wang, 1965 (collected pieces of theatrical criticism).

GADDIS, VINCENT. *Invisible Horizons*. Chilton, 1965 (stories about mysterious phenomena of sea and sky).

GALLAGHER, TERESA. *Give Joy to My Youth: A Memoir of Dr. Tom Dooley*. Farrar, 1965 (a volunteer who worked with Dr. Dooley tells of the man and his work).

GREBANIER, EDWARD. *The Great Shakespeare Forgery*. Norton, 1965 (fascinating tale of the exploits of William Henry Ireland, hapless but skilled forger of Shakespearean documents in the late eighteenth century).

GRZIMEK, BERNARD. *Rhinos Belong to Everybody*. Hill and Wang, 1965 (a collection of information and anecdotes about the national game preserves of Africa, with lavish photographic illustration).

HALACY, D. S., JR. *Cyborg: The Evolution of the Supermen*. Harper, 1965 (a discussion of recent scientific developments concerned with the improvement and repair of the human body).

HAN SUYIN. *The Crippled Tree*. Putnam, 1965 (the author describes her early years in China and presents her observations of the growth of Western influence there and the rise of the Kuomintang).

HAWKINS, GERALD S. *Stonehenge Decoded.* Doubleday, 1965 (facts about Stonehenge, an examination of previous theories about the significance of the stones, and a presentation of the author's personal thesis that the site was an early astronomical observatory).

HENTOFF, NAT. *Jazz Country.* Harper, 1965 (realistic novel about a teen-age boy who wants to become a jazz musician and faces difficult decisions about college and his personal course in life).

HEUVELMANS, BERNARD. *On the Track of Unknown Animals.* Hill and Wang, 1965 (an examination of reports of curious animals, from folklore and the accounts of historians and explorers).

HUXLEY, JULIAN, and KETTLEWELL, H. D. D. *Charles Darwin and His World.* Viking, 1965 (a biography of Darwin that also serves as an introduction to his theories).

INNES, HAMMOND. *The Strode Venturer.* Knopf, 1965 (an adventure tale involving London high finance, a primitive tribe on an island in the Indian Ocean, and suspense at sea).

KAYIRA, LEGSON. *I Will Try.* Doubleday, 1965 (the autobiography of a young African from Nyasaland who pursued his goal of an education in America with unusual determination and courage).

KEITH, AGNES NEWTON. *Children of Allah.* Little, Brown, 1965 (personal impressions of the people, social customs, and politics of Libya).

KINLOCK, BRUCE. *Sauce for the Mongoose: The Story of a Real-Life Rikki-Tikki-Tavi.* Knopf, 1965 (a game warden presents the personal history of a mongoose adopted by his family).

KNEBEL, FLETCHER. *Night at Camp David.* Harper, 1965 (a suspense novel concerned with the plight of a junior senator who is faced with the discovery that the President of the United States is insane).

KRAUSS, RUTH. *The Cantilever Rainbow.* Pantheon, 1965 (eighteen pieces of imaginative and unusual poetry, all concerned with the sun).

LAMONT, LANSING. *Day of Trinity.* Atheneum, 1965 (an account of the development of the first atomic bomb and the resulting moral dilemma facing the scientists involved).

LENARD, ALEXANDER. *The Valley of the Latin Bear.* Dutton, 1965 (eventful autobiography of the Hungarian physician who translated *Winnie-the-Pooh* into Latin).

LESSING, DORIS. *African Stories.* Simon & Schuster, 1965 (a collection of stories with an African motif).

LEWIS, HOWARD R. *With Every Breath You Take.* Crown, 1965 (discussion and possible solutions of the problem of air pollution).

LINDALL, EDWARD. *Northward the Coast.* Morrow, 1965 (an adventure novel set in Australia).

LITTLE, TOM. *High Dam at Aswan: The Subjugation of the Nile.* John Day, 1965 (an account of the building of the Aswan dam in Egypt).

LUCAS, RUTH. *Who Dare To Live.* Houghton, 1965 (a suspense novel about an Englishwoman who becomes active in the underground movement in Nazi Germany).

McCAGUE, JAMES. *The Fortune Road.* Harper, 1965 (a post–Civil War adventure tale about two children traveling across the country on their own).

MacDONALD, JULIE. *Almost Human; The Baboon: Wild and Tame — In Fact and in Legend.* Chilton, 1965 (a sculptress tells of her study of a live baboon and of her researches concerning this animal in other cultures and periods).

MacINNES, HELEN. *The Double Image.* Harcourt, 1966 (foreign intrigue, for mystery and suspense fans).

MARSH, NGAIO. *Black Beech and Honeydew.* Little, Brown, 1965 (a well-known mystery story author writes nostalgically of her New Zealand childhood, her wide theatrical experiences, and her professional development).

MAXWELL, GAVIN. *The House of Elrig.* Dutton, 1965 (the Author of *Ring of Bright Water* presents his autobiography).

MAYERSON, CHARLOTTE LEON (ed.). *Two Blocks Apart.* Holt, 1965 (the experiences and viewpoints of two New York boys from widely different economic backgrounds).

MEAD, MARGARET. *Family.* Macmillan, 1965 (an examination of family life in many cultures by an anthropologist and a photographer).

MERIWETHER, DAVID. *My Life in the Mountains and on the Plains.* University of Oklahoma Press, 1965 (the autobiography of a man who was associated with prominent figures of the American West in the early 1880's).

MICHENER, JAMES A. *The Source.* Random House, 1965 (the story of Israel built around each successive layer of a fictitious archeological site).

MILLER, MAXINE ADAMS. *Ali, a Persian Yankee.* Caxton, 1965 (the experiences of a young Persian of sheltered background who comes to the United States to study).

MOORE, TRUMAN E. *The Slaves We Rent.* Random House, 1965 (a study of migrant workers: their living conditions, economic role in society, and historical origin).

MURPHY, DERVLA. *Full Tilt: Ireland to India with a Bicycle.* Dutton, 1965 (observations of the people and places encountered during a bicycle trip from Ireland to India).

MURPHY, ROBERT. *The Golden Eagle.* Dutton, 1965 (a nature story concerned with the life cycle of a golden eagle).

MYDANS, SHELLY. *Thomas: A Novel of The Life, Passion, and Miracles of Becket.* Doubleday, 1965 (a fictionalized biography of Thomas à Becket).

NAIPUAL, V. S. *An Area of Darkness.* Macmillan, 1965 (a Hindu from Trinidad recounts his sensations on his first visit to India, the homeland of his ancestors).

NIMS, CHARLES F. *Thebes of the Pharaohs: Pattern for Every City.* Stein and Day, 1965 (Egyptologist recreates the daily life of ancient Thebes).

OLIVER, ROLAND and CAROLINE. *Africa in the Days of Exploration.* Prentice-Hall, 1965 (a collection of accounts from the journals of African explorers through the centuries).

PARKS, GORDON. *A Choice of Weapons.* Harper, 1965 (the autobiography of a Negro photographer who achieved success despite poverty and bigotry).

POPE, DUDLEY. *Ramage.* Lippincott, 1965 (historial fiction about events on the high seas at the time of the Napoleonic Wars).

PORTER, KATHERINE ANNE. *The Collected Stories of Katherine Anne Porter.* Harcourt, 1965 (a compilation of all of the available stories and short novels of Miss Porter).

RAND, CHRISTOPHER. *Mountains and Water.* Oxford University Press, 1965 (a collection of travel pieces about unusual journeys to far places).

RONSON, MAVIS. *We Never Meant To Go So Far.* Transatlantic Arts, 1965 (the story of the adventurous journey of two young British girls who worked their way through ports in Europe, the Middle East, and Asia).

ST. JOHN, ROBERT. *Roll Jordan Roll: The Life Story of a River and Its People.* Doubleday, 1965 (a study of the history and geography of the Jordan River and of the people who have inhabited its banks).

SANDERSON, IVAN T., and LOTH, DAVID. *Ivan Sanderson's Book of Great Jungles.* Messner, 1965 (profusely illustrated examination of tropical rain forests, their mysteries and splendors).

SCHLESINGER, ARTHUR M. *A Thousand Days; John F. Kennedy in the White House.* Houghton Mifflin, 1965 (personalized reconstruction of the Kennedy administration).

SHADBOLT, MAURICE. *Among the Cinders.* Atheneum, 1965 (a novel, rich in local color, about the growth to maturity of a New Zealand youth).

SILVERBERG, ROBERT. *The Old Ones.* New York Graphic, 1965 (a study of the Pueblo Indians and their ancient and contemporary cultures).

SMITH, VIAN. *A Second Chance.* Doubleday, 1966 (a novel about a young English delinquent who is given a chance to reconstruct his life through work in a racing stable).

SNOW, EDWARD ROWE. *Astounding Tales of the Sea.* Dodd, 1965 (a collection of true sea adventures).

SORENSEN, THEODORE C. *Kennedy.* Harper, 1965 (a memoir of the late President's years in office).

STEWART, MARY. *Airs above the Ground.* Morrow, 1965 (a mystery-suspense story with an Austrian setting).

STONE, IRVING. *Those Who Love: A Biographical Novel of Abigail and John Adams.* Doubleday, 1965 (a reconstruction of the courtship and career of the former President and his wife).

STRAINCHAMPS, ETHEL (REED). *Don't Never Say Cain't.* Doubleday, 1965 (the autobiography of a woman from the Ozarks who worked as a housemaid to pay her way in college and later became a teacher and writer).

STREATFIELD, NOEL. *On Tour: An Autobiographical Novel of the 20's.* Watts, 1965 (a description of the experiences of the author on theatrical tours of Australia and South Africa).

TROEBST, CORD CHRISTIAN. *The Art of Survival.* Doubleday, 1965 (tales of miraculous feats of survival and speculation about the traits of human character that made them possible).

TUPPER, HARMON. *To the Great Ocean: Siberia and the Trans-Siberian Railway*. Little, Brown, 1965 (an exciting account of the building of the Trans-Siberian railway, longest in the world).

TWAIN, MARK. *Susy and Mark Twain: Family Dialogues*. Harper, 1965 (an impression of Twain's domestic life from excerpts of letters and journals written by intimates of the author's household.

VARNEY, JOYCE. *A Welsh Story*. Bobbs-Merrill, 1965 (a sensitive autobiography depicting life in a Welsh mining town before World War II).

VON HAGEN, VICTOR W. *The Desert Kingdoms of Peru*. New York Graphic, 1965 (an archaeological account of the people who lived in Peru before the time of the Incas).

WAGENKECHT, EDWARD. *Harriet Beecher Stowe: The Known and the Unknown*. Oxford University Press, 1965 (a character study of the author of *Uncle Tom's Cabin*).

WELCH, GALBRAITH. *Africa before They Came: The Continent, North, South, East, and West, Preceding the Colonial Powers*. Morrow, 1965 (an examination of African culture in precolonial days).

WIBBERLEY, LEONARD. *The Island of Angels*. Morrow, 1965 (a lonely Mexican fisherman finds a new meaning in life when he helps a sick boy).

WILLIAMS, ELMA M. *Valley of Animals*. John Day, 1966 (a story of an unusual household in a Welsh valley where the author lives with an assortment of domestic animals).

WILLIAMS, LEONARD. *Samba and the Monkey Mind*. Norton, 1965 (the author presents his observations of animal behavior, based on study of a group of wooly monkeys).

WOLFF, RUTH. *A Crack in the Sidewalk*. John Day, 1965 (teen-age girl copes with tenement-life poverty and finds new hope for the future).

INDEX

*